Remembering...

A World War II Love Story

Remembering...

A World War II Love Story

Dorothea Fant McCollum

Acclaim Press
MORLEY, MISSOURI

Acclaim Press
— Your Next Great Book —
P.O. Box 238
Morley, MO 63767
(573) 472-9800
www.acclaimpress.com

Book Design: Ina Morse
Cover Design: M. Frene Melton

Library of Congress Cataloging-in-Publication Data

McCollum, Dorothea Fant, 1922-
Remembering-- a World War II love story / Dorothea Fant McCollum.
p. cm.
ISBN-13: 978-1-935001-77-5 (alk. paper)
ISBN-10: 1-935001-77-9 (alk. paper)
1. McCollum, Dorothea Fant, 1922---Correspondence. 2. McCollum, Marvin Frank, 1922-1991--Correspondence. 3. Soldiers--United States--Correspondence. 4. World War, 1939-1945--Personal narratives, American. I. Title.
D811.5.M317 2011
940.54'1273092--dc23
[B]

2011018044

First Printing: 2011
Printed in the United States of America
10 9 8 7 6 5 4 3 2 1

Contents

Dedication

To our children,
Buddy, Pam, and Melanie.

Acknowledgments

Special thanks go to Cy Fitton, who first prodded Bud to ask me for a date back in 1939, thus propelling into motion a romance which lasted 52 years – and in my mind, still endures to this day.

To the U.S. Marine Corps, which unwittingly taught me the virtue of patience.

To my granddaughter Holly Allen, who devoted so much time to retyping the letters which her grandfather and I exchanged. She must have wished at times that we'd been a little less prolific!

To Coleen Armstrong, inexpressible gratitude for her loving kindness and expertise as she guided the progress of this book.

And, of course, to Bud – who always said that he planned to write a book about us "someday." He wanted to title it, *I Love You.* I'm certain that he'd approve my going ahead and finishing it for him.

Cast of Characters

Parents – William and Elizabeth (Graf) Fant; Frank and Inez (Anstaett) McCollum.

Siblings – Ruth (Fant) Sizelove, Robert Fant and JoAnn (Fant) Burns. Martha (Mart) (McCollum) Brown, Galen (Gay), Bill, Jean (McCollum) Estes, June, Arlene, Ruth, Carroll (Kak), Asenath, Frank, Jr.

Ruth Ellen Bader – My Ross student on home instruction.

Mr. Robert Bogan – Our high school advisor and principal at Hanover.

Ed (Coop) Cooper – Bud's bunkmate. His uncle was a diamond salesman in Chicago. That's how Bud purchased my 51-point blue-white diamond engagement ring.

Koehler, Zim, Eggie, Chester – All Marine friends.

Uncle Claude – My father's youngest brother.

Aunt Emma – My mother's sister-in-law.

Mr. Homer Edington – A high school teacher and coach at Ohio State University.

Mr. Joseph Fichter – An English professor and vice president of Miami University. I worked for him. He was also master of the Ohio State Grange.

Mr. Fred Finkbine – Principal at Ross School.

Cy Fitton – Bud's Fairfield High School classmate.

Gay – Bud's brother, who was in the Coast Guard – older than Bill, who was in the Marines in the South Pacific.

Sid Gillman – Football coach at Miami University.

Don Graf – My cousin; son of Aunt Emma and Uncle Otto.

Dr. Guiler – My psychology professor at Miami.

Hanover – One of the local Butler County Schools.

Mr. C.T. Jenkins – A Miami administrator in charge of NYA (National Youth Administration) workers who received 25 cents per hour as they worked their way through college. This was one of President Roosevelt's initiatives to recover from The Great Depression.

Miss Jo – Cafeteria manager at Wake Forest College.

Johnny – Bud's youngest nephew, Jean's baby. His father was in the South Pacific.

Oscar Leiser, Jr. – Bud's best friend since elementary school; taught him to play basketball; son of local Probate Judge and an only child.

Aunt Lil and Uncle Russell – Mother's sister and her husband; Jim, their child, was my cousin.

Martha Waggoner – My roommate along with these friends: Midge, Brose, Ruthie, Eleanor (married to Jim), and Betty Pelle, whose name is the same as mine – Dorothea Elizabeth. And June – a Chinese-American living next door to us.

Dr. Wallace McConnell – My geography professor; he wrote books and taught at Miami.

Bill McDulin– Bud's best friend in the Marines. I had known him since childhood, since he lived across the alley from my cousin, Don.

Millie – Bill McDulin's wife.

Mr. P.R. Needles – Bud's high school teacher and basketball coach; principal at Seven Mile.

Mrs. Nelson – Landlady from whom Bud secured a room for me when I visited Morehead City; Bill and Millie lived there, too.

Petzold Platoon – A memorial platoon of local boys was organized in honor of Buzz Petzold who had been killed in an airplane crash in California; he was the son of a Hamilton hardware store owner.

Ross – One of the local Butler County Schools; I began my teaching career there.

Seven Mile – Village seven miles north of Hamilton, Ohio, where Bud began his teaching career.

Sis (Eleanor Sauerbeck) – Girlfriend of Gay; she became my sister-in-law.

Dr. Clyde Stafford – An Oxford doctor; our doctor until he died.

Matt Thompson – A Hamilton YMCA secretary who took Bud to Wake Forest College to be awarded a scholarship.

Woots and Bob – Sis' sister; Bob was a high school classmate.

Ray Wiggins – My cousin, who was overseas for three years; earned ten battle stars.

Miss Young – The English department critic teacher for whom both Martha and I did our practice teaching.

Preface

One cold winter day in 2008, I was suddenly seized by an impulse to pull down from the top shelf of my bedroom closet the love letters that my husband Bud had written to me before, during, and after World War II.

Whatever prompted this, I'm still not certain. I hadn't so much as looked at them since 1949, when we'd first moved into our new home. But nothing would satisfy me now except rediscovering what those letters contained – and what they would reveal about both of us some 65 years later.

I easily located the box containing Bud's letters to me. A surprise, however, was in store – to my astonishment, I also found another box that contained *my* letters to *him.* I hadn't realized he'd saved any of them.

Bud had organized mine according to date, and I had numbered his in sequence, so it was easy for me to review them in chronological order. His totaled nearly 500, stretching back to 1941, when he'd attended Wake Forest College on an athletic scholarship and continuing through 1946, the entire 44 months he was stationed in North Carolina with the U.S. Marine Corps. Mine numbered nearly as many, beginning in 1943, only when Bud finally decided that our relationship was serious, and he should start keeping them to comfort himself whenever he felt lonely. Previously, he admitted sheepishly, he'd been reading them once and then discarding them. In those days I hadn't felt entitled to take offense.

We'd known each other as high schoolers. Bud was an exceptionally talented, disciplined athlete who'd lettered in football, basketball, baseball, track, and tennis. He was also something of a poet and philosopher – extremely well-read, with high moral standards and a strong work ethic. No wonder he was voted "Most Likely To Succeed."

His early letters to me closed with "as ever," indicating not only a smooth, constant temperament, but also a person whose keen intellect and cool pragmatism would always rule his emotions. For a long time, although we dated, it seemed that he merely considered me a good friend. I was baffled by his unwillingness to declare any romantic feelings. I understand far better now. The future was at best a giant question mark. None of us knew where we'd be in a year, or later on, even a month. And Bud wasn't the sort of person who would intentionally lead anyone on.

So occasionally I prodded him gently to either make a commitment or else to stop wasting my time. But more often, I backed off. My focus, too, lay elsewhere. I was commuting to Miami University in Oxford, working as a secretary for two, sometimes three professors, studying, and trying to maintain my high grades. I was one of only two girls in my 1940 senior class (and the only person in my family) to attend college. Nineteen relatives would show up at my 1944 graduation to applaud!

Besides, my mother had repeatedly warned me: "Bud McCollum isn't interested in girls." I sensed that she was right.

But after I visited him one weekend on the base in 1943, something changed. Boom! It was as if we'd turned a page. Suddenly Bud was startling me with, "I love you!" Suddenly we were engaged – and he was asking, "How soon can we get married?"

He was also writing me some beautifully sensitive and passionate letters.

I was born on November 27, 1922, in an upstairs bedroom in my grandparents' home on a farm outside the village of Millville, Ohio, back a long lane across from the Millville Cemetery. My father, William Lucien Fant, and his father, James W. Fant, farmed the acreage from Boyle Road, Millville Avenue, and Minton Road – a triangular plot now occupied by the Queen of Peace Church and many private residences.

Aunt Ethel and Uncle Claude were teenagers living downstairs. They were delighted to have a new baby girl in the house. Their immense affection for me lasted until the day they died, and so it was with my grandma, Nancy Adeline Wiggins Fant.

When Grandpa sold the farm, we moved to a much smaller place along the river in Fairfield, just below the curved portion of Nilles Road, about two miles from Symmes Corner. My father worked at Fred J. Myers factory in Hamilton and later at Ford's; he was now only a part-time farmer.

We had cows. "Stay in the yard," admonished my mother, who was a city girl afraid of farm animals. "Those cows have horns." We had chickens. "That rooster will flop you with his spurs." And a horse. "That horse will step on you." And pigs. "Pigs eat little girls."

And a nearby river. "Don't go near it – you'll drown."

So I stayed in the big fenced-in yard, playing with my dolls and their fancy buggy, which Aunt Ethel had given me, swinging or climbing a high rope, and petting the horse only across the fence. My job was to pump water for the cows, but I soon tired of it. Those things just drank and drank and drank.

Both of my parents had only eighth grade educations – the standard for their day. My mother, Elizabeth Josephine Graf Fant, was sent to sewing school and to cooking school. She worked in a garment factory and later on the sorting line at Champion Paper down the hill from their Prytania Avenue residence. After marriage, she never held a job outside the home, also the standard for her day, but she was quite skilled in the homemaking arts. She read to us, played with us, and when I was older, she taught me to sew. My daughter Melanie still has her old treadle sewing machine.

When I was three years old, my sister Ruth was born; a third child (Helen Evelyn Fant) died at birth; my brother Bob arrived when I was nine, and my sister JoAnn when I was twelve. All of us were born at home with Dr. Georgina Williams in attendance. In those days a mother was confined to bed for ten days while an aunt or nanny took over household duties. My antique doll, made in Germany in 1894, was the playmate of our doctor, and for some reason she gave it to me.

At age five, I was enrolled in first grade at Symmes Corner School, located at the corner of River Road and Nilles Road about one-half mile west of Symmes Corner on Rt. 127. There were three grades in this one-room schoolhouse with a wonderful young teacher, Justina Bowling Ferguson. I still remember the big flash cards she used to teach us reading. There was a huge stove in the front center of the room. A "big" third grader, whose father served on the school board, arrived early to start the fire. Here, as at home, there was no indoor plumbing. For water, we'd take our collapsible cups from a special place inside our pencil boxes, go outside, and pump. There were two outhouses with the usual horrific smell. We were not allowed to play on the east side of the building – our teacher had a brand new Ford Roadster, and that's where she parked!

A student had brought a big chocolate bar to school one day, and someone had taken a big bite out of it. Our teacher sent us all outside, and then one by one she called us in to match the tooth marks. I was so afraid that she would think I had done it. When it was my turn to be matched, she took one look at me and said, "Honey, you didn't do it; you still have your baby teeth!"

In the spring of 1928, there was much bootlegging and gangster activity in our area, and Hamilton was nicknamed Little Chicago. I remember hearing about John Dillinger and Baby Face Nelson. One Saturday evening relatives from town came to visit with the news that law enforcement had warned them about gangsters gathering nearby. We were all frightened, but Daddy loaded his shotgun and kept watch most of the night. He had been a soldier during World War I, hauling ammunition via wagon-drawn mules, so whenever there was a disturbance outside, he relied on his gun.

On Monday morning there was much excitement at school. We found a big hole in the back door – the gangsters had had a shootout right there!

Fairfield Centralized School was completed in 1929; I attended from grades two to twelve. Symmes Corner School is now a residence painted white. Other one-room schools like Fair Play and Slade have been razed.

I was always the smallest in my class – and the most timid. But that would change.

Now, in retrospect, I see what wonderful, supportive parents I had. They were so complimentary of my achievements that I yearned to please them (and my teachers too) even more, so that I'd earn additional praise. My self-esteem was exceptionally healthy – enhanced by my habit of sharing with my parents everything I learned, so they could assimilate it into their own knowledge. This was especially true of English grammar.

In the 1870s and 1880s many Europeans immigrated to America to pursue a better life. Among them were my grandparents – John Jacob Graf and Elizabeth Fellman. Grandpa was an orphan from Berne, Switzerland, so I know nothing about his ancestry. He and Elizabeth did not meet until they were settled in this area.

Grandpa was about sixteen, leaving family behind, while Grandma, her two brothers, and a sister came here from Switzerland together. The total of Grandma's possessions was contained in a top-handled basket – the kind you've seen in history books. I still have it today.

Grandma's father was Catholic; her mother, Protestant. Before they married they decided that all girl children would be Protestant and all boys would be Catholic. My mother had many Catholic cousins.

The Graf family owned a dairy at 902 Prytania Avenue and sold milk all over the City of Hamilton. The children carried milk in small buckets to customers on the west side. Grandpa had a horse and wagon and delivered milk to customers on the east side of town.

One week in March, 1913, it rained and rained, and then rained even more. As the river rose, Grandpa loaded his wagon with milk and headed across the bridge – but flooding made it impossible for him to return. The bridge and many homes had been swept away; flood water by then had reached downtown's 9th and 10th Streets. Where he stayed that night, I do not know – perhaps he slept in his wagon or else bunked with friendly customers. Since communication was difficult, each day someone with a megaphone would shout across the river the names of survivors.

Grandma sent the older children to the riverbank several times to listen for news of Grandpa – none! The family did not know if he were alive or dead.

Two weeks later, he, his wagon, and horse traveled to Venice, where a bridge remained, and then toward the west side to his home. Only then did the family know he was still alive.

When my mother was eighteen, her oldest brother Otto gave her a wide-band pink gold ring as a friendship gift. It was engraved "from O to E 1914."

Once she had a wedding ring, however, she put the gift away. When we lived with Grandma and Grandpa Fant in Millville, Grandma lost her wedding ring one day in the garden. So my mother gave her the ring from Otto to wear as a replacement.

When I was five, just before Grandma died of cancer, she called me to her bed, took off the ring, and said, "Here is a remembrance of your mother and your grandmother." Once again the ring was put away for safekeeping. When I was older and more responsible, my mother gave it back to me.

Decades later, in October, 2000, when I broke my shoulder and my arm, shattering the bones, my first thought was to remove my rings before my hand could swell. I laid both my wedding ring and diamond engagement ring on my dresser.

Many months afterward, when I was able to wear my rings once more, the diamond was exactly where I had left it, but the wedding ring had disappeared. To this day I have not found it. And so, remembering that I still had a very special ring, I am now wearing the wide-banded pink gold as a keepsake – "in remembrance of your mother and grandmother."

I missed 60 days of school in first grade because I had whooping cough. My mother brought home my assignments, and when I returned to school, I was ahead of my class. Ruth, at age three, had memorized my reading book and even knew when to turn the pages.

Everything at Fairfield was so new and modern. We had indoor restrooms, water fountains, and electricity. Our superintendent, Mr. R.E. Augspurger, had selected most teachers with a strong Christian background. The Depression was at its worst – a plate lunch cost thirteen cents and milk was two cents. Most teachers had few dresses (no slacks were permitted); I can still visualize some of their dresses because they wore them so often. The men's suits had shiny rears. Students were in similar circumstances, wearing the same clothing day after day – that's just the way it was!

Times were so hard that there were months during which teachers received no pay. A decree went out that all married female teachers must resign. One income per family would help those with no income at all. Some of our best teachers had to quit or else divorce their husbands. Mrs. Duvall, my math teacher, fell into that category.

During The Depression my dad had a job with the WPA (Works Progress Administration). Their assignment was to build a new road, Rt. 127, from Hamilton to Symmes Corner. We, like most, were on Relief, which meant that we received free basic commodities (sugar, flour, cheese) and a small stipend for other groceries. Of course, thanks to the farm, we always had plenty of food – milk, eggs, meat, and a large garden. On weekends some of our city relatives came to visit and enjoy my mother's good cooking. She always sent them home with fresh produce.

I can still remember how good it felt on our bare feet as we trailed the horse and plow, which turned up cool soil to reveal potatoes. We kids gathered them like treasure hunters, then put them aside for winter storage in a special potato bin in the cellar.

On Saturdays my dad loaded his Ford, put a crate of squawking chickens on the rear, and headed to town and to his many customers. I liked to ride along. We sold dressed rabbits (which he raised) by order, live chickens, a big oats box full of eggs for 25 cents, and many vegetables. If a customer wanted him to kill a chicken for her, he'd get out his block and hatchet, chopping the head off right there in the gutter. We pulled, weighed, and tied rhubarb to sell at the Kirk Pie Bakery at the end of High Street.

The Depression was a time when everyone helped everyone else. Since everybody was in the same boat, we didn't know we were poor. I had one pair of shoes, polished for Sunday. My dad had a shoe last and glued precut rubber soles to our shoes – better than the cardboard we otherwise would have used.

Goods were cheap, but hardly anyone had any money. Aunt Lettie and Uncle Will lost their beautiful home on Elmo Avenue in Lindenwald because they couldn't pay the mortgage. The price of gasoline was only eight or ten cents a gallon, so it didn't take much to power a Model "T" Ford – but most people still couldn't afford it.

At home we still had no indoor plumbing or electricity. The radio ran on the same battery as the automobile. When the battery ran down, my dad switched it with the car's, and the generator charged it. He could always start the car, for it had a crank in front.

President Roosevelt had many novel ideas to extricate the nation from its Depression woes. The Rural Electrification Act was one of them. In 1936, when I was in ninth grade, my parents paid a small amount to extend an electrical line to our home and barns. It was the greatest thrill of my young life to come home from school and turn on every light in the house!

Every Saturday night we visited with my Fant grandparents; every Sunday night we visited with my Graf grandparents and all of my aunts, uncles and cousins. Grandma, who was only about five feet tall, fixed brown sugar and butter sandwiches for all of us kids, and then shut the kitchen door to contain the noise. We washed down the sweetness with water from the kitchen sink – no soda pop.

Grandma Graf always had homemade wine for her sons-in-law. Before she went to the cellar she would proclaim that this was the last of it. But somehow every Sunday she squeezed out more.

This was the time of Prohibition, when people made their own spirits at home. Whenever my parents made beer, they also made root beer for the kids. Both were sealed with a long-handled bottle capper. I recall visitors sitting around in a circle passing a single tin of beer. A handle on each side made for easy transfers. If a child wanted a taste, he could have it. Once was enough for me – I thought it tasted bitter. I've never had a beer since.

When Grandma Graf decided that too many grandchildren had not been Christened, she ordered all to come to her home where Rev. Vollbrecht held a mass Christening.

The Graf family returned to our home for a reunion. Aunt Lil baked a ham, and everyone else brought covered dishes. But Lil's husband sampled some ham as soon as it came out of the oven. When he became ill, they realized they could not attend, but they sent the ham anyway. Only after we'd finished it, word arrived that we shouldn't eat it because of possible ptomaine poisoning. Oops. Too late – some folks were already feeling terrible. They all hurried home, leaving Mother with two of us deathly sick, and with no telephone. Someone had eaten the sandwich Mother had fixed for herself, so fortunately she was fine.

Our next door neighbor called Dr. Williams, who stayed all night because my father was near death. As a last resort, she used what she called her "one-minute" remedy. It worked, but the lining of his stomach was so damaged that he had to eat baby food all summer long. I still have to wonder what the remedy contained.

It's quite possible that The Great Depression was what molded us into what came to be called "The Greatest Generation." World War II with its enormous sacrifices would follow, but I believe the economic hardships were even more influential than the War.

When I was in junior high, a member of the Fairfield school board offered my dad a real job – as a janitor! His pay was $100 per month, which sounded like a small fortune, but from that he paid $40 per month to an assistant. I helped too, by staying after school and going behind the sweepers with a dust rag for desks and window sills. There were three floors of classrooms, and I dusted every single one! That summer, as a reward Daddy took me to Petzold's East Hamilton Hardware on Grand Boulevard and bought me a blue, balloon-tired bike.

Ruth and I were both confirmed at St. Paul Church in 1938. At that time she was in the seventh grade, eligible for Confirmation, and I was three years older. We'd ride to Fairfield with Daddy and catch the Cincinnati bus to Hamilton for just ten cents. Rev. Vollbrecht would have a warm fire in the potbellied stove heating the little Sunday School room next to the kitchen. We sat around the stove studying the Heidelberg Catechism and other documents of the church. And we read the Apostles' Creed, "...to judge the quick and the dead."

"Dorothea, who are the *quick?"* he asked. And I didn't know! I have never forgotten that they are those still alive – why didn't I figure that out as the opposite of *dead*? Rev. Vollbrecht told me that my name meant "gift of God," and I've always remembered that, too. My confirmation verse was James Chapter 8, Verse 4: "Draw nigh to God, and He will draw nigh to you."

In one way it was good to have my dad at school. He was respected by both my teachers and my friends, for he did an excellent job. When it was below freezing in winter, he would go back to school after supper and stay all night, so the building would be warm in the morning when students arrived. Then at midmorning he'd go home for food and a nap.

The bad part about having my father know all of the students came when a boy would ask *him* if he could take me on a date. Sometimes he would say, "No," and I never knew anything about it.

President Roosevelt had many kinds of federal strategies intended to ease The Depression. Some students on this NYA (National Youth Administration) program helped my dad on Saturday mornings. One such NYA student was the most gifted athlete in Fairfield: Marvin "Bud" McCollum. His job? Scrubbing toilets. His pay? Twenty-five cents an hour. "A good worker," my dad nodded. Who would have guessed that he was speaking of his future son-in-law?

Marvin Frank McCollum was born on January 8, 1922, the second oldest of twelve children. His father was a maintenance superintendent and unordained minister. His mother was a no-nonsense housewife who could have a baby in the morning and be out of bed doing laundry by afternoon.

Frank and Inez McCollum gave their children a strict moral and religious upbringing – but they were sometimes generous to a fault. Bud remembered searching in vain for a favorite pair of socks or overalls as a child, only to learn that his mother had given them away to someone she deemed less fortunate.

As a teenager, Bud took odd jobs – pitching hay, shoveling coal, pouring cement. His father told him, "Son, always give a day's work for a day's pay." In those days, a day's pay was often a dollar. Bud cheerfully placed whatever money he earned on his mother's dining room table.

During the winter of 1939, the Hi-Y Club was having a party at Camp Campbell Gard – and Bud informed a friend that he was not going. He had no interest in weekend social affairs, only sports. Cy Fitton responded that if he didn't get a date, Cy would find one for him. Well, that irritated Bud. He was president of the organization; no one decided something that important except him. So he invited the first girl he spotted – me. "Would you like to go to the Hi-Y party?" he asked. I reluctantly answered, "Uh, huh."

My best friend had a date with a new boy in school, someone whom every girl had been panting to snag. When he asked her instead of me, I'd have gone with almost anyone else, just to show her she couldn't upstage me. Bud forgot to inquire where I lived or to tell me what time he'd arrive, but somehow he figured it out. Thanks, Cy.

Then, when the movie, *Gone with the Wind,* premiered in our area, the high school permitted students to leave school to view it. That afternoon my dad allowed Bud to drive his car and take me there. Not only was it one of our first dates, that's where I got the idea for Melanie's name.

Although Bud ate, slept, and dreamed athletics, he was also junior class president, he took leads in both junior and senior class plays, he joined the debating team, and he took art and music classes. His energy and commitment levels were astonishing. But the thing that impressed me most was his unfailing courtesy to others, something which would endure all of his life. Years later, I found that after using the bathroom in our own home, he'd polish both the washbowl and the faucets.

I still enjoyed school and tried hard to please my teachers. They rewarded me with an abundance of A's. I participated in debate and speech contests—receiving a bronze medal (third place in the county) in the Prince of Peace contest sponsored by area churches. I earned a Girl Reserve ring and was elected to the National

Honor Society during my tenth grade year. In a countywide math contest, I came out with a first-place ribbon in Algebra I. I earned parts in class plays during my junior and senior years, and as a senior was elected class secretary. (I am still arranging our annual reunion dinners 70 years later!) A unique class for seniors (especially in these days of ACLU) was called Effective Living, taught by our superintendent, who was also a Sunday School teacher. It combined philosophy and psychology, along with practical living principles based on Jesus' Sermon on the Mount.

I graduated from Fairfield High School on May 28, 1940, and entered Miami University that fall. During my freshman year I lived with Aunt Lil (Mother's sister) and Uncle Russell, and watched over my younger cousin, Jim Armstrong. His parents ran a bowling alley and were gone at odd hours. They came home very late and slept through the mornings. Jimmy and I shared a room with twin beds. I prepared his breakfast, and then we both headed off to school. Aunt Lil fixed lunch and supper, and I did the dishes, while she went back to work.

Jimmy and I did our homework, he practiced his tap dancing (he was very good), and then I taught him to type when he was still just a seventh grader. He used that skill his entire life in the Service. I also helped Aunt Lil to clean upstairs and change beds on Saturdays. We had four college boys living up there.

When my tuition bills arrived, my dad borrowed $100 from the bank. That paid for my books and enrollment for one semester. He gradually paid back the loan, and then when second semester came, he borrowed the same $100 again. And so on. When I earned my diploma in 1944, I had no college debt to repay.

Meanwhile, Bud graduated from Fairfield in June, 1941 – a year late because of a first-grade bout with whooping cough. Thus, he was able to complete twelve years of schooling at the same time as his brother, Galen.

As The Depression subsided, World War II began to loom in Europe. The United States tried to stay out of it, although preparations for defense increased opportunities for employment, and that was something welcomed by everyone.

We could not have guessed how soon the War would swallow all of us and put our lives on hold indefinitely.

Part One
1941-1942

*"We are no longer going steady.
There are no strings attached."*

One night in January, 1941, Bud asked if he could kiss me goodnight. I said, "No!" Feeling rejected, he was sorry he'd gotten up the courage to ask. Much later he revealed that he'd kicked himself all the way home.

The next time, he didn't ask.

But in April Bud suddenly informed me, "We are no longer going steady. There are no strings attached." I was encouraged to date other boys. He had me completely mixed up. Although I understood, sort of, that with years of college still ahead of us, his practical nature would not allow him to tie either of us down. My heart was broken.

One hot tear rolled down my cheek and touched his. Bud said not one word that night as I kissed him goodbye.

I saw nothing of him that entire summer. He worked the night shift at Champion Paper, then played baseball, golf and tennis and went bowling during the day. In September he left for Wake Forest College on a football-basketball-baseball scholarship, with a bus ticket in one hand and a single suitcase in the other.

Wake Forest was an all-boys' school in North Carolina. Bud worked in the cafeteria for his meals, and the manager, Miss Jo, asked him to drive her to the market three times a week. All of this, plus football practice and a heavy academic schedule made good grades impossible. He was just too tired to study.

He did write occasionally. In September: "Absence makes the heart grow fonder," and "Distance lends enchantment." Then: "I can't wait to come home for Christmas. Whoa, who said that? Me??"

I figured he was just homesick.

November, 1941

My complimentary close "As ever" means that I am playing it safe and not committing myself to any falsehoods with a complimentary close of "love."

Have you ever read about Martin Luther's feeling that his inner soul was not satisfied even when he was involved in the Protestant Reformation? That's the way I feel sometimes – as if I am never satisfied.

In December Bud hitchhiked home for Christmas.

December, 1941

Seeing you will be all the Christmas present I'll need.

It was a memorable holiday, but he confused me only more.

February, 1942

I might have to leave school. I like you better than any girl I ever knew. But I am completely lost. I can't figure myself out. My future is very uncertain, and I am too mentally weak to make up my own mind. I might be afraid to step out into the chilly bleakness of this old world.

I received no further mail until April.

April, 1942

I am mentally unable to explain why I have not written.

Once when he came to see me, my dad teased him by pointing his shotgun and ordering him out of the car! It scared Bud to death, but I knew Daddy was only kidding. What a poor joke!

Bud's drawing. Daddy with a shot gun. —Wake Forest

Patriotism had run high ever since Pearl Harbor. I remembered very well the morning of December 8, 1941. As a sophomore, I was no longer living with relatives; I was commuting to Oxford with my friend Woots and four other girls. We were parked on Spring Street, eating our home-packed frozen lunches, when Thad Powell, a boy from Riley, pulled up alongside our car. He had turned on his radio, and we listened as President Roosevelt announced the previous day's bombing and our entry into the war.

Many young men immediately enlisted, and even inspired faculty members to do the same. Our high school basketball coach, Mr. Needles, joined the Navy, and my typing teacher, Susan Marsch, joined the WAVES.

A memorial platoon was organized to honor Buzz Petzold, a Marine who had been killed on an air training mission in California. On October 3, 1942, Bud, his brother Bill, and many other boys from our high school joined the United

States Marine Corps. When Bud left for South Carolina right after the swearing-in ceremony on the steps of our downtown Memorial Monument, his best friend Leiser made me promise not to cry.

I didn't even go to the train station to see him off.

Bud's drawing. Pearl Harbor. —Wake Forest

October 9, 1942

We are headed for Parris Island where we shall get haircuts, shots, and an introduction to the Marine Corps.

October 18, 1942

I am still looking for a letter from you. The typhoid fever shot has made me very ill. I heard a good statement the other day – it applies to America and to friendships: "To live in harmony we must push aside our differences and think only of the things we have in common." Write soon.

I supposed Bud was lonesome, for he wrote often and even drew pictures of the boys marching, washing their clothes, soaking their tired feet, and awakening to a bugle.

October 27, 1942

Blues are the dress uniforms worn by Marines. Boot camp is that part of a person's training that changes him from a civilian to a fighting machine. You'll

have to figure *semper fidelis* out for yourself. In 12 days we shall go to the rifle range in New Bern, NC.

November 4, 1942

Our instructors have a job to do, and they do it. On the battlefield the response to orders must be a reflex – responding without thinking. "It is not ours to question or to reason why; it is only ours to do or die."

We received our dog tags and must wear them 24 hours a day. I was one of the 15 out of 31 who qualified with the bayonet the first time. My pay is $34 per month.

November 21, 1942

The rifle is the basic weapon of the Marines. Thanks to you and your mother for the delicious cookies and fudge. The fellows are begging for your address so they can receive some too. Your birthday will be coming soon – congratulations on the 20 successful years behind you. We are living in tents.

Please write soon; I would rather read your letters than those of anyone else.

November 30, 1942

I am now in the Aviation Engineering Squadron, Cherry Point, NC and am waiting to be sent to school. Why have you stopped writing to me? I made expert on the rifle range – only three of us made it; I shall have $5 added to my monthly pay.

Please explain – why do I think of you so much?

The Platoon broke up today; it was worse than leaving the train station for P.I. I could hardly say goodbye to them; we had been like brothers. There were many tears in our eyes.

I miss you more than ever. Taps – lights out.

December 2, 1942

I have been chosen to go to school, and I have the following choices: photography, aerology, sheet metal, aviation machinist mate, motor transport, yeoman mate, or radio. I think I shall choose aviation machinist mate. I want to learn something that will be valuable in civilian life.

December 7, 1942

The aviation machinist mate school is in Jacksonville, FL My grades on the P.I. tests have determined that I shall go to school and not into combat. I am just one step closer to my life-long ambition – to fly an airplane.

Do you know Bill McDulin?

December 10, 1942

What would you like for Christmas?

This is what my medals look like.

December 14, 1942

I will miss you at Christmastime – you, your tree, and your living room couch.

Yesterday we had a sham battle in a strange woods, and after a futile effort to break through the enemy lines, I was captured. I was happy to have advanced farther than any other man in my squad.

Do you remember what I told you about the movie, *Wake Island?* A man can get an awful lot of comfort recalling sweet memories.

December 17, 1942

I am having classes in small arms firing and chemical warfare – .45 cal. pistol, .45 Reising machine gun, and M-I rifle. In the evenings we study jujitsu – I'll take them on bare-handed now.

December 18, 1942

I think it would be better for you to have a full degree and a teaching permit. I can give you no sound advice.

Bill McDulin is here, and his wife, Millie, will join him soon. I have acquired no bad habits: I don't like cigarettes, liquor, cursing, or cabbage – so I don't eat cabbage! The Marine Corps takes boys and turns them into men, but I refuse to succumb to their philosophies or their metamorphosis. I appreciate your defense of my principles – I do have them, you know.

December 19, 1942

I went Christmas shopping today. I didn't find what I really wanted. I bought a pretty compact for you.

Part Two
1943-1944

"We are fighting for something bigger than you and me."

During my second year at Miami, I realized I wanted to become a business education teacher. I figured that if I didn't like teaching, I could always be a secretary, since I'd already been both. At that time not many professions were open to girls.

I worked for Mr. C.T. Jenkins and Joseph Fichter – an NYA job which paid 25 cents per hour. Later, as a senior, I also worked for Dr. McConnell, a professor who was writing geography books for elementary students. When he was out of town, I taught his classes – a group of V-12 Navy boys. Mr. Fichter taught freshman English; I subbed for him often and graded papers in addition to the secretarial work. Mr. Jenkins would sometimes ask me to escort prospective students and their parents around campus. I knew every building and its specialty – not so today; it's too big, and I'd get lost. These jobs provided money for incidentals.

I was pursuing a double major in business education and English, and a minor in social studies. I received all A's and B's, except for a C in sociology my senior year. I was glad for the C, for I told the teacher that if I went to student teaching as unprepared as he, I'd flunk! (Obviously, I was no longer the most timid in my class.)

In order to have enough money to stay in the dorm my senior year, I worked 93 days consecutively – at Herring-Hall Safe Company on Grand Boulevard at Erie Highway 5 1/2 days a week, and as a waitress at LeSourdsville Lake dining hall on Middletown Pike on Sundays.

My work at Herring-Hall was most interesting. Before being hired I was given an IQ test. At Miami I had just completed a course in Tests and Measurements, so when I saw the IQ test I noticed that it was identical to one we had been studying! I didn't even need to look at the directions, and all of the answers jumped out at me. A secretary graded my paper while I waited outside her office. There was quite a stir inside as she called her boss and others to look at my paper. I'd like to know now what my IQ was; for many decades students themselves were never told. Nevertheless, I got the job, and I kept my mouth shut concerning the test.

At that time, although I didn't know it, we were processing a component for the Atomic Bomb. My boss was Harvey Henkle; representatives from DuPont (an American chemical company founded in 1802) would arrive to confer with him. I was not permitted to let them in unless the letter they gave me was an exact duplicate of one that I retrieved from our files. I was fingerprinted and sworn to secrecy, but at that time I had no notion of what the secret was.

Another of my duties was to type the bill of lading for the material secretly processed upstairs while an armored Brink's truck waited in the alley. I had to type the height, width, and depth of these brick-like objects along with their weight. It did seem to me that these "bricks" were exceptionally heavy. A shipment went out every day. Only special employees were permitted upstairs; not me – I stayed in the office. We were no longer manufacturing safes; white medicine cabinets for hospital ships filled the manufacturing area.

After the War ended, employees were informed of what was really going on and even received awards for their work. I was back at Miami by then, so I received no award.

My senior year at Miami was delightful. I had a wonderful roommate, Martha Wagoner Hogg, now of Dayton, with whom I still correspond or visit several times a year. Dining at North Hall (now called Hamilton Hall in honor of our Dean of Women) was very formal. We made friends with Winnie, the head cook, and often he had something special for us.

I student taught in Typing I and English II – nine weeks each. Still, there was plenty of time for new friends and good times. We had open house at the dorm on weekends. All of the boys on campus were in the military – marching from class to class – but I wasn't much interested in any of *them.* My Marine caused quite a stir in the lobby as he waited for me in his dress blues. I had been to New Bern and Morehead City, North Carolina, just before school began that fall, so we knew that this was more than friendship. I was "verbally engaged" (Bud's words) after visiting him in Morehead City on September 6, 1943. It seemed that half the girls in the dorm were already flashing diamond rings and making plans.

My parents were butchering when I arrived home for Christmas vacation. As luck would have it, the weather turned very warm – into the 70s. The beef could not remain hanging in the barn for an extended time. We had no freezer; Mother canned the beef in large two-quart jars using her big pressure cooker. I was handed a big knife and a butchering guide booklet, and Daddy placed one-fourth of a beef on the kitchen table. I became an instant butcher – never before or since. As I cut the roasts and boned the steaks, Mother canned it all. They knew I could read, but what a bloody mess I made of that knife and booklet. I don't remember how many days we spent at this task, but somehow we did it.

As Christmas Eve approached, we planned to go to church, but Bob was ill, so I volunteered to stay home with him. We discovered later that he had scarlet fever – Mother contracted it, and so did I. My sister Ruth wrote to Bud explaining that no mail was to go from our house for a month.

An old family doctor came from Ross with a little black bag from which he took a couple of bottles of medicine. He mixed this with water, and that was our prescription. I missed a whole month of school, all my final exams, and the beginning of my last semester.

Bud telephoned me from Jacksonville, where he was wing leader. On January 8, he turned 21.

January 8, 1943

My chances of going to flying school are better than they have ever been.

One can never tell what future complications, if any, might arise to change the possible or even inevitable facts. The future is so uncertain that memories are the only sure and positive things that bring the satisfaction of having had or known happy and successful plans. I say plans, because everything is governed by a set pattern, either artificially or naturally. Just a little more of my philosophy – take it or leave it, as you please.

Memories are the past, present, and future for many men; it is all they have. I would even go so far as to say that memories are the motivating force for many adventures, whether their aims are worthy or unworthy. Revenge is often the active motive produced by memories. There are other motives which are put into action by memories – hate, love, sadness, pity.

January 13, 1943

I have 60 men to supervise as we go from class to class on time, for 12 hours a day. I dreamed that I saw your pretty blue eyes and that I held your soft hands (sigh). Good night, keep bright, and God bless you.

As ever (?),

Bud.

January 15, 1943

Our schedule begins with a bugle at 6:30 am. After classes and chow, we have to clean the barracks and attend classes until 12:30. From 2 to 5 there are more classes, chow, and at 6 pm more classes until 10 pm. Taps – 10:30. Every day is packed full – no time for ourselves.

January 18, 1943

The weekend – we went swimming at Jacksonville Beach. I have always wanted to swim in the Atlantic!

We won the Navy E yesterday for having the cleanest barracks in our area. It had made me very nervous to have been in charge of the cleanup, but I felt good when I saw the E flag in the front of our barracks!

January 19, 1943

I am now going to school eight hours a day and working eight hours a day – I am learning a lot. I am getting good grades – a 93% average so far.

January 25, 1943

Wars are not won peacefully, but there can be a truce of peace after the eventual end. We are fighting for something bigger than you and me.

February 6, 1943

I have been on the early shift – 4:30 am until 8:30 pm. I find that I know a great deal more about our Navy planes than I thought I did. I know them all – their characteristics, identification points, and their identification letters.

February 22, 1943

We have just completed a three-hour test over landing gears, C02, sanitation, first aid, etc. My head hurts!

Congratulations on your high semester grades! We in AMM School have yet to receive a furlough, although many others from the Petzold Platoon have.

I am learning how to handle these 60 men as individuals. Some want to take advantage of my good nature, and then I must be more military.

Thanks for all the letters you sent when you did not receive any from me.

Bud won a blue ribbon for a boxing championship. The Marines invaded St. Augustine – McDulin, McKnight, McGee, McCollum, Woedl, and Soapy Waters from Massachusetts.

March 8, 1943

I thought about how nice it would be if you could see everything I am seeing. It was nice to get letters from you daily.

March 12, 1943

I am receiving your gift of the *Reader's Digest* regularly. It is most interesting.

March 20, 1943

Right now my average in Engine Theory is 86%, but I hope to bring it up.

April 1, 1943

I have been studying even harder to bring up my average – it was 91% last week and 92% this week.

Thanks for the cookies and the dates.

April 7, 1943

I remember Christmas, 1941.

When I came home from Wake Forest College, I knocked on your door, and it opened. You let out a shriek and ran upstairs. Then you came back down after changing your clothes and fixing your hair – you were very surprised to see me. I was unpredictable! Pardon me while I laugh. I am just enjoying the memory.

April 21, 1943

We had another two-hour test over ignition, lubrication, and propeller. There are 3,000 parts in a propeller alone.

April 28, 1943

Thanks for the delicious box of goodies.

As ever,

Bud.

P.S. You're sweet.

May 25, 1943

Good luck on your semester exams. I have two more weeks of this school. It is hard to remember how long it has been since I was at home.

May 26, 1943

I applied for N.A.P. and have passed the flight physical. Will the board approve my application?

Even when I do not write, I am still thinking of you.

May 28, 1943

I think I love you, but I am not positive; I am trying to figure me out. Thanks for a beautiful letter.

PART OF ME

Part of me loves you,
Yet somewhere about
My heart, is a feeling
Of troublesome doubt.
Part of me wonders, I want to be fair...
How much I would miss you
If you were not there.
So I'm waiting to give
My answer to you,
Until I am sure
With the other part, too.

I do believe that it is the civilian populace who needs a lesson in morale. Throughout history many wars have been lost because civilians could not take it. This is probably the Germans' weak point. The English credit their success in this conflict, so far, to the determination and will of the people to carry on, no matter what the cost. Probably the only army not in this war morally is the Italian army.

It is not always the outward signs or expressions which portray the true feelings which lie within a man. Words are not designed to express or show real feelings. Were this so, a man or woman would merely say, "I am crying," or "I am laughing," and this would suffice. Emotions are not spoken – they are portrayed. Words are merely a means of helping the other person to understand.

All of this may sound silly to you, but it is a direct response to your last letter. In case you haven't guessed my point already, I shall be a little more explicit. I haven't written these words merely for protection, but to let you know what and how I feel – it is beyond my literary and mental ability to put it on paper. Only now do I realize how impossible it would be.

Last night I was lying on my bunk trying to figure myself out in relation to you. Because you are such a grand girl, and because you are so nice, and because I like you so very, very much, I wondered if I were worthy of such a grand person. Is that taking too much for granted? I could make everything so

simple if only I would say, "Dorothea, I love you." I believe I do, but then I'm not positive. My confounded mind has to have a complete solution – just like adding and subtracting to get one and only one answer. I am looking for that answer. It doesn't seem fair that this should be true in this one area of my life. It isn't true in regard to my athletic side, occupational side, or adventurous side.

Bud and Bill McDulin both advanced to the rank of Corporal.

June 3, 1943

One question the board asked me was, "Do you know where the Cat & Fiddle are?" I said, "Yes, Sir, but I have never been there," and as an afterthought I added, "My girlfriend doesn't approve of such places." They roared! The next question asked about the essential qualities which make up a good fighter pilot.

I am very happy and wish you were here, because then everything would be perfect – all of this is too much good luck for one person.

I'm glad you received such good grades, and I hope you like working at Herring-Hall's this summer.

June 6, 1943

I'll try to do my part to make your long wait for flight school pass more quickly. You say you feel like a "slacker." If some of the people around here felt the same way, maybe the War wouldn't last so long! Our servicemen are risking their necks for a bunch of people back here who aren't worth it! So many in the plants are just loafing.

You aren't the only one disgusted with the government – everything government does is time-consuming and uneconomical. Perhaps by the time you finish school the War will be over, and you will be most fortunate. So many girls have already lost boyfriends – I feel selfish, wishing you will never have to see active duty! When the peace comes, would you rather have the honor of serving actively and being dead??? In Shakespeare's *King Henry IV*, Jack Falstaff speaks on this very subject.

Woots and Bob will be married in Florida. She begged me to go with her to witness the marriage ceremony. No, thanks. I wouldn't like to be married away from all our friends and family.

In your letter you say that you wished I had gone to the station when the platoon left for the Marine Corps. I didn't go, because I thought you did not want me to.

Yes, Bud, you really surprised me with this letter. You said so many nice things that I never knew were true – it's hard to believe. I thought that you just didn't like me very much. You certainly gave me that impression. Now, my question: "I didn't want you to know I cared too much about you. I don't know why (yes, I do too), but I still feel that way." I want the answer for the "Yes, I do too" part.

I hope all our wishes come true – you hold the wand.
As ever,
Dorothea.

A letter from Bill McDulin arrived concerning me and Bud. It was signed: "My regards and Bud's love. Millie's husband, Bill."

June 10, 1943

I am becoming more and more interested in my mail. Your last two letters were the most delightful and nicest I have ever received. I enjoyed them immensely; I don't deserve all the nice things you said about me. I remember our walk along the river – the smell of honeysuckle and roses.

June 12, 1943

Say, did I ever tell what it is about you that makes me like you so? Maybe I was afraid to tell you all the nice things I was thinking about you. I think you are the most considerate, patient, most understanding (of me) and certainly one of the most likable persons one would ever want to know. I am proud to say to someone, "She is my girlfriend."

June 18, 1943

We are anxiously awaiting word from D.C. on our transfer to flight school. Last night I dreamed that you kissed me.

June 24, 1943

I am sitting beneath a Ping Pong table. I have been trying for a week to write you a letter, but I tear up each one as fast as I write it. I'll try another letter this afternoon.

Our barracks won the E flag again. I'm tired of lying around here waiting and doing nothing.

Bill calls me a jellyfish because I never make a positive statement concerning you and me. If I ever do, it will be to you and no one else! I don't think anyone but me knows exactly how I feel about you. You're sweet, and I adore you immensely. I'm sure I'll tell you someday, and I'm biding my time.

June 25, 1943

I leave for Cherry Point on Tuesday.

Until now Bud had not saved my letters. But now he began storing them, remarking, "My life began on June 25, 1943."

June 25, 1943

I have just finished a long letter to Bill. He thought it was strange that you would be writing to me about events created by God and man. You never sent it, but I know I would have enjoyed reading it. I've written to Bill trying to explain you to him. Maybe I told him too much, but I think he knows and likes you quite a bit. You may read it if you like.

I told Bill that I really enjoy those philosophical letters – to me they are you, as near as I can get with you a thousand miles away! We are together in spirit and in what we believe and think. After writing all this to Bill, I feel as close to you as if you were right here beside me in the porch swing, talking, looking at the flowers, the blue sky, and listening to the birds. There's a bluebird in the garden right now.

I said that that's why I like you – because of what you think about all those different things. But I added that he was wrong to think I'd laugh at your love letters – I wouldn't, unless you wrote impossibly silly things like Gay does.

It is loads of fun to remember – Woots' party, Coney Island with Osc, the picnic at Sharon Woods, the party at Camp Gard, the Negro dance we almost attended in Oxford, and the parties at the Needles home after the tournament games. I remember the fun we had with Osc and Pat, and the limburger cheese Bob Boies put on Bill Weiss' car. I cherish this gold basketball I am wearing – you played so hard, and I yelled my lungs out. How proud I was of you when you pitched those "no hitter" games (even the one we lost).

There's not much to remember about 1941 – but an anniversary is coming up. Did we really settle anything that day? We were no longer "going steady." Yes, I'm asking you.

I treated you very mean after that. I wish right now that I could just say, "Hi, Bud." But then I would hardly speak to you. That was the day you told me you were joining the Marines. I thought that if you wanted to get your head knocked off by joining such a dangerous outfit, then go ahead! I didn't care! But now, it seems that everything always works out for the best.

July 2, 1943

Our train ride from Jacksonville was dirty and monotonous. I may be here from one to six months waiting for pre-flight training while others are over there fighting. I feel as though I am a slacker, but I can do nothing about it.

I enjoyed your last letter immensely, thank you. I wish you could come down, but oh, well, what's the use of talking about it?

July 3, 1943

Did I ever tell you how wonderful you are? No, I don't guess I have. The truth of the matter is that I always thought nice things about you, but I don't believe I had the *backbone* to tell you. No, that's not the real reason. I think I never told you because I didn't want you to know I cared too much about you. I don't know why (yes, I do, too) but I'm afraid I still feel that way. You're sweet, understanding, and you never let me down. I can't think of any time that you have disappointed me in any capacity. You, I know, have been disappointed by many of my curious actions, and I'm sorry. You don't know how much I wanted

you to come to the station the day I left for the Marine Corps. It was an "awful" lot, even though I told you differently.

July 7, 1943

Today finds me a little more adapted to this new life. I miss the vigorous life I have always led. Aviation is a place for skilled men with dexterous hands and keen, imaginative minds. I may not be quick-witted enough for aviation. I do have one thing in my favor – natural senses which act cooperatively with my physical makeup (muscles). My biggest conflicts come from the combination of natural and created impulses. Your one guess is right. I am trying to find out more and more about me!

Say, did you ever stop to think how little I have seen you since September 5, 1941? I know you have remembered.

Today I was passenger on a bomber type that Doolittle used to bomb Tokyo.

Bud's drawing. You, me, car, home.

July 7, 1943

Your letter leaves me even more confused. I thought the answer to your "curious actions" was in the fact that you just didn't want to be bothered with such a silly thing as a girlfriend. That explanation made it very simple. But now you have me all confused. I still can't figure out why you gave me one impression when you really felt differently?? Maybe it's just because you've been away so long, that you tell me now. Please, Corporal McCollum, help me to be *unconfused!*

July 10, 1943

I like your drawings – you really do remember. Could you give me a clue concerning this guessing game of yours? "My biggest conflicts come from the combination of natural and created impulses." What one guess? I have no clue or guess. I need more clues!

I haven't thought about how little we've been together since 1941 for quite a while – that's been two years – a long time. You were away at college all winter, you worked nights at Hall's all summer, and then you joined the Marines.

July 9, 1943

You write that Woots and Bob are about to be married. It is all right, but I think there are many things working against it. Marriage is an uncertain proposition with the world as it is now.

You do not seem to understand that a man does not like to feel that someone else is doing his part while he stays over here in comparable comfort, always taking and never giving. We are going through a mental struggle with ourselves. In some instances cowardice creeps into the picture. Wars are not won on good intentions.

Bud remembered the day he said we would no longer "go steady." But now it was 1943, and he admitted that it was just an act, for now he confessed that when I kissed him goodbye, and one of my hot tears touched his check, he knew he loved me!! (Two years later, and NOW he tells me!)

July 12, 1943

I agree with your comments concerning Woots and Bob. Being married during a war is no time to try to make all the adjustments which marriage demands. When this War is over, the divorce courts will do a thriving business!

If the public had thoughts like yours about serving instead of getting and always taking, there might not even be a war in the first place. You have such high ideals – I know you are right. I am just selfish, wanting you to come back unhurt.

Just this spring I felt that I never wanted to tell the truth again. In my psychology class we were supposed to work 15 hours outside of class in the lab. No one did – I put in ten hours. When Dr. Guiler called each student to his office, they all said they had put in 15 hours. Some had two hours; others had none.

But at the dorm the girls said I was a "sap" for telling the truth. They made me angry.

The next day I went to Dr. Guiler and told him the whole story. I asked him if it had paid to tell the truth. When we finished talking, I was sure that it did, and I received an A in the course. Before the conversation ended, Dr. Guiler asked me to work as his assistant next year. But since I was already helping three other professors, I had to decline.

I know that your attitude was the only noble one, but I can't help being selfish and feeling glad you are waiting for school and are not in the middle of action.

July 14, 1943

The best part of my life is passing, and I can only wait. I am around the best planes in the world, and I am beginning to enjoy it. I should be getting a vocation and making plans to earn a living.

As I write this letter I am remembering all the little things which stimulate my memories and change my enjoyment from a passive to an active feeling.

Now it has been nine months, 11 1/2 days since I had the pleasure of seeing you, sigh, sigh! Furloughs are as scarce as wells on the Sahara Desert.

July 15, 1943

Of course, I remember everything about your house and yard – the cherry tree, the pump, the elm tree, and porch swing – and YOU. I remember the night before I left for Wake Forest College. I went to a party and then telephoned you at midnight. Believe me, that was one of the best decisions I ever made, except that it was to be 4 1/2 months before I would see you again.

July 16, 1943

***I have liked you since our very first date.* I would never tell a girl I loved her until I overcame the obstacles in my mind and reached my goal. *I believe I am in love with you,* but what a funny feeling.**

July 19, 1943

I am writing to a very sweet girl. I will end this letter with very pleasant thoughts of you.

I remember "Indian Summer."

July 19, 1943

Yes, I do remember the night before you left for Wake Forest. I never did figure out why you changed your mind, phoned me, and came down. Bud, you only confused me more than in 1941.

I don't know what to say about what you've told me about how you feel and have felt, except that it is very hard to believe – but I do believe you, because you tell me it's true. Your plan certainly worked, but now I am very surprised. There is so much I cannot understand. It seems to me it must have been very difficult for you to pretend and act as you did if you really did like me. I want to see you – I have a million questions!

What if I had followed the advice of many others, dated other boys, and forgotten about you? Why, I might have been married by now. Half a dozen boys with whom I refused dates are already married; one is married and divorced. Mother, Woots, and others said I was "crazy." What would you have thought of your little scheme if I had done as I should? But then, you never kissed my Mother or Woots or any of the others – only me. Your kisses betrayed your words. Your kisses said, "I love you" and caused my total confusion!

July 20, 1943

I just had to sit down and write to you because I have the queerest feeling I have ever had in my whole life. To tell you the truth, I believe you are the cause of my feeling. Bill and I took a long walk in the rain. We talked about feelings – never before have I expressed myself so completely as I have to Bill. Do you remember the times you used to ask me why I kissed you, and I would either keep quiet or say "I don't know"? I have asked myself the same thing, and up until a week ago I had no answer to what the reason might be. Not too long ago I wrote to you about the conflict with my sense of reasoning and my natural reactions. I could never answer, because my mind was fighting what I was actually feeling.

Once again, I believe my natural sense led my impulses onto the correct path. You will probably say, "How do you know all this? After being away from me for so long, you're just lonesome." Yes, I am lonesome – but only for *you*. Should you and I ever quit going together, I don't believe I would ever go with any other girls. Now more than ever, I feel that way.

I went to bed thinking of you, and I awoke still thinking of you. My stomach is full of butterflies, and I don't eat all my meals. Do you know what this might suggest? Well, I do. I am waiting for you to tell me!

Love (as ever),

Bud.

July 21, 1943

I feel (almost) as if every evening when I'm writing we are together. I'm out in the yard – just you, me, and a beautiful sunset. It is all red and pink, blue, purple, lavender, and white. Now the sky is a beautiful blue with ten big golden-pink streaks across it. Now a star is shining through. Let's make a wish: "Star light, star bright, first star I see tonight. I wish I may, I wish I might, have the wish I wish tonight!" It's needless to wish you were here; my wish is that you get to do all the things you've wanted – flying. Now what is your wish for me? The star is very bright now – don't forget to make that wish.

July 22, 1943

I look forward to this time of day when I can sit down and say something to you. I would rather tell you myself – things like, "You're sweet," or maybe, "The way I feel right now, I could hold you in my arms forever, Dorothea." You are the best ever; I am just remembering.

My first plane is a Curtis Commando – C-46. It has a top speed of 250 miles per hour and carries 1400 gallons of gasoline.

You have been working seven days a week all summer – this will be an

expensive year for you at Miami. If you ever need any financial help, I would be glad to help you, if I can. I want you to be able to do your very best your senior year. Don't you worry about money.

July 23, 1943

You thought I never wanted to see you. Oh, if you only knew how much I really wanted to see you. Remember how I used to tell you about those walks I used to take by myself down in Jacksonville? Every one of those walks was for the sole purpose of remembering you. I went by myself, because I did not want my thoughts to be interrupted, and I could pretend you were with me. One night I sat until 2:30, recalling all the memories about you that I hold dear to me. Please don't ever feel that I don't want to see you. More than anyone else, *you* are the one I would like to see. I can't stress my points enough, because I know you are wondering about me. Tell me something – do you think I was pretending when I kissed you? That was part of my feelings which I could not hide nor even cover up by acting.

I tried to tell Leiser how I felt, but he accused me of trying to be noble; so I never told anyone until a time when I could tell you. I am NOT fooling now!

If I could see you, I could tell you in no uncertain terms that I am serious and not fooling. Remember the time I told you to date other fellows? I didn't mean it, and I have thanked God more than once that I was still your boyfriend. Lucky me – I could kiss you and kiss you for staying as you did!

Was I being fair? NO. My apologies could never suffice for the hurt which I have caused you. To me, that was the greatest injustice – can you ever forgive me? I will say that I suffered from my own acts, but I felt I had no right to express my true feelings. A fellow can't be justly condemned for what he *believes* to be right. Goodnight, dear.

Love,

Bud.

P.S. When are you planning to quit work?

July 23, 1943

Bud, I'm not laughing at you; I'm smiling, because your letter makes me happy. I never intended to make anyone have butterflies in his stomach, and I can't imagine you not eating all your food. I didn't do anything, so don't blame me! And you expect me to tell you which or what might be wrong? It's very simple – I believe you really are in love with me. If you're waiting for me to tell you what's wrong, consider yourself told!

I never thought you would care about me any more than you pretended, and I was resigned to make the best of the situation. I couldn't imagine that Bud McCollum would ever let any girl interfere with any part of his life. I seem to be coming out of a fog – I always knew something was not just right. I was very confused! I knew you were not the type of boy who would act as if he liked me if he really didn't. I had that feeling somewhere inside me. I could never have let you kiss me without that inner feeling I had about you. Your sweet, soft kiss betrayed you.

With all my love,

Dorothea.

July 23, 1943

Yesterday I had read to me a letter that was beautifully written – written in such a manner and with so much thought that I could not help but admire the person who had sent it. Four times Bill read it to me. I knew that you knew me so well, but never did I expect to be discussed in such glowing terms. It represents your loyalty to me, and I devotedly thank you. It aroused in me feelings which I do not have the words to express and memories that I shall *never* forget. Only once can I recall an instance comparable.

Remember that afternoon we had taken a long ride in Galen's car – you thrilled me with your ability to say what you were thinking. So superbly sound was your thought that I could do nothing but sit there and admire you in my own *jellyfish* way.

When we stopped by the river, we were talking, and later you began to cry. When we first started dating, I told you I hated to see women cry, too. When you kissed me, I knew from that moment what love really is. It took hot sweet tears, nice lips, and beautiful and exacting words to tell me the truth. Just thinking about that day, I have a sensation which is indescribable – of falling through space, always groping, always reaching for something to hold on to. That day I found it, but I grasped it with only one hand – I'm still trying to reach it with my other hand. Your inspiring force is all that has given me the strength to hold on until such a time that my hold on life is secure.

To me, life is *you*. Our feelings are our inward expression of life and since life is a mystery, maybe that is the answer to my inability to sometimes express my feelings.

Yes, I have thought and thought, day and night, and have continually debated the issue – not the issue of my feelings toward you – that was settled in 1941. I have used the laws of comparison, laws of reason, and the laws of common sense and feeling. Lately I find myself thinking of feeling as the controlling force.

July 26, 1943

Bud, you tell me things that I never knew – I never guessed how you really felt when we took that ride in Gay's car and had that long talk. I thought you didn't have the nerve to tell me that you disliked me and didn't want to be bothered by me again. Now you tell me the truth – I thought we were being truthful to each other that day. You just kept quiet, and this made me think you were so disgusted with me you wouldn't talk! The day we decided to quit going together is the day you were sure you loved me. It doesn't make sense.

Since you've been gone I've felt somehow that you really did like me, but I didn't believe it for fear of disappointing myself.

No, Bud, I didn't think you were pretending whenever you kissed me. I was angry with myself for being such a fool, but somehow inside I knew you would not make a fool of me.

It's hard to believe all you write, but I know it is the truth. I'll feel that way until I see you and hear you tell me again what you have written.

I don't know how long I'll be working – maybe until school starts, or whenever I want to quit. Thanks for the offer of money for school – I'll be just fine. I'll be working for my geography professor in addition to the other two.

I should be very happy, but I don't feel as happy as I imagined I would whenever you decided to tell me how you felt – truthfully. I thought I'd be walking on air with butterflies, but I think I'm too busy for that. I'm happy, but I'm too tired to look happy or enjoy all the nice things you write me every day. Oh, I enjoy what you tell me, but I get so busy working that I forget to remember.

Goodnight, with a kiss on every wave (during a storm at sea).

Love, as ever,

Dorothea.

July 26, 1943

Bill is a great friend – he played an important part in making me realize the importance of happiness. You have helped me more than you know, and you were very sweet in doing it.

Today the memo from Washington, D.C. came approving me for N.A.P.

Love,

Bud.

July 26, 1943

They just played "You'll Never Know" on a Victrola here at the Morehead City USO. Dorothea, I would like very much to see you, and if it is the pecuniary angle that is holding you back, I think that something could be arranged.

July 26, 1943

I just remembered how angry you were when we were on a school bus, and I got your hair wet! I think you despised me that day; you were not at all attracted to me. Do you remember when you first began to like me?

July 27, 1943

You seem surprised that I would remember little things – sweet memories mean a lot to men in the Service. There are little sweet memories

like your dad coming out with his shotgun, ordering me out of the car, your saying, "Brownie, be quiet," or "Bud, you'd better go home," and all I would do was say, "Uh huh," but never move. I could have passed the rest of my life sitting with you on the porch swing or on the living room couch. Dorothea, once you asked me, "How would you act if you *really* loved a girl?" The answer: "Just as I acted then, because what I felt inside of me was exactly what I did not want you to know." I worried more about hurting you than you will ever know.

I saw Charles Lindbergh today; he flew in a new model F40, and we refueled it. Major Smith will test-hop the plane. Lindbergh shot down 19 Jap zeros! Lindbergh is only 38, but he looks old and tired. We were with him for about an hour – a very nice man.

How nice it is to know someone as well as we know each other. Our understanding is mutual, our love everlasting, and our hopes and prayers are one and the same.

July 27, 1943

Mother has often told me I shouldn't go with you, because you didn't like me. She said you just weren't interested in girls. Mother always liked you, but she said you are too thoughtless, too inconsiderate, and didn't appreciate me. She didn't want me to force myself on someone who didn't like me. But how could she know? She saw only how you treated me, and you never kissed Mother! That's the difference. Now Mother is wondering why I get so many letters all of a sudden. "Why the change?" she asks. "Someone must have hit him on his head and brought him to his senses."

My parents have always liked you a great deal, and when they see you being yourself without the "act," they shall be very pleased.

July 28, 1943

I think "You'll Never Know" is the prettiest song that has been written for a long time. It is first on the Hit Parade again.

I wonder why it took you so long to be sure of yourself? Yet any problem seems simple once you have the answer. I have often wondered how long it would take you to find the answer – a year, ten years, or when, if ever!

I like working for Mr. Hinkle. If you want me for a private secretary, all the other men in the world can hunt for someone else. So when that "someday" comes, let me know – I shall be very expensive. I have four years of college training in this field.

It is very sweet of you to ask me to come down to see you and to pay my way. If you want me to come down before school starts, I will come.

Bud copied the last verse of the poem, *Invictus.*

July 28, 1943

It matters not how strait the gait,
How charged with punishment the scroll.
I am the master of my fate
I am the captain of my soul.

In high school I was never interested in girls – they had no place in my athletic life. They had no place in my goals to be reached. These things were uppermost in my mind, and I had no time to complicate my ambitions with girls. I never stopped to consider what I would do after I reached my ambitions. I did not care, but one girl changed that – YOU.

Love,

Bud.

July 29, 1943

Yes, I was really angry the day you got my hair wet! But now, I wouldn't care if you soaked me, just as long as you were here. I didn't really like you then, and I don't remember when or why I began to like you. As I got to know you, it just happened gradually and has never stopped. Every day I love you more and more! On January 4, 1941, you asked if you could kiss me, and I said, "NO!" You were so scared and bashful.

July 29, 1943

Now I live from one mail call to the next.

I spent $2 to have my teeth cleaned in town.

I sent you a letter which I had torn up.

August 1, 1943

Will you come down to see me?

August 1, 1943

I prefer to tell you with my own lips.

July 29, 1943

Today the other girls grabbed me, pushed me into the kitchen sink, filled it with cold water, and then put ice down my back. It felt rather good – I was so hot. But only thing – they got my hair wet AND THAT MADE ME MAD!!! Remember?

July 30, 1943

What you tell me seems to be like a key, unlocking the reasons behind many things that once puzzled me, now helping me to see clearly and to understand. I used to think that Bud McCollum would never do anything to hurt or inconvenience himself – Bud came first, and others' feelings didn't matter.

August 1, 1943

POEM – So you won't be confused.

VICTORY

In the vast darkness lit by a light
A scratching pen, guided by thoughts of you,
Moves on to describe a fight
For an old love, born anew.
Few things are now of little consequence to me,
Other than thoughts of a sweet girl I know.
For in all her resplendent reverie,
Radiates personalities ever and ever aglow.

I received an eight-page letter of explanation.

August 4, 1943

In elementary school I did not think I was socially acceptable. I resented girls. I turned to athletics and was accepted as class president, in debate, dramatics, and other school activities. I was voted "Most Likely To Succeed" by my peers in the senior class.

August 7, 1943

A sub shot down a PBY and a blimp. Subs are near the New York coast. This was an emergency situation, and we were called out barefooted in our underwear to tie down the big planes and shove others into the hangar in a dark, cold rain.

August 11, 1943

Mr. Fichter wants me to go to Columbus with him. Now I have butterflies. How can I tell him, "NO"? It is the State Grange Convention.

August 12, 1943

What will we do after the War?

August 12, 1943

I can't eat.

What lies within a man is still isolated from his power to comprehend or solve – the mystery of life.

I have a furlough from September 5 to 14. *Will you come down?*

SLEEP

I'll fall to sleep
With you in my mind and
My love for you in my heart.

August 15, 1943

I am remembering "Indian Summer."

Bud was air sick again.

August 14, 1943

It has been almost a year since we have seen each other. What a year! I shall not send Flit for your butterflies – I'll send me!

August 23, 1943

SEEING YOU

I have just finished a letter
To the girl I love
I know of no way better
To spend my time, as above.
Pardon that last sentence
Yes, I do!
And I say without pretense
It's seeing you.

August 25, 1943

Good, better, best,
Never let it rest
Until your 'good' is 'better,'
And your 'better' is 'best.'

(Not an original; a poem in our grammar books to illustrate degrees of comparison.)

Neither of us could have predicted that years later this little rhyme would become Bud's most often quoted hallmark as a basketball coach!

August 27, 1943

This afternoon I rearranged all your letters beginning with June 25. I could write a book, or rather I should say a good book could be written with the beautiful thoughts that those letters contain.

Dorothea, there are two subjects about which we have never talked – engagement and marriage. We need to discuss these two very delicate subjects!

August 27, 1943

I just returned from a very interesting movie. No force can produce greater results on a person's nature than simple understanding by a simple portrayal of motive whether by words, sight, or material recognition of future developments. Women call it intuition. Great men have risen to great heights on their simple convictions. When we build a stronghold, we should make it simple. All this nonsense – a good retreat from serious thought and for a page and a half, I was very serious.

I am very serious when I say, "I love you." I definitely get my leave.

As I sat here thinking, or trying to think
Of a lyric or two,
My mind was so crowded
With the thought that I love you
I was unable to find
A line or two that suitably rhymed.

All my love,
Bud.

August 27, 1943

I'm back at work, and I just heard your dad's voice out in the hall. He sounds almost like you, but I know it is not you.

August 28, 1943

The plans for my visit to North Carolina are complete. Mother says it would be good if I could stay near Millie in case you couldn't be there at times. She wouldn't worry about me – she has known Bill for a long time. I shall quit working at the end of the month.

August 29, 1943

You wrote that the feeling within your heart is impossible to comprehend or express. That's the way it should be – love is an emotion and as such is portrayed. Don't worry about words. The song, "You'll Never Know" does a good job of explaining:

You'll never know just how much I miss you
You'll never know just how much I care.

And if I tried, I still couldn't hide
My love for you...

When you wrote, "But somewhere about lies a feeling of troublesome doubt," I thought you meant a doubt of your love for me. Now you explain that you really meant a doubt of your worthiness. If there is anyone in the world who is worthy, it is you.

Your dad let me read your brother Bill's letter from the South Pacific. Bill has not been properly informed; he thinks you and he both continue to be uninterested in girls.

August 31, 1943

I know that if I should fail to get through Flight School, it will not have been through a lack of initiative. Many men were just not meant to fly; if I am one of them, even though I shall feel hurt, I shall not be so downhearted as to become as a stagnant pool of water. I'd turn my efforts to another interest.

Once Woots said that if I go across I'll come back, because I just don't care, and I have nothing to come back for – little did she know!

August 31, 1943

I'm really busy at work; I have 150 production orders to prepare for the factory. Mr. Hinkle is still on vacation. I had to call a factory about some drill jigs. I didn't know what I was talking about, but I acted as if I did, and they shall send them. When I told the man I was calling for Mr. Hinkle, the guy said he wished he had a secretary who could take care of his business like that! He didn't know how little I knew about drill jigs!

Even if we don't receive letters every day, we can be sure that we love each other just the same. You want to be sure that I am happy? Just knowing you love me is enough to make me happy – I don't need anything more. Some girls want money and expensive clothes; me, I just want *you.*

I spent a week in Morehead City, North Carolina. Bud paid my bus fare and all expenses. I had a room in the house where Bill and Millie lived. Mrs. Nelson, our landlady, drove us to the beach. I had never seen the ocean before! Beautiful silvery moonlight topped the waves.

We became "verbally engaged" (as Bud's big words put it) on September 6, 1943.

September 13, 1943

As I write this, you are settled on your long bus ride home. I enjoyed every minute of your visit. It is wonderful loving someone as I love you. This past week will occupy a large space in my book of memories.

September 14, 1943

I need not tell you how happy I was to see you, but I'm not in the mood to go back to school and study again. I can think of nothing except our wonderful vacation; we talked about everything and understand each other so completely now.

September 16, 1943

Dorothea, you and I have so much to look forward to that it would be nice to stop our life ten years from now and really live. I miss you, and I love you.

A GOAL FOR WORDS

If words could speak
Or portray the love I feel,
I wager they would strain
Their ambitious goal.
For my love is so great
And words are so small
I doubt that no matter
How hard they would try
They would find an insurmountable wall.

September 17, 1943

I am deeply in love with a very sweet and lovely girl who has light brown hair, blue eyes, and is 20 years old – a senior at Miami!

A NOTE

Even though it may be
Only a line or two,
It contains all
My devoted love for you.
For no matter how flowery
A letter might be,
"I love you dearly,"
Best expresses me!

September 18, 1943

Bud, I love you and thank you again for being so very, very nice and sweet to me when I visited. I wish I were there right now.

I've gone through pay line, bought some books, visited Aunt Lil (she gave us some curtains for our dorm), and met with my critic teacher in typing. Martha and I are ready to go! I met June Yee, a sweet Chinese girl who lives next door. There are so many other nice girls here.

Woots wants to be "smart" and nasty about everything – even your Corporal's rating. I don't tell her a thing about us – no comment. When the sun comes up tomorrow and the earth is still going 'round and 'round, I shall remember your poem and your love.

September 18, 1943

SORROWS

As sure as the sun
Will come up tomorrow
As sure as the earth
Goes 'round and 'round
It is safe to imply
And you can reply,
On your love drowning my sorrow.

September 23, 1943

A GIRL

My mind's a whirl
And my heart's aflame
On account of a girl
Whose love is to blame!

September 25, 1943

Only one thing can surpass our memories – the actual thing before it becomes a memory.

September 25, 1943

Leiser wrote to me today – I enjoyed his "ribbing" me concerning my finally telling you the truth! Then he got serious and tried to tell me, of all persons, ME, what a wonderful girl you are.

EVENTUALLY

Days may seem long,
Weeks slowly creep by,
But it will be like a song
When we again discuss
Castles in the sky.

September 26, 1943

You thanked me for the box of goodies and wished you could say thanks with a kiss. You really did! Last night I dreamed of you and received two kisses. In my dream we discussed plans for after the War, and I felt very close to you.

September 26, 1943

Our dorm hosted the Open House tonight. I danced with some sailors and a couple Marines; I was not rude to any of those swabbies. Not one dances as nicely as you – I kept wishing I were at the USO in Morehead City.

September 27, 1943

IF

If life were but an empty bowl
And I could fill mine as I choose,
I'd need only your love,
Whose limits I cannot tell,
To fill it until it overflows.

September 28, 1943

I like your poems. Someday soon our "castles in the sky" will materialize – be real instead of dreams and plans.

September 28, 1943

You would be dumbfoundedly surprised if you knew how many men are in the Service against their will. They choose to remain in the pacifist shell they have built around themselves. Do they think that war is a game that we choose to play or not to play? Wars are created by men who are going to force their convictions upon us whether we oppose them peaceably or actively. Did Hitler stop at the borders of countries who had not warring ideas against Germany? NO! His ungodly acts showed no consideration whatsoever for those who objectively oppose war.

Hitler used this weak spot to strengthen his position or his theoretic convictions – his disregard for the laws of God only tend to make Hitler a pseudonym for the devil.

The government needs to adopt some method of determining fakes and true believers for those who object to war. Our courts are the nearest representative of justice in the U.S., but even they can be wrong. We, in our day

and age, have to fight for the preservation of our convictions. As free people, we in America should realize this more so than most countries. Our America was built on the sweat and blood of the fight for what we believed to be right, and we won. Now those established freedoms are threatened. It is time we make a few concessions in a few of those freedoms to preserve the many more that the War does not necessarily affect.

Looking down the rows of bunks here at the fellows writing letters as I am doing, playing cards, listening to the radio, and sleeping, I have no doubt that there is not one of them who wouldn't rather see their home and loved ones than the battlefront. They all would rather return to a free and sublime world. I speak not only for myself, but in the Service, men are much freer with their thoughts than they would ordinarily be.

September 30, 1943

APOLOGY IN VERSE

I'm sorry for all the things
I should have said, but didn't
I'm sorry for all the things
I said, but shouldn't.
But worst of all
In my eagerness,
I'm sorry for the thoughts
That brought you unhappiness.

October 2, 1943

A POEM

So with sleep in my eyes
And stringy old hair,
I will end this letter
In an amiable air.

October 3, 1943

THINKING

Do you ever wonder
If Fate will be cruel or kind?
I do, but I know
It would do me no good to mind.
For when She has made up Her mind
What to do,
I hardly think She stops to consider
Two infinite things like me and you.
But in Her mass
Created circumstance
She doesn't singularly try
To sway us from our life stance.

October 5, 1943

LIFE

Life in its inflexible inimitable way
Causes our minds to constantly fluctuate.
For love and kindness and all
Other moods that it may portray,
Are tools of life always
Tearing down, always building
At an unsteady gait.

October 6, 1943

Children are simple and subject to kindnesses and pleasantness. The impressions they gain when they are small are carried with them.

LOVE

We can't destroy
Something we cannot see.
That's why our love
Looks perpetual to me.
By the way that we use it,
In the time that we have,
Certainly should make us
Eternally glad.

I LOVE YOU

I love you
I love you not
Now that's a silly saying
I've heard since I was a tot.
I need no daisy,
As many people do,
To tell you, my dear,
That I love you.

October 7, 1943

It has been a year since we joined the Marine Corps – time for our booster shots. Yes, I am sick again from them. We had tetanus, typhoid, and malaria shots all at the same time. Bill McDulin and I are Sergeants now – we have really earned the new rank.

October 8, 1943

FUNNY?

Isn't it funny
How much pleasure we can get
From a bottle of ink?
Isn't it funny
How we can write

What we partly think?
Isn't it funny
How we can hope and pray
And can write what we would say?

October 10, 1943

I am student teaching in Typing I, carrying 12 semester hours of classes, and working at 25 cents an hour on NYA (National Youth Administration) for Mr. Jenkins and Mr. Fichter. I also work for Dr. McConnell, my geography professor. Yes, I am hurrying from place to place all day long.

October 11, 1943

Today I decided that I do *not* want to teach. I do not want to teach school even for one year. I have the worst critic teacher in the School of Education!! I am more discouraged and disgusted every day. He has taught for three weeks; I have taught for one week. He expects that I should teach them to type; that I should *make* them type. He gave them no foundation, but I can't tell him that that's what is wrong unless I want to "flunk." I felt a little better after I talked to Sis, but I still *never* want to teach school!

October 12, 1943

There is a difference between a woman's love and that of a man – women are more sensitive and therefore require more expressive thoughts of love than men. It doesn't make any difference to me whether you say, "I love you," or not. Just knowing that you love me is all that my inner self requires – just feeling your love is all that is required.

BIRDS AND BEES

Do you ever listen
To the birds in the trees?
Do you ever notice
The musical buzz of bumblebees?
How do they compare
With the sting of Cupid's dart?
They harmonize with the
Song of my heart.

October 15, 1943

Don't worry about your critic teacher; your students are the best judge of your work. If they like you, they will try hard to do good work. It matters not

what your critic teacher doesn't say; success depends on what you accomplish. I know you are doing good work; I can tell from your letters.

YOU CAN DO IT

Do you stop when you come to a hill?
No, I doubt if you ever will.
And we have to go up
Before we begin our downs.
So don't hesitate or change your mind
When you come to that inevitable grind.
For you can do it!

October 19, 1943

I know this will not fit in with your teaching schedule, but I have a furlough for ten days beginning November 4. It complicates things for my sister, Mart, also, but we have to take it when we can get it.

I got air sick again, and this has me worried. I am disgusted with myself – I want to get out of here and start school. If I am not to make it, I want to know before too many more days.

FATHER TIME

To me it is not the years that are long,
It's the days that go slowly by.
They carry with them
All things good and wrong.
And these are the memories
That we recall
That either make us happy or cry,
For these are the elements of Father Time.

October 19, 1943

Oh, how nice it is to know someone as well as we know each other. Our understanding is mutual, our love everlasting, and our hopes and plans are one and the same.

True blue,
Me, you.
That's the line
For just us two.

October 22, 1943

TO A TEACHER

"Oh, Teacher, I forgot my excuse.
Oh, Teacher, I can't hit the proper keys!"
Ah, ha, don't you blow a fuse,
Just think of those
Who are busy as bees.
Sometimes they make you glad;

Sometimes they make you mad!
But think of me
And fill your heart with glee;
For I am the boy
Who was the teacher's joy.
What! You think I'm kidding?
Well, you're right;
I was only ribbing.

October 22, 1943

I knew you were exaggerating your teaching plight – A-plus! You have the promise of being a great teacher.

I remember that we were excused from school to see *Gone with the Wind.* Your dad let me drive his car to take you to the movie.

I expect to leave for flight training before January or February.

Bud's drawing. Teaching school.

October 23, 1943

I shall be able to arrange my schedule at school – I have unlimited cuts in my classes, and I am working ahead now so as not to be behind. I cannot skip the student teaching at 10 am, but the Oxford bus leaves at 8, so I'll be just on time. My critic teacher has agreed to skip our conferences while you are home.

Your sister called me today to tell me about her marriage. If you would tell her you plan to be home Sunday, the 7th, she will plan to announce it that Sunday.

You should also tell your mother you will be home so she could be prepared. My mother wants you here for at least one meal or perhaps more. And JoAnn – is she ever happy – you'd think it was *her* boyfriend!

I am disgusted with student teaching, and you are disgusted with your situation – we can cheer each other up, just you wait and see!

October 25, 1943

GOODNIGHT

"Goodnight" is an easy thing to write
When you are so far away.
But I can recall many a night
When that word was so hard to say.
You used to remark
"Bud, you'd better go,"
And I would retaliate with
"No, Dorothea, no."
I knew that soon
I would have to leave
For Old Man Consideration
Kept tugging at my sleeve.
Then we would kiss, and you,
Playing the polite Miss,
Would say, "Goodnight, Bud,"
And two doors would close
With an ominous thud!

October 25, 1943

Remember what you told me last week when I was discouraged?

I am excited inside; I can imagine how you must feel after having been away for such a long time.

I was just informed that I have been elected to Kappa Delta Pi – a National Education honorary right next to Phi Beta Kappa. My A-plus was not from my critic teacher – it was from a different man in another course. Today my critic teacher interrupted my teaching with some papers to be filled out concerning the "dumbest" pupil in class. He made me all confused!

October 26, 1943

It has been thirteen months since I saw my family. I will want to spend a lot of time with them. Don't plan two full weeks of just you and me. My parents

have suffered much with three boys in the Service. I shall try to calm their fears for us.

McDulin wants to meet all of your girl friends at the dorm. But me – maybe I am too shy around girls, and my shy attitude will not withstand their roving eyes!

A COIN

It has always been important
In many, many ways.
And it has decided many conflicts
For years and months and days.
In Latin they call it "pecunia,"
It made King Midas say "Ah-ha,"
I have flipped it into the air
To decide a problem for a pal and me.
If I yelled "tails," and he yelled "heads,"
And heads it turned out to be,
We'd continue with a satisfied air
For we knew that a simple coin
Had decided it fair.

October 28, 1943

Two boys who had passed the flight physical first time, failed this last time – I am worried.

October 29, 1943

Bud, I do love you even more because you are so considerate of your family. I wasn't planning to be so selfish as to take you away from them. You are so considerate of the family you love; it proves that you will be that considerate of me when that "someday" comes. I hope to see your family, too. I haven't seen your dad since I quit work, and it's been quite a while since I saw the others. I just spent more than a week alone with you – surely it's their turn. It's your furlough; make your own plans.

I have only pleasant memories of Morehead City – I remember everything about the town. I remember how blue the sky was and later how the moon looked on the waves and water. Mrs. Nelson drove us to the beach; you asked me how deep the ocean was, and how high the sky was – that's how much we love each other. Don't you think that a situation like that makes a person more aware of the presence of God? In our religion class, Dr. Wickenden expressed the thought that the presence of God may manifest itself in friendship and love – one is made aware of a higher power than man.

What a beautiful poem – "Goodnight." Once again, the poem will be true on your furlough!

October 30, 1943

I've been working ahead – spent from 1 to 5 o'clock studying, and I have lesson plans ahead for two weeks! The girls said you must be some *motivation* for me to study this much. The girls said to tell you they wouldn't hurt you or even stare at you. They are probably not the kind that Bill would like to meet. They say that they'd like to meet him, too.

Bud, this time next week you will be HOME! Aren't you excited? I am!

Bud's furlough ended on November 14.

November 14, 1943

I am glad I choose the sea and sky to remind me of you – they're always there, and that is just where I want you to be. I say to myself, "Dorothea, I love you," and for some strange reason I feel as though you hear me.

I enjoyed meeting all the girls at the dorm; they are really nice girls. Tomorrow I will be on the rifle range for two weeks. It hardly seems possible that I could make "expert" two years in a row – but I'll try.

What a wonderful furlough – but it was too short. My pen may finish this letter to you, but my memories remain as a constant reminder of my deep love for you.

November 14, 1943

Bud, I figured it up – you had about 182 hours of furlough time, and we were together 103 of those hours! No wonder I miss you so much now. Your family probably thinks I'm just a crybaby, but I couldn't stop crying even after the train left the station. I telephoned your dad to tell him your telegram indicated your safe arrival back to the base.

Miss Page, our housemother, asked if I were back to stay. She is very nice to all of us and asked quite a few questions about your work in the Service. She thinks the War will be over soon; I think she's just trying to keep up our morale.

June Yee came over to see my "ring." She asked, "What's his feeble trouble?" She had a date with a Marine last night and returned with a ham sandwich, candy bar, and potato chips.

I was never so happy in my whole life; you were so kind, sweet, and considerate – there are so many sweet things to remember, except that you were not able to wink with your right eye!

You were with me at the station one minute, and the next you were gone. You did spend a lot of time with your family, and I hope they didn't mind having me there so much, too.

November 15, 1943

I am back on earth as a Marine! I enjoy being at the firing range – reminds me of boot camp. I shall have the same firing coach that I had last year, and I'll be firing on the same day one year later. That year seems so long ago; so much has happened in 1943. We are both much happier; I am looking forward to my next furlough.

I know what I would like to give you for your birthday, but I am saving that for a special occasion. Do you remember the night we were "verbally engaged?" So do I, so please be patient.

There are so many things I want to do; maybe I should go back to college, or concentrate on aviation. You play a very important part in my decision – I do not want to disappoint you.

Goodnight, Dorothea. May every prayer that you say come true; I love you.

WINK

When I wink at you
My heart begins to beat;
When you wink at me,
You knock me off my feet.
Oh, if you really did know
How much I love you!

Bud's drawing. Winking.

November 15, 1943

Mrs. Fichter telephoned me to ask me to take her husband's two English classes. I like doing that. Now I have 3,000 spelling words to grade! I have only four more days of teaching typing. Your late hours did not exhaust me – I have all my pep and energy as usual.

November 17, 1943

Your beautiful letter telling me I should be with my family during my furlough time convinced me I should be with *you* as much as possible. I kept you up too late while I slept in, and you went back to teach typing in Oxford – I'm sorry. I hope you are not too tired.

There is an old saying, "All good things must come to an end." Good things never end, do they?

Do good things really end?
We always have memories
To keep alive the good things
Long after they have stopped.

November 17, 1943

It's hard for me, too, to get back in the routine of classes and teaching. Your letter was so sweet that I just sat on my bed and cried! I, too, have that warm feeling when I am with you – so secure and content.

My exams are starting.

I hope you make "expert" again at the firing range.

November 22, 1943

That feeling of warmth was exactly the feeling I had, but I couldn't explain it. Were I capable of choosing one wish, of the many I have, I would wish that my life and feelings toward and with you would be everlasting.

November 22, 1943

I'm not student teaching anymore!!! Mr. Fichter wants me to go to Cincinnati with him to the State Grange Convention December 13-16. I think I'll go. He paid me for teaching his English classes, and he'll pay me for the Convention.

The Kappa Delta Pi initiation is tomorrow. Did I tell you that Mrs. Tully paid for my membership? She is very good to me.

Thanksgiving Day is coming – I'm thankful that we have each other to love.

November 23, 1943

You need not worry about causing me problems with my studying for exams. I have an A in religion, A- in business law, B in sociology, and the highest grade in the class in special methods. Thanks for teaching me to appreciate lovely things in life – friendship, happiness, memories, laughter, and tiny incidents too numerous to mention. I guess we have taught each other to appreciate these things.

November 24, 1943

Thanks for your postwar concerns. With your inspiration I know we'll work everything out. You have made me feel much better about the future.

November 26, 1943

I made "expert" on the firing range for the 2nd time in a row!

On November 27, 1943, I received flowers for my 21st birthday.

November 28, 1943

Thank you for the beautiful pink roses. All the girls wanted to know who sent them and why. Millie is spending the weekend along with nine other girls. We went to a movie and then picked up my birthday cake which Aunt Lil had brought from Mother. We had oodles of food – almost ate ourselves sick. We tied our beds together and slept crosswise until 11 am Sunday. We took a long walk in the afternoon. I love you with all my heart. You said that you love a person with all your nervous system – I don't know; who is right?

November 29, 1943

Dorothea, I don't want to write to you. I want to see you, talk to you, and just be near you – but then there is a War going on, and we have to give up these things. I must be content to write.

Thanks for the cookies; thank your mother for the Christmas cards I can mail to my friends.

Thanksgiving – I am most thankful for you. Nothing ever took as complete possession of me as you have – I enjoy it, I love it; I hope I can retain some of my other ambitions.

November 29, 1943

I am going with Mr. Fichter to Cincinnati for four days. All my expenses will be paid at the Hotel Gibson. I shall be paid besides. Tomorrow I start working for Dr. McConnell – $22.50 per month – 45 cents per hour. Everyone is so very nice to me.

Mrs. Tully was impressed with your good manners when I took you to visit her.

November 30, 1943

I was flying again today, and I am feeling weak and very ill. My hands, my feet, and my mind are all a void as far as their use over this weakness. I just don't know what to do. I certainly will not be able to fly if such a condition continues. I'll just keep trying until it stops me. Maybe I can find a way to overcome it, or at least I tried.

I would never go AWOL to come home – don't worry about it.

Do you recall the night (when I was on my last furlough) that we were discussing the time I asked to kiss you, and you said, "No!"? I was a very embarrassed boy, and my ego was greatly deflated! When I turned away to walk to my car, I could hardly keep from running. All the way home I kept telling myself what a terrible fool I had been. After that, I didn't dare to ask or even attempt to kiss you for such a long time. Oh, that night the joke was on me. I'm glad you never knew how I felt.

This morning I was standing on the ramp to the hangar – the sky was solid with black clouds. Suddenly there was a clear place in all those dark clouds, and that hole was filled with a beautiful light blue. I needed no other invitation to think of you.

November 30, 1943

Dr. McConnell dictated for about an hour on the subject of Arabia. It took me another hour and a half to transcribe the notes. I hope I can read them.

Those roses still smell good, but they are withered and dried. You never sent me flowers before. Thanks again. Last year is so different from this year. I didn't get my birthday gift until six months late last year.

December 1, 1943

Thanks for the cookies – the fellows thank you, too. Sometimes I can have such a warm feeling that I can fold my arms and almost feel that you are there.

December 2, 1943

Congratulations on making "expert rifleman" again. I said a little prayer for you to make it, and I believed that you would – it was as easy as that! I hope everything will always be easy – having faith in something or someone makes wishes, dreams, and prayers come true.

I worked 6 1/2 hours for Dr. McConnell today – grading V-12 papers. There are swabbies and Marines in the class, studying the geography of Great Britain.

December 5, 1943

Christmas is coming – what would you like for Christmas? I like Christmas, but I hate to go shopping for Mom and Dad and the others. What does the photographer tell you about your picture? I need it here in front of me as I write to you.

December 5, 1943

We won the basketball game last night. Glen Kessler played for Miami. Isn't he the one who traveled to Wake Forest with you to consider a scholarship?

We surprised Martha with a party for her birthday. What a spread!

I hope to receive our pictures before Christmas.

December 6, 1943

Today I was flying and didn't get sick! We saw several fishing boats down there; they were really hauling them in; their position prevented us from making our 45-degree approach from the south.

Tomorrow is December 7 – the day that was to change the destinies of so many of us or even the destiny of the United States.

My complimentary close is written in invisible ink, just like my love. I can't see it, but it's there.

December 6, 1943

I suppose I'll have to send you wrapping paper and string if I want to receive any more gifts for my birthday.

You need not be sorry about telling me your troubles. Telling someone always lessens their importance, so tell me, and I'll try to say something which will help.

I don't know why I am unable to remember the first time you wanted to kiss me, and I wouldn't let you. I don't remember, but I'm glad. I always had the idea that kissing someone was too, shall I say, sacred to go around kissing everyone or anyone, and you know that then I wasn't sure at all that you liked me very much. But, maybe if I had let you kiss me, I would have made up my mind more quickly than I did to love you. (Or did my mind have anything to do with it?) Maybe? You did wait a very long time before trying again. Here's a promise: I'll never say, "No" – not *ever* again.

I don't have to try very hard to feel your arms around me, and when I shut my eyes I can recall the things we've done, places we've been, and things we said and didn't need to say. I fall asleep remembering.

December 8, 1943

I don't really know what love is, but it's a wonderful feeling, no matter what, isn't it?

December 9, 1943

I will be glad to do your Christmas shopping if you send me the money and an idea of what to purchase. I'll have plenty of time during vacation.

Gay spent an hour with me at the dorm while Sis was in class. He had a million questions about you. He doesn't want me to go the USO here in Oxford. The V-12's that I am teaching are really college boys in uniform, but Gay still doesn't trust them. He doesn't know what a good time I've seen Sis have with them at open house! Gay knows a lot about gunnery, but how will that ever help him in civilian life?

December 9, 1943

I am completely disgusted with myself – I got air sick again today. Never have I inflicted such punishment on myself as I have since I began my determined efforts to overcome air sickness. Even if I lose 50 pounds, I am going to keep trying. I want to have the satisfaction of knowing that I at least tried.

Thanks for your promise never to say "No" anymore! I feel very small when I consider what I would like to do for you and for myself. I just shake my head and wonder about the uncertain future. I would like to go back to school, but in what capacity? There are other things to consider now – you, my age, and changes after this War. I think college would be unfair to you, and several other things would be unjust to you. Now I know you will ask for an explanation of "other things."

December 12, 1943

I've been grading V-12 papers from 6 to 11 pm. Some of these boys are so dumb. The government is wasting money on them. I'll probably leave for Cincy with Mr. and Mrs. Fichter tomorrow. His regular secretary will be rooming with me – Miss Van Gordon.

A girl just down the hall got word that her fiancé was killed. He visited here in October; they were to be married at Christmastime. The whole dorm is in mourning. It's so sad; I don't want to see her.

December 12, 1943

Lately I seem to be more easily angered – I don't like that feeling concerning some things that happen.

I find myself arguing in a loud, bombastic way – me, the quiet one. Being around all these men, one cannot expect to obtain many good qualities – we are exposed to more bad qualities. There is only one answer to all my self-analysis – I must be growing up! Once you told me that I seem to be older. I have learned a great deal since I have talked to so many different fellows. But the more I talk with some of them, the more disgusted I get. I don't like their uncivilized modes of thinking, their immoral attitudes, their inability to recognize the rights of all men, and their attitudes towards this, their own country. I feel that I have a just and fair attitude toward my fellowmen whether they be black, red, or yellow. I have a stubborn attitude; I for one refuse to follow these buddies (?) through their most common faults. Civilized!!! Are we really – sometimes I wonder.

Christmas is drawing near, and I shall miss you.

December 13, 1943

I am to teach Mr. Fichter's two English classes tomorrow and then take the bus to Cincinnati. He has everything arranged there.

December 14, 1943

Your Aunt Lettie sent me a photo of you. It's small and far away, but it gives me a wonderful feeling. What will your big picture do to me?

Thanks for the offer of buying Christmas presents. I am sending you $20 – try to find something for Mom.

Does the element of time bother you much? I think of it incessantly, and I can't help but feel that you are wondering about you and me as far as the future is concerned. Everything is so indefinite with me. If you ever get tired of waiting for me, I would have only myself to blame. We are both very young (?)

Symmes Corner School, 1928-1929. First grade. I am third from the left. Note the high number of students, all ages. Unthinkable today!

Galen, Frank Sr., and Bud McCollum, 1943.

Bud with Bill McDulin, 1943.

Together again. April, 1943.

Bud and me in Moorhead City, NC, 1943, during one of my visits.

In 1944, Bud wrote, "I had my picture taken with you." I was mystified until I saw this.

Bud (center) with friends at Cherry Point.

Bud (right) just hanging out.

Morning wash-up at Cherry Point. It was done as a group, out of doors, and using pails!

The McCollum men: Gay, Frank Sr., Frank Jr., Bud, Bill and Kak.

Our wedding day, finally! July 5, 1946.

Bud's graduation from Miami University, 1948. Although I'd graduated in 1944, I borrowed a cap and gown to illustrate that we both now had college degrees. We're standing in front of our Vet Vil unit.

Bud's early coaching job was in football in Seven Mile, 1950. His friend and assistant coach Gene Steed is on his left.

Housing Units Erected At Miami

Shown above are the first 15 two-family units for G.I. couples attending Miami university, set up between Campus avenue and Oak street, in the south part of Oxford.

The "veterans village" had its first residents this week as 30 couples and their children moved into the homes, brought from Willow Run, Detroit, Mich.

One room, measuring 10 by 20 feet, with the bedroom and tiny bathroom in each unit divided by a curtain, the unit rents for $22.50 or $30 (if the wife works) a month. The university provides water, electric, oil for heating, gasoline for cooking, and furniture.

Believed to be one of the largest villages of its kind of campuses in the midwest, 100 units are to be

A newspaper photo of the buildings at Veterans' Village. They were made of heavy, pressed cardboard! When the wind blew, the walls wobbled. And each unit measured a mere 10 by 20 feet, including the bathroom – so we were living in close quarters indeed.

Our new home. I still live there today.

yet I feel old when I consider time and realize how much of our lives are being spent apart. I want you, and I love you.

Love always,

Bud.

December 16, 1943

At last the Convention is over. I've been typing news releases and Convention resolutions. The place is swarming with reporters, and I'M TIRED. My steno pay amounted to $18, meals and bus fare were $7, for a total $25, and I earned every cent of it.

December 16, 1943

Dorothea, I say a lot of silly things at times, but I am never more serious than when I say I have a very deep and warm feeling because I know I love you. I may work and like it, I may participate in sports and love it, but none gives me the sweet and nice feeling that I get when I lie here and think of you and all the memories that go to make our love so very wonderful.

December 19, 1943

I'm home from the Convention. Mother has needed me to help her. She is ill – all broken out, with a face that is swollen. Doctor said an acid condition.

There is absolutely nothing I can do about your air sickness except remind you that that's the way it is supposed to be, and that it is all for the best in the end. Perhaps someday we'll see a reason that we can't understand now.

Woots bought Gay a ring with his initial on it. Gay wanted to give Sis an engagement ring for Christmas, but your sister talked him into waiting a year. She's having too much fun with other boys. June knew all this gossip. June had just curled Asenath's hair, and she said, "Hi, Dorsey!" over the telephone.

I have no fear that you will acquire any bad habits in the Marine Corps, no matter what kind of men you must be associated with in your dorm – pardon me, barracks.

I will be thinking of you as we decorate the tree. Mother needs me now.

December 21, 1943

I am very deeply concerned about my flight physical. I have almost everything that a normal happy person should have – eyes, ears, five senses,

the most wonderful girl a fellow could want, a whole family loving me, and a world of opportunity ahead. What more could a fellow ask besides the end of this terrible War which has destroyed physically "Peace on Earth." Only a man like Hitler can destroy that, mentally.

December 21, 1943

Your mother wants to wait for the new dress until springtime; I'll find something else for now.

Bud, whatever could make you think I'd be tired of waiting for you – I didn't get tired even when I wasn't sure you loved me! I don't think of time, except that each day brings us closer to the day you'll be home, and we'll be together for always! I am not wondering about you and me and the future, because I know that we'll be very happy. No one can be certain about anything these days, but we can be certain of our love for each other. It's the War which makes everything so uncertain; our plans will come. Please don't think I'll be tired of waiting for you.

December 23, 1943

Never before have I been so mentally depressed as I am now. The only pleasure I shall get out of Christmas is thinking about you. If I could only talk to you, I know you would make me feel better. You always do. I love you, and no matter how miserable I feel, that part of me does not change.

December 24, 1943

Everyone went to church tonight, but I stayed home with Bob – he is quite ill. Mother has returned home, and she feels miserable, too. Mother used the money you sent to buy me a black purse and gloves and beads to replace those from Mrs. Tully that were broken. Thanks for everything. I do hope that next Christmas will be a merrier one.

December 24, 1943

This Christmas can still be one of the best ever, because I know that there are many happier ones to follow. This Christmas you know how very much I love you, and I get a great deal of satisfaction out of the fact that I have opened my heart and told you truthfully how I feel.

Bill has just handed me a letter – if we both go to flight school, if one goes and the other does not; there are many "ifs." Bill and I are like brothers; I can't

imagine life in the Corps without him. He is a friend that I am never sorry to have known.

I'm feeling better than yesterday's letter would indicate. I realize that you mean more to me than any ambition I might have, and I am devotedly grateful for having you. You have already helped my morale 100% by writing so many reassuring and nice letters.

December 27, 1943

Several weeks ago eight of us were called into the NCO's office. We were to leave for flight school on January 20. There was a catch – a six-months physical was given before we would leave. I passed eye, ear, and a host of other tests with flying colors. My pulse was very good, but my blood pressure was a little high – 42 points above normal of 122.

I am thankful that I have you. I'm remembering what you said, "for the best." Coaching was always my 2nd choice, but nothing is definite.

December 28, 1943

General Eisenhower predicts that the War will be over in 1944. I hope he is right. We are frozen here – indispensible.

December 31, 1943

Oscar is home and came to see me Christmas Day. He couldn't come in because Bob has scarlet fever. I sat in his car and talked with him. He is always so sad, and he looks so thin. He had one last date with Pat; he thinks that this is the end! All the other fellows receive mail from girls – except him. He can't believe that you are really *you*, but he's happy for us. I think he likes to talk to me because of you, his very best friend in all the world.

Our county superintendent wants to talk to me about a teaching position for next year. It's time to think about it; what do you think?

Now I am living at Aunt Emma's so I won't get scarlet fever, because I need to go back to Miami next week. Aunt Emma is Don's mom.

I am very sorry you didn't pass the physical. No matter what happens, what you do, where you are, you know I'll always be here waiting for you and loving you more and more each day.

December 31, 1943

Dorothea, my only wish for the new year is that our love will find us even more grateful. I love you and wish for you the best in life, love, and happiness.

December 31, 1943

I know how much you wanted to fly, but now you must have to do something else. My Shakespeare prof said we should count ourselves lucky if 50% of the breaks in life come our way. Don't we believe that God has a plan for not letting you pass? We think it is bad, but someday we'll understand that it is good – that God has something else planned for your life.

How about the idea, "World, I'm not licked! There are plenty of other things I can do, *and I'm going to do them.*" I know you can; I have all my faith in you. Remember REASON and EMOTION? Let REASON do your thinking now, and everything will be all right.

"There is always a possibility that you may lose me. But there is one thing definite – you won't lose my love."

January 2, 1944

My dear, I'm sorry you are ill. I wanted to telephone you but had no opportunity to do so. Do you know what I would prescribe? A pretty blue dress and a big hunk of Marine with a very big place in his heart for you, a nice, warm moonlit night, a porch swing for rhythm, and a topic concerning two people very much in love. We could talk about all the things we like to remember, speak of our love for each other, and then dream together of the future and of the days that will find peace and happiness being practiced in the world. Goodnight. My prayer this night will be for you.

January 3, 1944

Thank you, my darling, for the two very nice and reassuring letters. Dorothea, I'm not so down in the dumps that I forgot all about the many other things I have to be thankful for. It should be my total efforts with one thought in mind – where can I do the Corps the most good. I have *my interests* foremost in my mind, and that, my dear, is very, very greedy. Individuals will never win the War even though individual initiative and self-interest are assets which make the American soldier one of the best in the world. From here on I shall let my course wend its way without any interference from yours truly. It seems that Fate was always my best guide anyway – at least She produced the best results.

SMILE? Why, Dorothea, can you imagine me not smiling? I have an ironic habit of being able to find humor in the most morbid and depressing circumstances.

Please D-O-N'-T worry – I'm ok now and in complete charge of all my faculties. *Reason* never left the driver's seat. He's just traveling on a bumpy road at the present. I miss Bill an awful lot, but then this is War, and there is no place for sentiment on the bloody hand of Mars.

January 4, 1944

Are you back at school? I don't know where to send this letter. I am receiving no letter from you. Are you ill? I want to hear your voice. Are you at home or at school?

January 7, 1944

Today I received a letter from your sister, Ruth Marie. I didn't know where or what or when or anything. I was very confused. Knowing that you have scarlet fever, I am very much concerned about you.

Every now and then I try to recall when I first knew you or began to notice you. I can only remember you as far back as bookkeeping class. But so much of me loves you that it feels as though I grew up, and you grew right along with me. The day I asked you for that first date will live in my memory forever. That was undoubtedly the greatest venture I ever attempted, and no matter what other ones confront me, I know that I will not be as gratefully rewarded.

Dorothea, do you remember the night you breathed a prayer for you and me? Tonight my prayer is for your speedy convalescence.

January 9, 1944

Today I saw a movie called *Three Cheers for Miss Bishop*. With three chances for marriage, she remained a very good school teacher. I stopped to think, "Dorothea could be sweet and sacrificing as Miss Bishop had been, but she isn't going to be – NOT IF I CAN HELP IT."

I am enclosing some snapshots taken when you were in Morehead City – sweet and pleasant memories. It is getting nearer and nearer to the time Bill will leave me for flight school. He's leaving, you're ill – playing basketball is one means of clearing my mind of all those things.

I miss your letters terribly – it seems ages since I heard from you. Today I was walking along with my forehead furrowed deep in thought and a voice said, "Bud, don't do that." Remember that phrase?

Bud sent me flowers.

January 12, 1944

Today I received two very nice letters from Martha, your roommate, and from Midge Taylor. I miss your letters! My brother Galen and I are planning to meet in Washington, D.C. on the weekend. Right now Bill and I are at the USO in Morehead City. We hope to eat a chicken dinner and corn sticks before the restaurant closes.

January 13, 1944

Last night was a very chilly affair from the happy nights we spent in Morehead City. Without you it was like Coney Island in the winter. Why, the chicken did not even taste the same.

Your sister Ruth has been considerate and nice to write to me – she says you are much better and that makes me feel better, also. Your roommate misses you almost as much as I do. She writes some very nice things about you. Midge told me that all the girls talked to you on the phone.

I only know that I am a Sergeant in the Marine Corps who is very much in love with the sweetest girl in the world, and I miss her very much. At the moment, I am creating a parade – mentally, of course. Shall I give you a short resumé and example of a few of the things that are passing in review? I see a very beautiful pair of blue eyes. OH! What's this? One of them winked. Ok, I'll be sociable and return the optical handshake or expression of love, whichever the case may be.

Next, I see a small pair of pretty white hands buttoning my coat, and I am proud to know that someone is taking care of my appearance. Now her head is on my shoulder, her hand in mine, my joy at being near her, and all of the many things both big and little that I associate with her. These are the acts of my mental parade. I hope they bring you as much enjoyment as they bring me. Don't you wink with your right eye, either, or I'll refuse to wink back. What – you say I couldn't wink if I wanted to – well, maybe you are right, but I never had any use for winking until I met you. Remember – I love you, and I'm still praying for your speedy recovery.

January 18, 1944

I feel sorry that I haven't written to you for several days. I had the very good fortune of being with Galen this past weekend. We walked around, talked, and ate. We played Ping Pong at the Y. The talking never ceased. I telephoned Betty Lou Shaver, a girl I had met when some of us from Wake Forest were invited to a ball in Virginia. We went to her home and met her parents. She lived in D.C. all her life; she was a perfect tour guide. The Congressional Library was most impressive. The place seemed to be alive with all the spirits of all the people who live in this great country of ours. My only regret of my trip was that you were not there. As I stood there reading the Constitution, I couldn't help but be duly impressed. Betty's mother fixed a home-cooked supper for us, and then we later went to a movie– *Marie Curie*. Mrs. Shaver fixed a bed for me in her father's den and after a good night's sleep and a very appetizing breakfast, I caught the train back to Cherry Point. Do you mind my telling you about my trip?

Dorothea, you mean so much to me that I'm just not all here without some sort of contact with you. I am looking forward to the day when I shall start receiving your sweet and reassuring letters again.

Goodnight. I know you will be well soon, because we have God on our side.

Bud telephoned me from Washington, D.C. He was playing and coaching the Cherry Point Marines basketball team. Flight orders gave him $120 per month.

January 20, 1944

The quarantine sign comes off our house tomorrow. I received your telephone call this afternoon, and I just had to write today! It has been very hard for me *not* to write. I'd read your letter, think of a million questions and replies, lie here and think about you, and just fall asleep. These 28 days have passed quickly (I wasn't even bored) because I spent them thinking of you and of us and how happy we shall be.

You think you sent pink roses – they had to substitute pink carnations. That doesn't matter to me – just knowing that you sent flowers made me almost completely well. And then today when you telephoned me – well, I am fully recovered. When I was too ill to comb my hair, Mother braided it into two pigtails. Today I shall wash and curl it.

I've had cards and letters every day during my illness, counting yours, of course.

The connection was very poor on your telephone call. Then when you said, "Goodbye," I lay here and thought, "Well, this is one time I didn't cry when he called." But before I finished the thought, I was crying as if I had just left you at the train terminal.

I called your mother; she had been very worried about you after you failed your flight physical. They thought you'd be too depressed. I assured them you are really all right.

I want to go back to school, but it will be difficult to make up three weeks of work, a semester of reviewing and exams.

I missed your birthday – you're getting old, Bud – 22! The older you get, the more I love you.

January 21, 1944

Your phone call did the trick – I've been up all day. We cleaned and aired the house and put all the bedding outside on the clothes line. I enjoyed looking at the pictures we took in North Carolina. I looked terrible, but you looked so happy in all the pictures. I never knew I could make anyone so happy, and I was surprised at your joy and excitement when I arrived in Morehead City – I knew you'd be glad to see me, but I never knew you'd be *that* glad.

January 22, 1944

Today I went uptown and spent the remainder of the money you sent me for Christmas – pajamas and a new house coat *and* a frame for my picture, if it ever comes.

When my roommate and the girls asked if I were allowed to write you, it was their decision to try to take my letter-writing place.

January 22, 1944

I feel much better now that I know you are well enough to talk on the phone. With the bad connection, I was trying to tell you that our basketball

team won its first game 44-36. We played against a very good team, and I was lucky enough to be high scorer with 16 points. As of January 12 my pay will be $120 per month – I have partially made up for my recent loss.

Dorothea, coaching, playing, and finding time to practice is about a full-time job outside of my regular duties. You probably know from the very mention of the word *basketball* why I have not written more often in the past few weeks.

It is Sunday, and I have duty. The sky is blue – I don't need it to remind me of you. You have no idea how often I think of you, and nothing is more pleasing to me in this faraway place. I will be sincerely happy when I receive my first letter from you.

January 23, 1944

The doctor came today; I talked him into letting me go back to school. I didn't tell him my tonsils hurt, and my neck was swollen, but it'll be all right.

January 25, 1944

Yesterday I received that long-awaited first letter from you – it gave me the best feeling I have had in months. You are kind and considerate; I like your faith in mankind. Dorothea, I *like* you, and when you like someone you *love, that* is wonderful. I could write pages on the reasons I love you so very much, but too much at once becomes monotonous.

When I joined the Marines, I wanted to get all out of this outfit that I could. McCollum – that's who I was thinking of. Since then I believe (I'm not sure) that my attitude has changed. If it hasn't changed, it has definitely become more or less unstable. If we are to win the War, each and every one of us must put aside our personal interests and begin to think of what we can do to help – not what the Service can do to help us. Maybe it can do both. It is certain that the job I am doing is very necessary, and someone has to do it.

You are so self-conscious about your hair. If your hair were in pigtails, I'm positive that my love would not be changed! I am remembering the day I surprised you coming from Wake Forest. (I'm laughing.) I'll always remember that you opened the door, saw me, screamed, and ran upstairs to change and comb your hair, leaving me to greet your father instead of you. I can still see you!

A new order from D.C. states that all men with 18 months or more in the States are eligible for transfer to active combat. Don't worry about it – it would be many months before I would be transferred. I am a man, and men do have consciences, you know. I would at least like to know that a plane I worked on was dishing out a little trouble to our common enemy. Yes, I would be just as lonely, but at least I would know that I would be sacrificing a little more for victory's sake.

Thanks for the two very nice letters. They are the best things that have happened to me in such a long time – September 6, 1943.

January 26, 1944

I'm back at school and just finished my sociology exam; I have office management at 10:30. I studied all day yesterday, and right now I am very tired. I have hives or something itchy, and my hands and wrists are so swollen I can hardly write. I have an appointment to see the doctor here in Oxford. If I die, I'll send you a telegram.

January 27, 1944

I'm feeling much better today. I saw Dr. Stafford – not the University doctor. He said scarlet fever can affect your heart, ears, and kidneys. He said my heart sounded good and that I should try to slow down and take it easy. Me? Take it easy? I have some pills and awful medicine.

All my profs have been so very nice to me; I have four more exams next week. I have a "peach" of a schedule for second semester. So if you have a chance to come home, I think I'd have a *little* time to see you.

$120 per month – you'd better save most of it – but I don't need to tell you, because you already know it may come in handy.

January 28, 1944

Please don't rush your convalescence. Don't expect to accomplish in a few days what took millions of germs weeks to destroy. Remember, you are very young and have a full life ahead of you – there is plenty of time to make up your schoolwork, even though you may not think so.

Dorothea, I do know that I love you, and your interests are *my* interests, so please be careful. Today the sky was clear and *blue*, and I immediately thought of you. I like remembering all the things we used to do; I am just content to lie on my bunk and dream rather than write, but then that isn't fair to you. "Stardust" is being played on the radio; it seems so short and yet so long ago that we sat and listened to "Indian Summer."

January 28, 1944

I am feeling much better – the hives are almost gone. Martha and I walked over to watch the basketball game. We beat Cincy 68-52; Glenn Kessler played for Miami. Everyone has finished exams – except me. I studied all afternoon and shall study all day tomorrow. I know you are very prejudiced in your opinion of me, but I guess I do like to hear you say it. And you added, "When you like someone you love, that is wonderful." Why had that thought never occurred to me before you told me?

Your job is very important – we can't all be heroes by bombing Berlin or Tokyo. Someone has to do the work behind the scenes. They seem to be doing not very much, but in reality they are very necessary for the heroes to carry out their jobs.

I'm glad you met Gay in D.C. Betty Shaver was very nice to you; her mother made your visit even more special with her dinner and lodging for you. Be sure to write her a note.

Do I have to ask what happened on September 6? Shame on me! The scarlet fever must have affected my brain!

January 30, 1944

I have almost decided that I would like to be a coach. Sports are probably the most interesting of all occupations. It is hard for me to forget them. Here at Cherry Point I have a lot of opportunities to participate.

January 30, 1944

My religion exam was an oral one. I'm sure of a B or maybe an A. The card you sent is cute, but I never think of you as a worm. When you miss a few days I just worry about you – are you just very busy or are you unhappy?

Oh, Bud, I just escaped from a "wolf." Protect me, please! Mark Barkley came to the dorm and I spent 20 minutes trying to convince him that I would not go anywhere with him while he is home on furlough! I suppose I said "No," about 20 times, and he finally left. As I shook hands with him, I smelled the alcohol on his breath. Now I don't feel so bad about having hurt his feelings.

February 1, 1944

Last night we played Mitchell Field in New Bern, and we were victorious, 45-38. What a rough game!! At the half, one of my players (I was coaching the team) remarked that he would like to take a crack at his opponent if things continued so rough. So Coach McCollum speaks up: "Fellows, we have a good team, and we can only be a winning combination if each and every man on our team keeps our purpose in mind. Our little individual grievances should be disregarded for the rest of the team. When we begin to think of ways of getting even, we are not concentrating on the ball, but rather on the man. If the other team can make us angry, then they have us 2/3rds beaten. We are playing right into their hands if we let them know that their psychology is effective. While they are playing psychic games, we will play basketball – and therein lies the victory."

We went back onto the floor, built up a good lead, and then the second team went in to play. With two minutes left, the first team entered the game. It was rough – too rough for my placid state of mind. So-o-o I intentionally fouled a man and asked the referee in a sarcastic sort of way how he knew,

and he slapped a technical foul on me. The game ended just as I was preparing to take a swing at a fellow! The moral of this story is PRACTICE WHAT YOU PREACH.

Our C.O. laughed at me all the way back to the base. He congratulated me on my fine half-time pep talk and didn't mind reminding me of it. Did you ever see me angry like that before? NO. That, my darling, is a spark of what I term a changing attitude. I don't like to be like that! I like being able to control my emotions, no matter what happens. SO many things have made me more or less rebellious – not getting N.A.P., being air sick, having high blood pressure, your illness, and my inability to eat and write all the letters I would like to. I seem to have a continual confused state of mind. I am tired of this life. Postwar problems worry me. Oh, I don't know how I feel. It is only when I read your nice letters, play basketball, read, or work that I am ok. As long as I have any time at all on my hands, I am radically indifferent toward my present attitude. Dorothea, I don't like it, but I can't stop feeling as I do. I don't want to change – I want to stay as I have always been.

Dorothea, I just read the letter you wrote after my trip to D.C. First, I did *not go* to Washington to see Betty. I went there to see Galen. It was only after Galen and I talked our heads off that I suggested talking to Betty. As for staying there all night, I'm sorry if it seems wrong to you. What if your father had a den downstairs and a comfortable cot, would you offer it to a friend when conditions are as they are in Washington? Oh, I could probably have found a place to sleep, but I did not know the Capital, and at that time of night everything is filled up.

My dear, if *you* don't trust me, then who does? How do you think I feel that you have suggested the thought of trust? What you think means everything in the world to me. If you consider taking advantage of a hospitable act as wrong, then I can only say once more that I'm sorry I stayed there.

I did thank Mrs. Shaver for the nice meals and warm bed. I know plenty of Servicemen who would have been more than envious of that bed. I hope I don't seem sarcastic; it is just that I am a bit hurt at your disapproval.

My sympathies go with you when you tell me how some friends (?) rubbed *it* in. I can imagine some of the things they said, even though you did not choose to tell me about them. Their attitude toward you concerning my trip is the only part of it that I regret.

It's so hard to write my feelings about this, so, my darling, if you were in my arms, and I could see your pretty blue eyes, I would tell you how much you mean to me and how much your love means to me.

Love ever,

Bud.

February 2, 1944

We are both very busy – I have been flying around from work, to class, to teaching, to taking makeup exams, and studying. Please write to your mother! This is a very short letter. I'm taking your advice and trying to get lots of sleep.

February 2, 1944

I have only 20 minutes in which to write a note to let you know I'm thinking of you. This is my most placid moment of the day – writing and thinking of you. You are doing a swell job of catching up on your work.

Thinking about my trip to Washington – my thoughts are kicking me in the pants! I can't help but feel your disapproval. You are entirely right – I know now how I would have felt if I had been you. I'm sorry if my actions (innocent as they may have been) hurt you. This is the last time I shall mention that trip.

February 3, 1944

I received two of my grades: sociology, C; office management, B. I was furious about the C, but I can do nothing about it. My last semester should be easy: 11 hours of classes plus teaching and geography, sociology, English methods, school administration, and religion.

I also heard "Indian Summer" the night before I received your letter about having heard it. Remember when we had noon-hour dancing at high school? Cy announced that that song was dedicated to *us.*

The part of your letter – *no good for anything* – is all wrong. If you're no good for anything else, you're good for me!

Exams are all completed; I'd sleep late tomorrow, but Dr. McConnell needs me to work. I just spent five hours grading papers for him. All our roommates are out of town, so Brose and I are going to a movie for relaxation.

The show was entitled *Odd Acquaintance* – good and different without a happy ending. "Love at first sight" is hard for me to believe. Then the show embodied the theory that you might love someone one day and wake up the next morning *not* loving him. I don't believe it, but if I did, I would be afraid it might happen to us. My emotions were strained at the movie – could that happen to us? I hope it is merely the influence of the show that has me wondering.

I joined a girls' chorus yesterday – for a change. Oh, yes, the first song we sang the first day was "Carolina Moon," and I remembered a real Carolina moon I had seen with you not so many months ago when you said, "verbally engaged!"

You wrote that the only thing you are sure of is that you love me – well, that's a lot! I remember when you wouldn't tell me, and I wasn't sure you did love me. Last year at this time I was still wondering!

February 5, 1944

Coach McCollum must be a good coach – even if he does not "practice what he preaches!" You didn't really strike anyone, did you? He was lucky the clock saved him from the boxing champ of Jacksonville. It's hard for me to believe you could be so angry, but with the whole world fighting, it seems natural that you want to sock someone. The idea of Parris Island boot camp was to make you *mean* with a fighting spirit for War. It is the military influence, but not a permanent change. Sociology – we are influenced by heredity and environment. You are enough like your kind, mild dad not to have a fighting nature.

I have explained my reasoning as to why you didn't make N.A.P. God has another plan for your life. Here is another way of looking at disappointments: After we go through such experiences, we come out really much finer people. Things like that build character. At times it may seem easier to just stop altogether than to go on, but only the weak do that. Most of us just get up and keep on slugging away, smiling, and maybe being knocked down again and again. We are much finer persons after the fight! Do you believe this? Well, then, stop worrying. You know that worrying never changes events.

I had a lot of time to think when I was in bed with scarlet fever. If I worried about all my exams and back work, nothing would happen that was positive. So when I returned to school, I made an appointment with each professor. I then knew what work I needed to make up, the definite day for each exam, and what to study for each exam. I had a religion exam Monday, so I spent Sunday studying *only* for it. On Tuesday I had a methods exam, so I spent Monday studying *only* for it. So you see, I forgot about all the others, except the one on which I needed to concentrate. One by one I crossed each off my schedule, and now I am finished! How does that apply to you? Well, you are worried and confused about postwar problems. What can you do about them? Nothing. Just wait until they are real. We can't cross the bridge until we come to it, and then if there are any postwar problems, we'll just line them up and solve them one at a time. It would be hard for you to knock out 20 fellows at once, but it wouldn't be hard for you to take them on one at a time. We'll take them on one by one, and soon there won't be any. Yes, Bud, I'll be there helping you, and I'm not a bit worried about how we'll come out. You said you value my opinion – my opinion is that there is no finer or stronger person than you in this whole world! You have proven this in so many ways. These War years and days are not normal times.

Can you take another opinion? I don't think I could have anyone nicer any place loving me! When I hear about or see some of the girls' husbands or boyfriends, I feel sorry for them and remember how very lucky I am.

I dislike writing to you about Washington just as much as you do, but I need to make you understand. I knew you went to D.C. to see Gay, not Betty. I remembered that she had invited you to come to see her if you were ever in Washington. You knew no one else there. I am very, very sorry if I gave you the impression that I did not trust you. *You know better than that.* That is not at all why I thought you should not have stayed there. It was very kind of the Shavers to have been so hospitable. But you don't understand *girls*. I don't know her, but I do know girls.

I know she has been writing to you for a couple of years – I can't blame her if she sees someone she likes. Her intentions may be perfectly innocent; I know girls, and your staying there may have meant a lot to her, for girls are always jumping to conclusions. Perhaps she told a friend that a Marine spent the night at her home; girls are always ready to read into the story that you and she must be more than friends. This may not be true of Betty, but it would be true of many girls I know. My opinion had nothing to do with my *trust in you*; but I don't trust GIRLS. Do you understand?

Most couples could be in a terrible fight over something like this. Our not quarreling proves again to me the strength and depth of our love. Yes, Bud, I'd be very happy to be in your arms, hearing you tell me all that is in your heart; maybe we won't have to wait too much longer.

Love always,

Dorothea.

February 7, 1944

I remember well those noon-hour dances at high school. I clearly recall the day Cy announced "Indian Summer" was dedicated to us.

You were disturbed by the movie; allow me to ease your mind. Have you forgotten that Marvin McCollum is the boy who makes up his own mind, the one who plays the situations of life only if he is *sure* of them, and he is the one who loves you? If I had the strength to keep my love for you to myself for such a long time, do you think I would have told you the truth were I not *sure* of that love? Love is not a feeling that we can turn off or on as we would a light. It is a feeling encased in an impenetrable enclosure safe from all the momentary fluctuations of life.

There is always a possibility that you may lose me – that is only natural – and works just as well in reverse. But there is one thing definite – you won't lose my love. Love isn't something we measure in cups or any other form of measurement inside the depths of infinity. I sincerely and truthfully believe that this feeling is the superior of all our feelings. We can neither add nor detract.

Love is the highest level reached in our regard for a person. Day after day, week after week, and month after month my love remains.

I'd better stop and read what I said, for my feelings may have run away with my pen and dribbled into nothing at all. I hope that this will ease your fear that I might stop loving you.

I shall not adopt those military pugilistic traits; I have not changed. Fellows around here know me as a mother's dream because I don't smoke, drink, swear, play cards, or do any of the things of which she might disapprove. Never in my life have fellows admired those traits as they do here. It is hard to associate with fellows who do just the opposite. I have talked with many of them individually, and they have changed since coming into the Corps. I can still respect humanity for the good in spite of all the malfunctions of it.

Businessmen who were former athletes still try to keep an active heart by playing golf, etc. Their athletic hearts need to remain active and vigorous.

You are completely right about postwar problems, so I'll take your advice and wait until they present themselves. Who knows – maybe there won't be any, and if there are, I'll enjoy working them out.

Yes, my dear, I do understand your feelings about Washington – it wasn't *I*, it was *Betty*. Once Millie wrote concerning how much Bill and I liked each other. She said that girls never felt that way about girlfriends – girls are too catty.

It is with respect and thanks that I accept many of your theories and explanations. You prove to me more and more what a wonderful person loves me and is loved by me.

February 8, 1944

No letter came today from you, but I have another boyfriend who sent me a letter – my brother, Bob. I didn't know he even knew how to write!

He tells me that you have a brand new baby brother – Frank, Jr. Are you surprised? I wasn't expecting him until the end of the month. I am anxious to go home so I can go out to see him.

February 9, 1944

You seem to be back to normal with all your usual pep and energy – I can tell from your letters that you are growing stronger – even full of humor. I laughed about your encounter with the "wolf." I live with a pack of them. You gave a commendable account of yourself.

My basketball team beat one of the best teams in the tournament by a score of 49-23. I slopped in 15 points to be high-point man again. We are tourney favorites, but we play for another month and a half. Maybe I can win another basketball for you.

Thanks for the box of cookies – a very nice Valentine. Could you bundle yourself up in a box and send it to me?

February 10, 1944

I shall be a real school teacher for one week – the commercial teacher at Hanover is very ill, and several of us who are seniors in Bus. Ed. will take turns as weekly subs! Mr. Bogan is the superintendent. He was glad to know that I'd be first. I'm happy and excited! I shall teach Shorthand I and II, bookkeeping (your favorite class), and 8th grade math. I shall also supervise two study halls.

Sis and I attended assembly together – she was extremely nice and pleasant. I told her about the baby – she did not know.

February 13, 1944

I worked six hours for Dr. McConnell today. I cannot work again all week. We are paid $6.50 per day for teaching at Hanover. Ruth Lampe will sub next week.

February 15, 1944

I know what the X's stand for, but what do the zeros mean? Do I get a zero for not writing more often?

February 20, 1944

Today it is rainy – no flying – so I have plenty of time to lie in my bunk and daydream, think, and dream. Would you like to hear some of my daydreams? I dream of being home and playing ball with the guys from high school. I'd be the coach, and I'd place each man in his position, work out each individual's part in the play. When the play goes wrong, I'd explain it all again. We would have a man-to-man defense, switching when screens are in progress. On offense I would work off a triple pivot. There are hundreds of details I have worked out for my teams if I ever become a coach. It's fun pretending, isn't it? I'm thinking with a mind trained and experienced in this field. You are probably as lost as I would be if you conversed with me concerning office management. My dreams concern teaching high school lads and even, perhaps, my own son someday. I'd teach him every trick I knew and encourage his liking for sports.

I dream of aviation and adventuring. Every man, I don't care who he is, has ambitions of a journey – he actually travels that trip many times in his life, creating adventures and beautiful places, ending that trip a much wiser and more contented man. No, I know he doesn't really do it, but you would be goggle-eyed if you could share with us all the wondrous things that we see and do on those trips. At some time or other every man is a Richard Haliburton, Sinbad the Sailor, or Marco Polo, and almost always there is an intervening and overpowering force – his love for the girl of his dreams!

This brings me to my next dream of mental and synonymical solitude. Dreams must be in the fourth dimension, because even though I can't see them, I can feel them. If you're laughing, I'm laughing with you.

When I drift into the realms of love, I feel very dreamy-eyed with a wonderful feeling in my heart. I think girls are more frank than men about certain things, so if I, in my own modest way, do not elaborate on this subject, you can supply your own conclusions to fit your dreams.

Girls don't go adventuring, do they? I believe they build houses, have beautiful weddings, and go on nice honeymoons.

Am I right? A man is happier to share *after* he has satisfied his lifelong fictional ambitions. Happiness is the basis of the success of all our ambitions – that's probably why I am so contented on a basketball court, loving you, and knowing that you love me.

If this letter is silly and without content, please accept my last few words as true and factual and truly expressive of past, present, and future feelings – I love you, Dorothea.

Love ever,

Bud.

February 20, 1944

Our former high school principal came to see me at Hanover; he offered me a job in Franklin, Ohio. He was really surprised to see me subbing there. He asked about a boyfriend, and when I told him it was you, he was very pleased. He even asked if we were to be married. Tomorrow is my last day at Hanover – I am almost sorry to leave. I am no longer tired after school – getting used to it.

February 21, 1944

We saw the movie *Iron Major,* the story of Frank Cavanaugh, football coach. I liked it except he had nine children – too many for me! I'd like very much to be the wife of a coach.

It has been more than four months since I was with you in North Caroline. The news showed some women Marines marching on the beach there. I had never seen the ocean before, and seeing it with my hand in yours was very wonderful.

Didn't you know that the O's were hugs? Here's a few more for you:

X O X O X O X O X O etc.

February 22, 1944

I have been involved in a very lengthy discussion. The odds must have been 100 to 1 (me). I knew that I was correct and thus never wavered from my path. The question: Men are privileged to date other women after marriage, but such is not the case with the wife. I was the only one who said that marriage is more than a legal agreement. It is a corporation involving trust, faith, understanding, and love.

When all was said and done, we understood each other, but whether anyone's opinion changed is another question.

Good night, dear teacher! You certainly did a wonderful job of *teaching me* to love you!

February 23, 1944

I'm supervising Mr. Fichter's English classes today while they write themes for him, thus the poor paper. Yesterday in this very room I proctored the V-12 for Dr. McConnell. There were four Marines and eight sailors there, and Dr. McConnell had the others. These fellows will be shipping out from Norfolk soon. I felt like a one-cent piece waiting for change when the boys came into my room. I heard their remarks – poor psychology, for how could they concentrate with *me* in the room? I pretended not to hear them, but a few minutes later Dr. McConnell came in and informed me in a loud voice that the rest of the class wished to be in *this* room! The fellows roared and cheered; I could have chased Dr. McConnell, but he was just having a good joke while torturing me. Now I'm grading their papers.

I checked with the Registrar's Office – I have another A, this time in special methods for teaching business subjects.

I needed no special Valentine – I already have your heart. You gave it to me when I was in Morehead City, and I brought it back with me!

February 24, 1944

I enjoyed very much hearing about your daydreams; I enjoy hearing you talk about basketball, even though I understand very little. I'd like having you become a coach; I know you'll teach your son everything you know about sports. After the War we'll concentrate on making your coaching dreams come true.

I never knew you dreamed of being Marco Polo, etc. I dreamed when I had scarlet fever, but my dreams were never about going on adventures and trips to faraway places. Who told you what girls dream? You are right, but they like to have a solid foundation backing their dreams.

Your letter isn't silly; in fact, I like it. All your big words and adventures are YOU, and I love you for who and what you are!

I finally received all my grades: Business Law, A; Special Methods, A; and Marketing, B. You already know the others.

February 25, 1944

Yes, I saw the *Iron Major* movie. I'd like to lead a life like that. Last night my team won over Mitchell Field, 62-33. I know you will ask – I made 17 points.

I am glad to know what the O's are. I thought they were subtractions from the X's for not writing more often.

The night at the ocean was one of the nicest nights of my whole life, and I shall never forget how strong my feeling for you was at that time. The water in all of its beautiful vastness with the dancing moonlight said to me as it came crashing on the beach, "You lucky guy," and I held you close and thought how very true that was. You seemed to be a part of all the natural beauties, and you were that part of the picture that is really the theme of life. Thanks for reminding me of those precious moments. I'm becoming homesick, so I'll end before I become mentally depressed.

So you like teaching and plan to teach for 15-20 years. Let's see – what could I do while you are teaching? I could stay in the Marines – NO. I could travel all over the world, and then write a book on the adventures of a modern nomad, try my hand at farming in Alaska, promoting aviation in China, or go prospecting for oil. I could go to South America and put my Spanish to use. After 20 years, I should be ready to live with a certain girl who has been teaching that same 20 years!

Maybe we should have made a different decision in our youth. I hope you recognized the satire involved in my adventures while you were teaching for 20 years.

February 26, 1944

Dr. Vallance asked me to go to Hanover for another two or three days, but I cannot miss any more classes or work time with Dr. McConnell. I have only $28.10 left for my week's work after taxes – 20% is called a Victory Tax.

Keep up the argument with the others about marriage rights and duties! Where do they expect to find a girl who would put up with that situation? I could give them a lecture myself!

I didn't *teach* you to love me; you did it all by yourself. There are some things we don't need to be taught.

February 27, 1944

My basketball team is depleted – illness, and some are shipped out. On March 1, 80 men in Squadron 46 will be transferred for preparation for fighting active duty. Squadron 46 will never again be as I know it. I think the War will end before I have an opportunity to be where the battles are won. The ground crew is *too valuable* to participate in combat. We, like mice, would be scrambling for shelter every time an enemy scare would present itself. I can see myself sitting calmly by while some nearby outfit is taking a beating as we protect the arm that protects them.

February 29, 1944

I suddenly realized that this is Leap Year, but this privilege (women's) I reserve for myself!!! There is a lot implied; therefore, there is no need for more discussion.

March 5, 1944

Tomorrow night we play for the championship. I made 23 points against Beaufort; this brings my three-game total to 56. I want to telephone you, but how would I do it?

March 5, 1944

Mother met me in Hamilton, and we went shopping. I have a new pair of shoes, four new dresses, and some stockings. I had time only to telephone your mother; she's always so sweet and understanding. She has your nice long letter about the new baby. If you ever stop writing me, I am to call her, for then she'd know something was wrong with you!

March 13, 1944

I am enclosing some photos which Betty Pelle took of me; I'm wearing my new lavender dress that Mother bought.

March 13, 1944

Ed Cooper and I visited Washington for four days. We met with Galen; we visited all the sights I had missed the first time. But I'm glad the trip is over – something was missing. I made mental notes of all I would want to show you – *someday*.

Don't worry about my health – I am ok. The doctor told me the high blood pressure was nothing to worry about.

You have brought me many wonderful and glorious thoughts and feelings – thank you, my dear.

March 16, 1944

Mid-semester exams are coming up – I'm studying more than usual. Speakers on the radio are reviewing two plans for returning Servicemen. One plan in Congress is to give $3 for each day spent in the Service stateside and $4 for each day spent overseas. The second plan proposes to give aid in rehabilitation – education, $1000 loans to build homes, purchase a farm or farming equipment, or for starting a business. All the talk concerns "after the War." We need to keep the peace, prevent a depression, readjust Servicemen to civilian life, and make a living. There is little emphasis on winning the War.

While Martha has been gone, I have rearranged the room for the umpteenth time. She can't find the light, the alarm clock, or even her bed. Do you think I shall confuse you when I move our furniture around?

March 16, 1944

My bunkie thinks I'm crazy as I sit here and stare at your snapshot – you look so healthy, happy, and sweet I can't help feeling that I am the luckiest

fellow on earth. That's a cute dress you're wearing. Did I ever tell you that you are a very attractive girl?

There are so many places I want to take and share with you – dreaming and planning is so much fun. One of the nicest things in life is sharing an abundance of happiness with someone you love dearly.

In Washington I saw a mural, "Reading maketh a full man; conference, a ready man; and writing, an exact man." I could use a bit more exactness.

I like the way you express yourself – with a touch of humor while restraining the seriousness of the situation. You have spared me many unhappy moments due to my own negligence by your ability to put across your point without any bitterness. I really should write more, but it is too easy to just lie here and dream.

We are one step closer to the championship. I have been picked for an all-star team; we'll play an exhibition game tomorrow night. While playing Beaufort, I scored 65 total points in four games. There I go, bragging again, when I have no right to do so.

When my heart plays such a wonderful tune if you are near, I am positive that it is in par excellence shape.

March 18, 1944

The all-stars were beaten by the best team I have ever played against; I scored 16 points. My airplane crashed today; no one was seriously hurt. A woman Marine was on a photo hop; she certainly earned her diploma. The women Marines in photography must make a pattern picture of Cherry Point from 10,000 feet. My plane is a photo ship. Now I must put on a new wing, new propeller, and get it back into flying shape.

Two good men were taken off my plane and replaced with women Marines – women mechanics. I told my group leader I was violently opposed to feminine mechs and refused to work with them. He talked me into working on my plane and trying it for two weeks with these mechs. I don't like it! I never, never intend to get along with women who choose to play the part of men even to the point of profanity! I am not the least impressed by their swearing, and I shall not tolerate any while they are on my crew! I am still peeved, but what's done is done, and I'll have to be patient – but how long can I be?

March 18, 1944

What a busy day! We played Chinese checkers with the boys at the USO at 6:30; then it was time for us to sing. There was a group singing after that. We skipped out and went to a concert by the university symphony orchestra. The USO was very different from the one in Morehead City. There is one large room, filled with sailors and smoke. My hair and clothes smell of cigarette smoke – I HATE IT.

It is so cold that all the buses from Oxford and Cincy have stopped running – ice is everywhere.

I was so cold in bed that I dreamed I was Santa Claus passing out Christmas presents on the corner of 3rd and High Street. That's no lie! I really dreamed it. I woke up and decided if I were that cold, I needed to put on another blanket.

Thanks for your beautiful letter; I read it three times; do you see I was really impressed? If that's what staring at a photo of me can do, I shall enclose another with this letter. You make me feel that you are right here saying all those things as you do on your furlough.

You're right about happiness – I agree. The way to be happy is to make others happy. If I make you happy, then I'm happy. We'll have to be happy just dreaming and planning – not daydreams, but real dreams we hope to make come true.

I'm very proud of those 65 points and all-star status; I wish I could have seen you play!!

March 19, 1944

It's a bleak, dismal day here and raining. I've been thinking of all the things we could be doing on a day like this. But now I recall all the nice things we could do if it were not raining. Remember when we had a long stroll down along the river behind your home? I can still hear the water rippling in the quietness of a summer setting sun. You didn't know then how I felt, but I knew, and my mind was really whirling. My heart was playing a contradictory tune to several of my thoughts, but I didn't mind, for it was so wonderful.

If I would write everything I recall, it would take all night – squeaking porch swing, little cherry tree, Brownie barking, and the nice cool breeze ruffling the leaves of your big elm tree – and all topped off by your warm and pleasant presence. I could write a letter much faster if I did not dream so much. David was a dreamer, so I guess it is all right if I dream a little.

March 21, 1944

Today the days and nights are of equal length all over the world – from the equator to the poles. That's what we're teaching the V-12s in geography class, and they aren't too brilliant on the subject. I recite geographic principles to Martha explaining very commonplace things. She's not too interested, but to me it is very interesting.

I am always happy when I see a white envelope with your familiar handwriting in my mailbox. I carried it unopened to the dining room, for it would have been impolite to read it at lunch. I hurried through lunch and when I read it, you told me how you rushed through lunch to check with the mail clerk. Here we were – both rushing through a meal in order to read a letter.

Try to be patient with those women mechs; maybe they won't be as bad as you imagine.

Won't it be wonderful when letters are no longer necessary as a means of expressing our love?

March 21, 1944

Believe me, my not writing was not to be *mean* to you – I knew you might think that. Now that basketball is over, I shall have more time to write a halfway nice letter to you because I am reliving a great part of our wonderful friendship. That gives letter writing top honors.

Do you realize how long it has been since I last saw you? We had a great time on my last furlough. I spent much time at home with my family, and you were there with me. I hated to come back here.

Poor Martha – she can't even find her bed after you have cleaned house and moved everything. I don't intend to spend my life with you moving furniture.

So it rained, and your hair got wet. Does that remind you of one of our first encounters? I was angry, too, at the way you acted. We have both come a long way since that day on the school bus.

March 23, 1944

Don't be shocked, but it is no longer February – it is March. Your letters have been headed "Feb." Oh, there are lots of things we could do on a rainy day. We could put on some old clothes and take a long walk in the rain. We could go for a ride in a car in the rain. It always seemed so warm and cozy with the rain beating down outside. I like to hear you tell me all the things you were thinking about. Later I'd have to tell you it was time to go home, and you'd just say, "Uh huh," and never make a move to leave. About an hour later, you'd decide you really had better go, but then it was I who wouldn't insist that you leave. And then you cracked your head on the wooden roof above our kitchen door!

I'll never forget our walk down by the river. You told me you were going to college in North Carolina; I didn't want you to go so far away. I began to cry, but you went anyway. You've spent most of your life since then in North Carolina. When we returned from our walk, I was afraid of stepping on a snake in the tall grass, so in the spirit of Sir Walter Raleigh, you carried me through the grass. I remember that, too.

You waited and waited for your brother to come to pick you up, but he never came. Daddy got out of bed to take you home.

I have received another letter from Mark. He has a furlough before he goes across. Frankly, I hope he doesn't get one, for I have no more excuses. Do you have any suggestions?

The girls in our dorm have a thrilling topic of conversation. The mailman brought an insured package for Marge Walt. What was in it? A DIAMOND RING!! What a unique way of receiving an engagement ring, but she thinks it's just as nice as any other way.

March 23, 1944

Have you gained so much weight that you could be Santa Claus? Your dreams always are so vivid.

We played our final game last night and won 49-21. The Cherry Point Marines are the champs! Now I plan to have more time for letter writing.

We ask not for happiness nor love in our dreams. We already have that! We only hope, dream, and pray for a chance to share what we already possess. Christmas has probably been the most outstanding holiday since the birth of Christ for the simple reason that people enjoy sharing and giving in a spirit of mutual happiness.

Marriage is an institution that requires mutual harmony; I am utterly at a loss to explain how important it is to me. I hope I never disappoint or undermine your faith in me. As I look out the window and up at my bunkie, I feel a sense of loneliness for which there is only one cure – YOU.

March 15, 1944

This is a letter I forgot to mail – I found it today when I was housecleaning. Have you not been home since you had scarlet fever? I know you have been busy catching up on your school work and working for those three professors.

May is the month when you shall graduate from college. You will be very important in the postwar world. The War has drained many men; the immediate need for educators will rest on the present-day women students. Women will come out of this War a much stronger and influential sex than they were before the War.

Women's control and equality are new, and their self-ego has undoubtedly taken a step forward. Too many women will fail in their past responsibilities, but many will wish to continue in their present capacities. My attitude may be idealistic and old-fashioned, but I am not trying to belittle the capabilities of women nor their ability to do a job as well as a man. I sincerely believe that life should be run on a cooperative basis, with women doing feminine duties and males resigned to the masculine or rugged duties.

Intellectually both men and women have equal rights and privileges. From Adam and Eve to Mom and Dad, women have been feminine. Down through the ages when a man dated a girl he didn't expect her to be his buddy, but he wanted her to be girl, all girl. I have the proud pleasure to say you are *all girl*, and I love you for it.

I want you to have a good time at college, so if you want to attend dances and parties, do not refrain from enjoying yourself because of me. Goodnight, I shall go to sleep with the warm feeling that we are closer than the distance separating us would indicate.

March 24, 1944

We are doing our spring housecleaning. I am washing and ironing the curtains while Martha washes the windows. I am confused about where to teach next year. The job at Hanover pays $1400 a year. Should I live at home and teach in the county, or go away to some other part of the state? What should I do? I really want your opinion. You can always reason things out so clearly and rationally. I only know I do not want to teach English. I'd like to teach commercial and geography.

I am not looking forward to spring vacation, because I shall begin practice teaching in seventh grade English. My critic teacher will make me write lesson plans in "pupil-teacher" conversation. How do I know what the students will say??? It is confusing to go from proctoring Mr. Fichter's English class to being a pupil myself in geography class.

March 24, 1944

There is a lot of work to keep my shoes up to Marine standards. We brush and shine, saddle soap them, wash off the saddle soap, brush them, dye, brush, and then apply polish and a whole lot of elbow grease. It has taken me three hours to fix three pair of shoes.

We eat snacks about 9:30 every evening. We are enjoying food just like you enjoy your spreads. I remember when you gave me the strawberry shortcake that Ruth had been saving for herself. I can't blame her for being peeved at you – but I didn't know it was hers.

I have been thinking about how long I may be needed in the service of my country. I have come to the conclusion that it may be longer than I had believed. I often think I am being unfair to myself and to you. We have agreed that we should wait until after the War before we make a move involving our most mutual and common interest – our future happiness together. Can you help me, or must I go on wondering, waiting, and hoping? I have a curious feeling, fleeting though it may be, of being afraid. Of what, I don't know. It's like when someone throws me a baseball, and I wasn't completely expecting it.

I am so irresponsible, and you are so efficient – just the opposite. My high school coach once told me that this difference is the bond between opposites because each has something the other does not have. Both share the same eagerness through friendship and understanding.

Maybe this is why we both love each other so very much. You are so much stronger than I in so many ways that I feel a need for your strength. I'm sorry, but "I can't give you anything but love," or so the song says.

March 24, 1944

I'm sorry I called you "mean" for not writing to me more often. I should never have sent that letter, but I hadn't received a letter for nine days! I know you would never do anything intentionally to hurt me. It takes me a long time to answer your letters, too, because there are so many dreams behind the words.

Your last furlough was special. I had intended to let you spend most of your time with your family – not with me alone. The first night on leave you took me home with you. What a swell idea you had – you were with your family (I was, too), and you were also with me.

Why do you think I picked such a big, strong, husky man if it wasn't to move furniture around at my every whim? Did you think I had any other reason?

Graduation at Miami is May 29, at 10 am. Why do you want to know? I wish you could be here for it.

March 26, 1944

A TOUCH OF SPRING FEVER – one of the nicest days so far this year. The very atmosphere is soothing the possible turbulence of our War-wracked minds. Mother Nature seems to be playing a tune in harmony with our very souls. Did you ever stop to listen to the birds and feel that they were the very essence of happiness that God gave to us as our contact between ourselves and nature? Maybe He meant for them to set an example, and in my mind, He has succeeded very well. All the beautiful birds have an instinctive love of life. They travel with the sunshine North, East, South, and West; where we have sunshine, we have life. In biology they call it photosynthesis; I call it beautiful and wonderful. I have experienced the quietness of a spring day on Sunday at sunset. Everything has recognized the day of rest. Thoughts are so clear and undisturbed except for the beating of our own hearts.

I want to be there for your graduation, but I can't even ask for a leave yet. I enjoyed reading all your thoughts about the rain; I remember it all, too. You think you're smart because you can wink with your right eye. I watched your every movement and said to myself, "Aren't you the lucky one!" I believe I have a permanent knot on my head from the porch roof.

You asked how to get rid of a pest – how about Flit? Or you could use your father's shotgun. I could suggest some cruder Marine tactics, but they're a little harsh. He is being impolite, and you should treat him in like manner. What you do should be a creation of your own – whether it be accepting or declining his invitation. Do not let me stop you from doing something that you might want to do. I don't believe that you need me at a time like this.

Exciting – a thrill that should come but once in a lifetime. You say that perhaps it does not seem very exciting for me. Probably it is more exciting than you realize. Imagine – a life's dream so nearly realized and a woman's most cherished goal, marriage. This is a very positive step and one which should be taken with an almost total realization of the problems involved.

Remember the night in Morehead City when we arrived at a mutual understanding of our future interests? I did not want my selfish feelings to control my action. I said that I had no engagement ring, but something you

said seemed to make everything ok. Engagement is a prelude to marriage, a period of preparation in so many ways. It takes two people to make this single decision. I wish I were talking to you rather than writing.

March 26, 1944

You'd better give up any hope of ever getting the picture I had taken in October. The government is suing the picture studio because they had purchased materials on the black market. The company has been dissolved. I lost $6.13 on that deal. Never again will a business ed. person pay in advance. I'm MAD!

I'm moving the furniture around again. Martha refuses to help me.

March 28, 1944

My heart is broken because you are planning to use me for your spring cleaning. Phooey! And to think that I had always hoped that you could care for me in a deeper sort of way. Popeye would say, "I can't understant womink." You're sweet, and I enjoy your delightful sense of humor. You are newly exciting; so alive and energetic. Has my expression of love had anything to do with your happy attitude?

Tonight I was amused by the response of my fellow Marines. I made a picturesque speech in the USO on "The Hot Dog as a Vital and Necessary War Food." I need an outlet for my abundance of happiness (because I love you so very much), so I gave a scene-by-scene description of Washington, D.C., complete with an historic background.

When I was a lowly freshman at Wake Forest I contemplated my future. But now, with your interests in mind, the question takes on a more serious aspect. I need to think of what you like and dislike. If I were to choose an occupation and if I had at my command qualities and qualifications which would allow me an elastic choice, then I would choose a job in which I would be happy and satisfied. Choosing a job is most important for a man, because it would be a lifelong undertaking. For most women, a job is temporary during normal times, but these are not normal times.

I am not familiar with pay differences outside our county, but how much does salary mean to you? You might gain more experience teaching outside our county, but do you really want that experience? No matter where you choose to teach, you will be an asset to some lucky school district.

I can't give you a good answer. Am I letting Bud influence my decision too much? All of these questions are only food for thought. I have some selfish conclusions, but they are very unfair to you. You have spent four hard years preparing to be a teacher. Do you intend to make a profession of it? Dorothea, I want you more than anything else in all this world, but I do not want to make all of your training seem a waste of time. I am frowning because this bothers

me very much, and I know that everything I say comes back to one thing – I love you very much.

March 28, 1944

Thanks for the *Cherry Point News* concerning the big championship game. I have not been home since I had scarlet fever, but I am going home Thursday and hope to see your new brother.

It is interesting to read what you think of women after the War. They want no "buddy." I remember a song you used to sing – "I only want a buddy, not a sweetheart." That was a long time ago, too. Many girls on campus wear boys' clothes, shirts, jackets, and slacks. Our profs speak of it – they don't like it. The Navy chaplain asked the girls to dress in feminine attire when in the company of our Servicemen.

I have NO desire to go to a university dance unless it is with you. Don't think I sit here alone while all the other girls are out dancing. Half of the girls don't go, and we are never lonesome. We really have good times here in the dorm.

Dickens said, "These are the best of times." I shall never again have girl friends like these!

I agree with you with all my heart – we want only a chance to share what we already possess. You confuse me by fearing you might disappoint me or undermine my faith in you when we are married. Impossible! Stop worrying. I am *absolutely* sure of you in every way.

I do not intend to be a wife who is angry and pouts, leaving the poor husband to try to figure out her problem (or his problem). We'll just be frank and tell each other what we think. Erase those silly ideas from your head.

If the War were to last three or four more years, I know we should not wait that long to be married. It is already too unfair to both of us. We are very alike in some qualities but very different in others. I shall add to your personality, and you shall add to mine those traits which you possess and I lack. Together we shall make one perfect union.

It isn't true that you "can't give me anything but love." There is so much in your character that I lack; I am weaker in so many ways in which you are strong. I've been reading a book on marriage; the psychologist writes of needing each other for support and that this interdependence is very important to a happy and lasting marriage. Each should have something the other lacks. I think we already knew that.

March 31, 1944

I'm glad you do not feel left out when you do not attend the dances at the university. We have dancing three nights a week, but I have never gone because I enjoy myself at the barracks.

Your letter has given me sufficient reason to erase my unsure attitude. My expression of doubt in myself will cease as of tonight. I shall put that silly idea out of my head. You seem to understand what I am trying to say and can say it with all the expression of my thoughts.

Your letter is so uplifting. I like the term "interdependence" and its effect upon a lasting and happy marriage. I am completely satisfied with all your conclusions. Paper and pen are partly responsible for all my ambiguity and confusing thoughts.

Some letters do not appear in sequence because Bud forgot to mail them.

March 29, 1944

I am hopping mad about that picture. I hope the studio is punished. I had a nice letter from Mom. She said that you and she understand each other. She thinks you are "tops," and I love her even more for that. You know what Dad thinks of you, since you worked at the same place. I can't tell you how much it means to me that all my little brothers and sisters "go for you."

I am glad that your sister JoAnn and I are friends. She is so cute and energetic.

Did you hear what Henry Ford said about the War? I hope he is right.

You wrote that it is a pretty day and asked what we might do on a day like this. I'd like to make up for something I did on another beautiful day. We could take a ride over the same roads that you and I traveled but with a much different attitude than that one. Instead of stumbling and fumbling around the words to tell you I wasn't sure of myself, I would tell you how much I am looking forward to a continuation of love and happiness. You understood, but didn't. I remember only too vividly how hurt you seemed. You did not want to cry, and it hurt me seeing you try to hold back the tears. Then a large tear rolled down your cheek, and you kissed me goodbye. As you did, one of your hot tears dropped onto my cheek. To me, that was probably the most decisive day in my (hidden) love for you. I realized how very sweet and understanding you were, and I only hoped that I could someday consider myself *worthy* of such a wonderful person as you. Up until this day I have not gotten over that feeling, but you deserve to be told how much I love you and how very deserving I think you are.

Now I sound conceited, but the thought of losing your love is much more a point against me than for me. You have given me more confidence than I have ever had before in my whole life. For that I am thankful.

What I want to tell you, now, is that I am very confident that I have done the right thing in telling you how I feel about you.

March 30, 1944

I'm supposed to be on spring vacation, but I have V-12 papers to grade for Dr. McConnell. Bud, I have a date with – guess who. No, definitely not Marc. It is with Mr. Frank McCollum. Your mother has invited me to come for supper, and he will pick me up at 5:45. I am very happy to go there and see everyone. It has been three months since I saw them all. I bought booties and a sweater for your baby brother. The Needles have a baby girl, and I have something for her, too. I shall fix you an Easter box – there will be no more chocolate eggs for the duration.

March 31, 1944

Your father didn't keep me out as late as his son has so many times. It is 11 o'clock, and I am ready for bed. He didn't come *late*, either!

Your mother had a delicious supper, but she went to too much trouble for me. The baby is darling; he is so active and strong. He has dark eyes and hair – I think he looks like Gay and Jean. We talked and talked about you three boys in particular. Ruth showed me the Easter clothes she and Asenath and the baby have. Asenath will look like a baby doll in her new blue coat and hat. They still remember my name, and Asenath wants me to swing her the way I did when you were home. I helped June with her arithmetic, and I almost taught Kak how to tie his shoes. They all showed me things, asked questions, and all tried to sit next to me. I am glad they all like me – it makes me very happy. Your mother showed me the dress she bought with your Christmas money. Your dad brought me up-to-date on news from the shop. I had a very enjoyable time – your mom and dad are so very nice to me. I don't know how I can ever thank them.

April 2, 1944

I have my nine-weeks' grades – 51 right out of 60 for second highest in the class. My roommate has only 43. I have a B plus in English methods; in sociology I was second high. I have an A in geography and a B in religion. My student teaching in seventh grade English begins Tuesday while I watch Miss Young for two weeks. I'd rather not teach English, but I shall.

April 3, 1944

I'm trying to decide where to teach in the fall. You know good and well that I don't intend to have teaching as a *lifetime* profession. For the few years I do teach I want to be satisfied, happy, and making some money which I can save. Springboro offers a job at $1600 per year teaching all commercial subjects. The Hanover job has no vacancy now. There is a vacancy at Ross for $1500. If I say the word, it is mine. I *do* want your opinion to influence me, and I feel you would rather have me close to home. That's where I want to be, too.

My training will never have been a waste of time. These four years have passed so quickly and pleasantly, and I have no debts to pay for my education. I have learned so many other things besides my education for teaching – no one could take that away. I'll always be able to teach, if I want to. Don't worry about my training being a waste of time when we are married.

April 4, 1944

I'm sorry I broke your heart by wanting and loving you only because your strong back could move furniture for me! Your idea of having tracks around the room for moving things does not appeal to me. Every time I think I have a bright idea to tease you, you turn the tables on me and ruin my plan to tease you. That's one thing – life will not be dull!! I'm always teasing Martha. Whenever something happens, I am the first one suspected of the *crime.*

We all teased Dr. Vallance the other day. He had complained of not feeling well because he ate brains for breakfast on Sunday. I bought a get well card, and we sent it to him – he wasn't really ill. I added, "Don't eat brains for breakfast anymore." We signed it "Your dear children," for that is what he calls us. He still doesn't know who sent it, but he told our class about it the next day.

April 5, 1944

I really enjoyed my visit with your family. You do marry *one* person, but in a way you "marry" his whole family, for you will be in contact with them for the remainder of your life. You know that Mother and Daddy think there's no one nicer than you. My loving you has not taken you away from your family – you love them even more for loving me.

When we take that long ride again, as you suggest, *I'm* going to be the one to sit there not saying a word but listening to you as you say all the nice things you've been thinking for the past seven or eight months.

I don't like it when you talk of not being worthy of me. I thought we had all that settled, but here you go again. I am the judge of that, and I am sure you are the most wonderful person I know. I am satisfied, and it is silly for you to think of not being worthy.

Easter, 1944. Bud's furlough was April 7 through 11.

April 11, 1944

When you came to my dorm in your dress blues, all the girls wanted to know who the Marine was, and when they heard my name they could only say, "Oh." All my girl friends have been telling me how handsome, sweet, gentle, humorous, and nice you are – just to mention a few of their adjectives. I am so very proud of you, and all the nice things the girls are saying make me love and appreciate you even more. They tell me how lucky I am, and they're right.

We had a wonderful time when you were home – too wonderful to express. I am very happy, but I am also very sad. I *almost* didn't cry last night when you left, but I couldn't help it. Your sister Mart put her arm around me and said, "He always comes back," but I was never sure she liked me enough for me to marry you. And then she kissed me and was so very nice to me.

April 12, 1944

This teaching and lesson plans are getting me down. I have spent ten hours since this morning, and I am nearly "nuts!"

They measured us for our caps and gowns today. My Easter corsage still smells sweet; I wore it down to dinner. It reminds me of our wonderful Easter. Goodnight, Bud. I'm thinking of all the pleasant memories we associate with "goodnight."

April 12, 1944

It has been only a day and a half since I last saw you, but already I am feeling at a loss for your company. I can't help but feel that I am not all here. Just being able to look into your eyes and hold you in my arms made me feel so wonderfully and gloriously alive.

I arrived back at Cherry Point at 4 a.m., and today I had a lot of work to do, so you see, I didn't get much rest. I am writing this letter at 11 pm, and I have duty tonight. Even though I feel numb all over, I find a feeling of enlightenment and satisfaction in writing to you.

YOU

Of all the people I have met
None can compare with you, as yet.
There will never, never be
Any other girl but you, for me.

April 12, 1944

I've lost all ambition for worldly acclaim, I just want to be with the one I love – Oh, what a wonderful feeling, oh, what a beautiful day. I have a wonderful feeling that everything's sweet and ok. If I were a musician and could compose, then tonight the greatest love song of all times would be born.

Coop and I are both writing and enjoying the cookies. Bob Hope is on the radio; he is so loud that I can hardly think.

Those nights when we were talking and planning the future are full of hope. I am not sorry about present world conditions because I know that I am serving and sharing in a program that will make our future happiness a reality. I love you for caring enough about me to cry when I left for Cherry Point again.

April 14, 1944

The weekend passed so quickly – time always passes quickly when we are happy or busy. I'm remembering you, what you did, what you said, what we thought, and what we talked about. Now I am very busy catching up on sleep, teaching, writing lesson plans, and then rewriting them. In between I've been studying for a sociology exam, and I have helped Dr. McConnell.

We are having graduation pictures taken tonight; perhaps you'll receive one of them soon. Sis told me that Gay will be home for two weeks – that's better than three days.

We made the gossip column in our school paper. I've never been mentioned before; I suppose a Marine in dress blues did the trick. I'm still hearing some very nice compliments about you from some girls who are pretty choicy and popular coeds.

April 14, 1944

I just had a wrestling match with my bunkie. We begin by having fun kidding each other, and we always end up wrestling! I think the girls were impressed with my *blues* more than with me.

Your roommate and friends were very nice to me; I like them all and they like you. Can you imagine how many questions the fellows had for me? Did you have a good time? They all think I should be married. I appreciate their interest.

Nothing could make me happier than knowing that my sister was so kind and understanding. That is the Mart I love and adore. So many do not know her for her nice qualities. She is very eager to see that we boys are happy, and I do believe she would become very rebellious were she to learn that someone was deceiving us. I'm glad you told me of your experience with Mart at the terminal. My days at home are like something out of a storybook – it is hard to realize that I was really there; it is almost like a dream.

April 16, 1944

My chances for being home for your graduation are practically nil.

April 17, 1944

I've been writing lesson plans from 1 pm until 10:30 p.m., and they are *terrible*. On Sunday I wrote from 2 p.m. until 9 and didn't finish even one. In six weeks we'll be preparing for graduation. Exams are only four weeks away. We are required to teach through exams even on the 26th. I shall rejoice when practice teaching is over. All my classes next year at Ross won't be as much work as this *one* is.

April 17, 1944

Don't worry about my lesson plans; I can always manage to get by somehow. Whenever a huge task comes up or I have an unpleasant job to do, I seem to have the philosophy, "You'll live through it!" I shouldn't have bothered you with all my lesson plans, but that was my excuse for not writing after the wonderful leave we had when you were here. Each time I am with you, each letter I receive from you, each new experience we have together makes me love you more and more.

I read parts of your letter to the girls. Ruthie insists on writing a note to you. I've been so busy since you left that I haven't had time to think about our talking of the future. Sometimes I am too busy to appreciate our happiness, but it is always there in the back of my mind. One thing about the scarlet fever – it gave me plenty of time to lie there and think and dream and be happy knowing that you love me.

Bud, I didn't cry much at the station until you disappeared beyond the door. Your family must be used to having their sons come and go again so quickly. When you are gone I feel very alone even though I am with your family. Someday I hope to meet you at the station, and you will never have to leave again.

April 18, 1944

At last I think I am on the right side of my critic teacher. This is her compliment on my paper: "You have a real art in this type of work. Very few students have this ability to help pupils to plan through use of concrete ideas."

I suppose the fellows think we're not married because I don't love you. I hope you understand what I meant when you asked me *when*. I want to make sure that reason is deciding when (?) instead of emotion. Emotion would say, "NOW!! Right this minute!" We need a combination of reason and emotion.

April 18, 1944

I still can't find the letter I wrote you wishing I could be home for Easter and go to church with you. Last evening I cleaned house and arranged all your letters in order. I have only those since June 1943.

April 19, 1944

I love you very much, but I am not complaining about my being so far away because I know that we have a lifetime of happiness ahead of us. I think of a home and all that goes with it.

April 21, 1944

My time here is not my own; I had good intentions of writing last night, but we received a new plane, and I had to pull the acceptance check.

You asked me a question – do I think it is possible for us to be this happy *all the time*? I was always happy at home, and our happiness exceeds anything I have yet experienced. Our present happiness is only a sample of what the future holds. I believe that it will reach a higher and higher degree of comradeship and mutual understanding. If the faith I have is proof enough, then we are in for a very beautiful life.

I am like a huge soap bubble – so full of air you can see through me as plainly as though I were a window. It seems impossible that our love, happiness, or whatever you choose to call it, could increase. But it has.

I do understand what you told me when I asked you *when* (?). I cannot convince you one way or the other for I, too, am undecided. Leaving it up to reason sounds too mechanical, but it is a safe philosophy. I have no control of time since I came into the Marine Corps. Marriage isn't something to be worked

out like a math problem. Therefore, I am depending very much on my natural instinct and Fate to choose the right time. I don't know exactly where or when I would like to be married, but I do know that there will be a proper time.

If we are to depend too much on reason, it will hold us apart for a much longer time than either of us would choose. Service life is cheating so many married people of happiness which they had heretofore experienced; but there are others who chose not to wait but to brave the obstacles that were working against them. Their marriage was a *commendable enterprise*. You can see that I am very undecided, and my ideas are not concrete; therefore they are subject to change. If time were mine, we would already have passed that day when you and I say, "I do."

April 22, 1944

My contract came today, and I signed it. I'll be paid $165 per month; I hope I have done the right thing. If regular teaching is as hard as this practice teaching has been, I shall not teach very long.

Just as I was ready to hop into bed, Sis and Fritzie came. Gay and Fritzie's boyfriend were downstairs. We talked about five minutes, and then they went back to the dance. Sis and Gay seemed to be getting along just fine – I'm glad for his sake.

I moved the furniture around again today, and Martha is confused again. She threatens to write to you to warm you of my weakness – moving furniture.

If you were here tonight and asked me when we should be married, I'd agree with "Now!" I think I was too reasonable and rational when we talked about it. Tonight I don't feel very rational – perhaps it's a good thing you are not here, or maybe it would be better if you *were* here.

April 23, 1944

Last night I arranged all the letters you have written to me since June 6, 1943. I picked one from each month, and I was surprised to find that you haven't changed very much. Many letters seemed as if they were written only yesterday.

I could not find the letter you wrote to Bill McDulin in my defense. I suppose he kept it. You wrote that letter not yet knowing the fullness of my love for you. To have left you playing a guessing game would have been an injustice for you. I sit here writing, and I open my mouth but can't say anything, because there are no words to tell you what an impression you make on my very soul. Maybe that is why I can't express myself, for my soul is the holder and absorber of all my love. After all, the soul is the living part of us, and if we can't explain our soul then neither can we explain the texture of our love which exists there.

At the train station I wanted very much to be alone with you to tell you how much I loved you and how very glad and happy I was having you loving me. I shall *never* forget the night you spoke a prayer for me, or I should say, for us. I wanted to hold you in my arms forever and forget all about the train, but that would have been a very unwise choice.

How would you like a little poem?

MY SOUL

There lies within my soul
A power of incomprehensible pleasure.
I call it love, and it has no equal
That up to it will measure.
Some say it with paint,
Others with notes so concealing.
I don't say it really,
But, oh, what a wonderful feeling!
I love you with all my heart and soul.

Bud.

April 23, 1944

I forgot to tell you – I like yellow gold, *not white* gold. You asked which I think is prettier. Dr. McConnell is lecturing in Boston and in the East. While he is gone for two weeks Ruth Lampe and I are to give tests, and I have to teach one day for him.

Sis was to go to your home for dinner with Gay. I wonder how she acted; Mart and Ralph were to come home, too. Gay says that Asenath calls him "Bud." Sigma Nu fraternity just serenaded one of the girls in our dorm. Will you bring Squadron 46 home with you and sing "The Marines' Hymn" below my window?

April 25, 1944

I have a new airplane; it belongs to Colonel Conrad the CO (Commanding Officer) of this base. He likes my plane; I am in charge of three other planes. Colonel Conrad flew my plane this afternoon, and when he came back he thanked me, which is very out of the ordinary. He made me feel as if I had done him a favor.

April 26, 1944

It seems that all I do is complain, and I'm always tired lately. Maybe it's the scarlet fever; I am scheduled for a physical at the hospital tomorrow. I almost had a fight with my roommate at noon today. Teaching with Miss Young has made us both irritable. I just left the room; everything is ok now.

April 26, 1944

There are times when I, too, become disgusted and unhappy here with wasted time. We must absorb the shocks of life's journey.

I will not be home for your graduation. You have reached a stepping stone in life for which you have been working, and I am so proud of you and your accomplishments. Do you remember in high school when you first decided to go to college?

April 26, 1944

Thank you for the wonderful letter, Bud. I came home from teaching and a conference feeling tired and disgusted, and then I saw your four-page letter in my box, just waiting to be read. I've been happy ever since, and even wrote a lesson plan for next week. Thanks for your inspiration – you have helped me write these plans even if you are so far away.

I didn't really want an answer to my questions as to whether we shall always be as happy as we are now. But our happiness seems almost too good to be true or too good to last, but I'm sure we'll always be happier and happier as each day goes by.

Don't worry about depending on reason as to when we should be married. I'm not as reasonable *really* as I think I am. If the War is over soon, there will be no problem; if it isn't we can still solve our problem rather easily. Others are doing it; so can we!

April 27, 1944

I am happy to know that you are feeling better, and that my letter was able to give you some moment of relaxation.

Sometimes our thoughts are a parasitic drain on our happiness. Confusion is so repressive.

April 28, 1944

I am tired and nervous. I do not like teaching 7th grade English. My critic teacher is TOO demanding. Martha and I are both writing three days of lesson plans every night – one for tomorrow, the one we have to rewrite, and the one for two weeks from now!

I have a first-time appointment with Dr. Stafford. Am I feeling the effects of scarlet fever even now? University Hospital gave me an exam, x-ray, and TB test. That doctor said I was just fine. Little he knows!

April 29, 1944

Since your girl friends are going home this weekend, what do you say to an invitation to take a nice walk with a very ardent and fond admirer? We will enjoy the scenery, but the most wonderful thing to both of us will be our topic of conversation. As we stroll along, hand in hand, I can squeeze your hand and you could retaliate with a soft and tender squeeze. Here is a nice place – shall we sit by the water and talk of all the wonderful times we have in store for us, or shall we talk of our common and mutually pleasant memories? I dare say, that before our walk is over, we shall have talked about both, so let's let our gibberish tongues flow where they may.

I recall very vividly the evening Mrs. Nelson drove us out to the beach. It was such a beautiful night, and we were so happy. I can even now feel that "up in the clouds" feeling that I experienced. You were so soft and wonderfully warm and close as the moonbeams dancing on the water. My love was so refreshing and alive as the very wind that came in on the waves. I am reminded of the porch swing at Mrs. Nelson's and at your home – these memories are "out of this world."

I am reminded of the afternoon you and I took that walk along the river – remember? It is getting dark; I think we had better discontinue our walk and get back to the present and reality.

April 30, 1944

I'm going to the doctor tomorrow. Mother thinks I have just been working too hard with classes, student teaching, and working for those three professors. I shall tell the doctor about the scarlet fever. Several of us took a long walk through the Western College campus and then to the formal gardens. We ended our walk with a Coke at Tuffy's (where they serve those delicious toasted rolls).

I have another letter from Marc – that makes five or six, which I haven't answered. He expects to be home on furlough before he is shipped overseas. I hope he doesn't expect me to build up his morale before he ships out!

I asked the girls to write to Ed; I won't have time until after graduation.

May 1, 1944

Some animals are more wonderful than some humans. I just saw the movie, *Lassie, Come Home*.

May 1, 1944

I'm sorry to write to you about how I feel; every letter for a week has said nothing except that I don't feel well. I was fine until student teaching began. My critic teacher said my lesson went fine today; she doesn't know that I am ill. I felt fine when you were home.

The university doctor doesn't know much. He said the streptococcus infection from my scarlet fever and the flu *probably* settled in my chest and is causing me to feel like this. He gave me a TB test.

He was so indefinite that I came to Dr. Stafford's office. It has been over two hours and he is not back yet. I am first when he does come – IT'S MY TURN.

Dr. Stafford said it is all nerves and that I am working too hard. He gave me two kinds of pills and some vitamins. I had a thorough exam for $6.50. Maybe my letter was a little too pessimistic at the beginning. He says there is nothing wrong with me from the scarlet fever – I'm so very glad! I feel better after talking to him.

May 3, 1944

I am feeling much, much better. Dr. Stafford assured me that there is nothing seriously wrong with me. The worrying about it made me as sick as did the physical feeling. He said that being nervous and worn out is a result of scarlet fever. My TB shot from the university doctor is negative, so there is nothing to worry about there.

I have another letter from Marc; he's getting to be a pest. I don't answer his letters.

You're right in saying we probably won't want to wait until the War is over to be married. I'm not going to be stubborn with you – I want to make you happy. If waiting will make you unhappy, then I'll do my best to make you happy!

May 3, 1944

Do you realize that we girls were taking a long walk the very same time you had invited me to take an imaginary walk with you?

Your mother has your dress blues pictures for me, but I am not going home this weekend. I think I'd better stay here and rest. We're ordering our graduation announcements tomorrow. I'm not sure to whom I should send one. Any suggestions?

Yes, you are a worry wart. I can't imagine "woman-hater McCollum" afraid of losing me!!

May 5, 1944

The new wing for my airplane came in, and I have been working long

hours trying to get it back in flying shape. Tomorrow it will be test hopped; hope it will come back ok.

Spring at Miami is more beautiful than it is here. Here the seasons seem to run into each other, and we do not have the chance to experience the fullness of the change from the dullness of winter to the living aliveness of beautiful spring.

I still remember you sitting across from me in bookkeeping class. That was when I first knew you. All of the time we were together and so very close, and we didn't even know each other. Gee, what a shame!

Please try to take it easy!

Memories are like water – we can't live on them alone. We need something more substantial and vitalizing. I had a very depressing, morbid thought the other day. I have never before had such a thought. I wondered how I would feel if something serious happened, and you were not there anymore. I almost began to cry and shake all over. My reaction was one of such loneliness that life would be completely empty without you, if not unbearable. I do believe I would cease to care about anything. I made myself stop thinking such thoughts by starting to wrestle with Ed, my bunkie. *Don't you ever leave me.*

May 6, 1944

I'm trying to clean our room, and Martha and Ruthie are dancing. They are scattering my *mound of dirt*. I am feeling much better; I think the doctor's pills keep me from feeling tired and nervous. I have only 13 more lessons plans to write – I shall make it! I dreamed they were sending you to China, and you had just five minutes to say goodbye. Why do I dream such crazy stuff?

May 7, 1944

The weekend was very restful. We had a picnic on Saturday afternoon, and on the way home we picked a bouquet of dandelions and violets for Dr. Vallance. It's hard to see such a nice prof ill in bed. His wife put them in a vase; he laughed and told us jokes. He was very happy that we had come to see him.

Just after I had left the dorm your mother called to see how I was feeling. My roommate talked to her. She gave your picture to my mother who will bring it to me when she comes for the weekend of Mother's Day.

Ruthie and I played Chinese Checkers with a sailor from Mississippi and another from Iowa. I danced with a Marine for about five minutes; he wanted to walk me home, but I had no problem telling him, "No."

"Moon River," the radio program, is on WLW. Pretend we're listening in your car. I'm sleepy and tired. Are you still here with me listening to "Moon River?" That's good. My head is on your shoulder; my hand is in yours; I feel so safe and warm here with you. Here's a goodnight kiss – wait a minute – only *one?*

May 8, 1944

We had the test flight of my plane. It passed, but I was air sick again. I am disgusted and feel as if I never want to see another plane again, but I know that isn't true. The airplane is as important in tomorrow's development as was the covered wagon. You know its possibilities, but I don't think you feel the romantic wonders of those possibilities.

All 71-hour passes have been eliminated because my squadron personnel have been increased. Now my chances of seeing you become less and less.

Yesterday Koehler, Cooper, and I went paddling in a canoe up some beautiful lagoons. Few people are in the swamps of North Carolina, so we had an uninterrupted and quiet afternoon by ourselves. So many times I thought how nice it would be if you could be there with me enjoying all of nature's natural beauty.

Your graduation is getting nearer and nearer, and I can see a huge strong wall with a small door, and you have earned the key to its lock. I envy you, Dorothea. I'm glad you suggested sending an invitation to Mart and Ralph. Send one to me, for I know with all my heart that no matter how near I am to your graduation, I will be so very proud of you.

May 9, 1944

I have only eleven more days of student teaching. I have applied for my teaching certificate. I shall not be a coed or a student teacher much longer. "Take it easy" is a laugh. I have a term paper to write for religion class, other assignments for class, and lesson plans to write for Miss Young. It is certainly a relief to know that Dr. Stafford says there are no complications from scarlet fever. I'm working very little for Dr. McConnell. Don't worry about me; I'll be all right. Mother doesn't want me to work this summer.

Gay had a great time on furlough, but he spent most of his time with Sauerbecks – even stayed all night. He had been home several days before your dad even saw him. Your whole family was hurt. Your sisters told JoAnn that you loved your mother and father too much to stay away during your furlough. They love you for being so considerate, and *so do I.*

May 9, 1944

It seems ages ago since I last saw you; I might just as well be on a South Pacific island as in this faraway place.

Far away in distance reckoned
Yet how near you seem to me!
Separated, yet together
In the realms of memory.

Here in thought
The miles between us melt away.
Parted, yet in spirit meeting
Every hour of every day.

May 12, 1944

I shall not be able to come to your graduation. Your mother is right. You should *not* work this summer. Do you realize that you have been going full steam for four whole years?

I can't picture you driving a car. If you do buy a car, you need to *learn to swim* before you learn to drive. There is much water between your home and Ross school, and you might run into the river. One of our planes crashed into the ocean only 300 yards off shore. Of the six on board, only three survived. The other three could not swim. I can assure you that any children we may have will definitely know how to swim. Twice in my childhood I had to have artificial respiration administered to me simply because I could not swim!

WAITING FOR A LETTER

Waiting for a letter
How long the time may be,
Looking for the postman
Watching anxiously.
My sweetheart and my mother
Just live from day to day
Hoping for a letter
A little line to say, "All's well."
For that is sufficient
When loved ones are apart
To banish fear and worry
And cheer the lonely heart.

May 14, 1944

I feel so utterly helpless and disgusted because I cannot plan or hope for anything definite. This War may be over within the next year, but my enlistment papers say, "For the duration and six months after the *national emergency*." That can be a very indefinite period of time. You have told me that now is not the time to be married. Under these circumstances it would be totally unfair to you for me to ask you to subject yourself to these conditions.

Even if I were to pick up where I left off before I entered the Service, where was I? Nowhere. I actually believe I am going backward instead of forward. Even though I feel as I do, I wanted to tell someone.

May 16, 1944

So much is happening around here as we begin to complete our education and head for exams. Midge is in the hospital with a boil on the end of her spine caused by a bad bump. Eleanor cut my hair about an inch. How would you like to have a curl?

I am not ill. I have stopped taking the pills and feel just fine. The problem is that I can't work hard all day, study, and work until midnight or later, and then get up early to race from place to place continuously. I'll sleep until ten tomorrow.

You think I'd drive a car into the river? I am not a moron! You can't picture me driving a car, huh? Just you wait and see. You think I'm not too good with mechanical things, but a typewriter is a mechanical device! You'll be surprised the next time you come home. Your doubting my driving ability makes me even more determined.

Did you write the poem, "Waiting for a Letter"? It is so good that I wonder if you found it in a book.

May 16, 1944

Two weeks ago I bought a Mothers' Day gift, and I have not yet sent it! Do you know why? I have no string. Why can't I be more prompt and dependable?

You have weathered many hardships during these four years, but you have had so many nice experiences and met so many good people. You have gained a goal which I shall never have the opportunity to reach. I wanted to fly – that's all over. I wanted to graduate from college – that's interrupted. Now where am I – in the Marine Corps. What do I have – only my self-respect, your love, and a world of opportunities (?). I can't survive on these substances.

May 16, 1944

Mother came for Mothers' Day; we went to the sorority serenade for mothers. We attended a university play and had a spread in the room before bedtime. After church we visited Aunt Lil, and Uncle Russell drove her home – a very tired mother from so much walking. The tint on one photo does not do justice to the Marine uniform. One photo looks so real it almost scares me, for I think it's actually you.

I WISH WE COULD SEE THE END OF THE WAR!

May 16, 1944

When several fellows ask me how it feels to be in love, I tell them in such glowing terms that they always come back for more.

We're going to Atlantic Beach for the weekend. It will be fun swimming in the ocean. I wish you could be here. I miss you more and more as each day goes by. I need to see you and talk to you; everything seems so empty without you.

May 18, 1944

It is strange to switch from teaching one hour for Dr. McConnell and then being a student the following hour. The strain of writing lesson plans and student teaching is almost over – Martha and I are giddy – just plain silly – it is over!

Mildred is out of the hospital, but it hurts her to walk. I sent out 22 initiations.

Right now we can see no end to the War – but it can't last forever! Six months after the national emergency could mean anything – who knows when they will declare the end of the emergency? I know it bothers you that I said wartime is not the time to be married. In a way that's true, but I'm not going to wait for many more years. What's a war compared with two people in love?

May 18, 1944

If one of my pictures is so real it scares you, then how do you keep from becoming hysterical when you actually see me? Don't answer that. I'm glad that your mother finally got to meet Mom and Dad. I know our mothers have talked on the phone many times. There is no need to tell you to take it easy as you prepare for exams – it is like asking me to stop playing basketball. I shut my eyes, and my arms can feel your warmth, because I love you so much. We're separated, yet together in the realms of memory.

May 19, 1944

Poor Bud. No string to send your mother's gift. I'm sending you some now! I'll be happy to take care of such details for you. We have been studying for hours and hours. You see, we have just one book. We have giggled all night; my stomach hurts from so much laughing. I think we are so silly tonight, because this is the first night we have not had to write lesson plans.

Please don't say you'll never graduate from college. It is quite likely that you shall – I plan for you to go to college. You say you have only self-respect, my love, and a world of opportunities. Many people don't have even these three things.

I'll pick up my graduation picture tomorrow. You shall have it soon. It looks much better than the proofs – thank goodness! Your picture is here as I write this letter. It looks so real – as if you could step from behind the glass and speak to me!

I remember how your letters changed last May.

May 20, 1944

I read in yesterday's newspaper that 13 Marines were killed in a Navy patrol plane which crashed near Cherry Point. Did you know about it? Please don't fly anymore than you are required to do so. Please be careful. I don't want anything to spoil our happiness, because I love you very, very much!

One more week and it will all be over. I suppose I'll be unhappy to leave the dorm and these good friends, but I'll be going into another phase of my life. Eleanor cut about an inch off my hair; I am sending you one curl.

May 20, 1944

Tonight I am in Morehead City at the USO. I can't say I am having a wonderful time tonight, for I have only memories of your having been here with me. Tomorrow you will be taking exams, and I shall be busy getting a sunburn.

May 22, 1944

Cherry Point is a world all its own – I am so tired of not being able to see beyond a clump of trees. If I had two problems figured out, I would not ever again have feelings of disgust:

1. **A job after the War to supply us with a living. This worries me.**
2. **Being able to keep the faith that you have in me.**

I don't believe that Fate is playing a foul ball with us. I am sorry to have given you that impression. I worry about the conflicts that marriage now would create in your work. I need to be talking to you, not writing my thoughts in a letter. I love you more than a gallon of gasoline. That's not what I intended to say! I love you more than anything in all the world.

May 23, 1944

I had geography and sociology exams today. I was able to answer everything correctly in geography, and in sociology I answered 125 true-false questions in 20 minutes. Every senior in the School of Education had to take the school administration exam. I am glad to tell you that I had the highest grade in the entire class – even beat the Phi Betas and my roommate! My conference with my critic teacher went well, and I received a very good rating.

May 25, 1944

We took our critic teacher out for dinner, and then we took her back to the dorm, so she could see our room. When she saw your picture, she wanted to know who was dating a Marine. "I am," I confessed. Her reply surprised me. "Oh, I just love Marines! Why didn't you tell me you were dating a Marine?" Maybe she wouldn't have been so demanding of my lesson plans???

Thanks for the Marine head scarf and handkerchief.

May 25, 1944

Saturday night here in Morehead I devoted it all to you by walking up and down the beach just as we had done. I had beautiful thoughts and memories.

I was hoping that you would not see the accident in the newspaper. Yes, I knew about the 13 Marines who lost their lives. Do you remember that I told you our squadron is the base squadron? I had duty that night, and at about 2 am I had to get up and have the crash plane ready. We located the crash from the air. Our planes do all that type of work – air rescue, crash location, etc. So you see, we are busy on every crash that happens within 200 miles of the base.

May 28, 1944

I awoke this morning knowing that it is your graduation day. I am very proud of you.

May 28, 1944

Graduation from Miami!

I am the first of our entire family to graduate from college; 17 relatives came to Oxford for the occasion. Their gifts totaled $19.00. Mr. Fichter gave me $5, and Mrs. Tully gave me two $25 war bonds. Your mother gave me blue satin pajamas, but they are too pretty to wear. Uncle Claude gave me $5 and this note: "I have loved you since the day you were born, and I have followed with interest your very rapid rise from one grade to the other, and now today is the climax of your school career. Darling, I know you have lots of sense, but always be careful, and if you ever need a true friend, always remember your loving uncle, Claude."

Everyone has always been so good to me!

May 29, 1944

Many of my aunts and uncles whom you have never met came to graduation. They finally lined us up – faculty in one line and graduates in another. Sailors with flags led the procession which was many blocks long. The faculty followed the seniors, and as we approached Withrow Court the sailors split our line and proceeded to the rear to bring up the faculty in the center of our line and into the building.

The speaker was a member of the Norwegian Parliament and a member of the League of Nations. After an hour and a half, I received my sheepskin. Uncle Claude was the most proud – you *must* meet him. He was about 12 years old when I was born upstairs in his family home. He has always been my favorite uncle.

May 29, 1944

HOME!!

No more lesson plans.

No more teaching for Dr. McConnell and Mr. Fichter.

No more grading their students' papers.

No more studying.

No more exams.

No more picnics, spreads, or walks with my wonderful roommate and college friends.

May 30, 1944

Now that I have time to think, I have some suggestions as you contemplate a job and the future. I think we should make some plans now so that when the War is over, we'll be ready to go!

I have learned there are four steps to follow:

1. Proposing
2. Planning
3. Executing
4. Evaluating

List the thing you would like to do and then

1. Compare
2. Choose a preference
3. Is it interesting or enjoyable?
4. Salary?

You already have college credits. Two more years plus two summers should be enough hours for a degree.

Would you like to go back to Wake Forest? Ohio State? Miami? Or would you like to skip school and find a job in aviation? You are already skilled in that field.

May 30, 1944

There are no rules which keep married teachers from teaching. I don't know what rules you are talking about. Since the War, they're glad to hire anyone, and many teachers have returned from retirement.

Sometimes I, too, wonder about what job you will choose in the future. I only wonder; I do not worry. Never do I worry about losing faith in you; nothing can ever cause that! As for after the War, let's think about it and begin to make plans now. I had said we should wait until the War is over and then think about it. I'VE CHANGED MY MIND. (Maybe it is the result of all those lesson *plans* I had to make for student teaching!) You'll feel much better about a future job if we begin to plan now. Just as soon as you take off that Marine uniform, we will already know what you are to do the very next day.

May 31, 1944

I don't feel bad about leaving college; there was so much work connected with it. I'll still be able to remain in contact with all my Miami friends.

May 31, 1944

I have been working 14 hours a day. It doesn't leave much time for writing.

June 1, 1944

True happiness comes from making someone else happy.

June 2, 1944

I have no letter from you today, but I have a letter from Marc. You can read it for yourself. I need your advice!

My photo should be in the mail; Ruth mailed it for me. I put all of your letters in order and fell asleep rereading some of them.

June 2, 1944

Thanks for the details of your graduation. Do you really have more aunts and uncle than I have met? There were so many cousins to meet at Easter that I have had nightmares about them!

June 4, 1944

Thank you for starting me toward a planned postwar goal. I have considered coaching and aviation. Ohio is a state which will see aviation advance as any other state. That is just a minor factor. If I go back to college, I do not think it would be Wake Forest. I'd rather be closer to old friends. However, I am ready to stray from that thought if the situation should present itself. I won't try to cram all my thoughts into one letter. I am so happy that I love you.

June 5, 1944

I'm doing nothing; finally relaxing. I picked some strawberries, and Mother is making a cake. I'll eat an extra piece for you, or should we give it to Ruth to make up for the piece you ate?

I had such a good time in North Carolina. During wartime people learn to appreciate life in terms of days, and days are so very important.

It is all right that you could not come for graduation. There were so many friends and relatives there, I could not have given you all my attention.

June 5, 1944

Sometimes it seems that I have loved you all of my life. But I didn't know

that you were *the one* until we took that long ride, and I decided we would no longer go steady. At that time I did not think it was fair to you for me to tell you that I was in love with you! That one hot tear on my cheek confirmed my feelings, but I was silent.

Last June I did finally tell you, because I knew I was cheating you. It was like a flower bursting into all its wondrous beauty.

Now, what to tell Marc? I'm prejudiced, so I can't give a good answer. You'd have to decide. The polite thing to do would be to accept his invitation. He is a Serviceman; he is going overseas. That would hurt me. If you were to tell him a positive "No," that would make me happy. Tell him what you think, without *any influence* from me. I wish I were the one who would be home on furlough.

I hope your picture arrives tomorrow!

D-Day, June 6, 1944

Your letter reminding me that "the way to a man's heart is through his stomach" has me baking cookies all afternoon.

All we hear on the radio is concerning the invasion of Europe. President Roosevelt has been on the radio all day. We are happy and at the same time fearful because of the boys who will be killed.

June 6, 1944

Your picture is beautiful, and you are actually looking at me! I'm afraid to look into your eyes too long, for you might wink at me. I love you dearly for loving me in the manner that you do. D-Day has been overshadowed by the receiving of your sweet gift.

June 6, 1944

We in the Service are not elated over D-Day; we accept it as just another phase of the War. If it goes right, it will be only another step toward the eventual end. We shall leave the rejoicing to those who have a little better than a spectator's interest. We realize what lies ahead for those in the so-called invasion. When peace is signed, then truly will we show our rise in patriotism.

I ramble on and on; it is just like a strawberry cream pie. The cream is just the filler, and the strawberries are what really make the pie. When I write a letter, and tell you how much I love you and how much I miss you, with all my emotions acting in harmony to verify what I am trying to say, then, to put it simply, I am down to the strawberries.

June 7, 1944

Today I have been sewing some drapes for my room. Your mother telephoned me about your transfer to Arkansas.

June 7, 1944

You are sitting right here, looking at me. I always liked that dress you are wearing because it is so soft.

These fellows are arguing with a dictatorial attitude toward the people we are fighting with and against. To hear them talk, you'd think Great Britain was our enemy; they hate the English. They want to keep *all* the islands we are fighting to win. Maybe according to the law of survival of the fittest this may be right; to me the only right law is *human rights.* It makes me angry all over to know that the very thing which we are fighting against is exactly what these fellows propose.

June 8, 1944

Isn't it a coincidence! On Sunday you wrote a letter begging for cookies. Not knowing of your request, I baked cookies for you on Tuesday and mailed them on Wednesday. Today, on Thursday, I received your letter asking for cookies. I sent them before I knew you had asked. Do you think we could exist on love and cookies when we are married? You know I can't cook.

June 8, 1944

We have been searching all day for a plane lost with four people aboard. It was returning from South Carolina. Our squadron has been having a great deal of bad luck recently. Last Saturday a GH burned to a crisp after cracking up on takeoff. I have a 6:15 flight tomorrow morning to go to Goldsboro, NC, about 300 miles from here. I have worked on my plane so long and know its characteristics so well that I would not be afraid to go anywhere in it, provided I had checked it and put my ok on the flight clearance sheet. The pilot who was flying this last plane was one swell guy. Oh, well, that is the War on this side, and I suppose nothing can be done about it. Nothing I can say will alter what Fate has in store for those who cross Her path or come within Her focus.

June 9, 1944

I had made up my mind about Marc before I received your letter – I shall NOT go with him! Your mother and dad were here bringing my graduation gift.

Five of the children came along and enjoyed playing with JoAnn and Bobby. The baby is growing so fast. Asenath talked my ear off. She was looking for you; she thinks you are always with me.

June 12, 1944

I am just one of seven million victims of this War machine. I shall continue working in this dull, monotonous place.

June 12, 1944

I'll be glad to fix you some strawberry shortcake with whipped cream, too.

June 13, 1944

I hope Asenath didn't really talk your ear off. I look forward to the day she will be right, and I shall be with you all the time.

June 13, 1944

We're all going back to Oxford next weekend. June, Eleanor, and Stewart are in summer school, so we'll stay with them. I miss them all and will be glad to see them again.

Here is some information concerning the Pacific Islands; Dr. McConnell has taught us this:

In 1944 the War was on everyone's mind. It is important for Japan not to control or own the Pacific Islands. We have Hawaii and Alaska as outposts, but we need more. We need islands in the Pacific to protect our outposts, too.

After the First World War Japan suggested that she be given a mandate over the Marianas - except Guam, the largest and best which we wanted, along with the Marshall Islands and the Carolinas.

We were friendly with Japan and too blind to see what such control meant to Japan and how valuable they were to her. The island of Yap is especially valuable since it is close to the Philippines. More than a thousand islands were given to Japan without any consideration. Japan has had more than twenty years to fortify them.

That's why it is so important that we take them now. The other islands which belong to the Dutch and Britain, but which the Japs took, don't mean as much in a military way as the islands which Japan has held for twenty years. To take these from the Japs is an important gain.

June 14, 1944

The best part of our whole story is the part you played in recognizing the potential qualities of our friendship. I'm so happy that my first plan failed in the discontinuance of our steady courtship. But the new and grand love that was that day recognized by me is something for which I shall ever be grateful.

The War may last two more years! THAT'S TERRIBLE!!

P.S. I feel that something terrible is about to happen.

June 15, 1944

It did happen; our squadron is all fouled up.

June 16, 1944

The War in the Pacific is going well – those Japs are running for home! Perhaps soon you can come home, and I promise to make your life anything but boring!

June 18, 1944

Today I had my photo taken with you. You'll understand when you receive the picture. All my friends know you. Coop would like to find a girl like you. We had some time off and went sailing.

June 19, 1944

I have saved $200, but I won't have it long.

June 21, 1944

I'm tired of writing letters; this War *must* be over soon!!

June 21, 1944

Today I was so air sick that I wished I were dead. I shut my eyes and tried putting my hands over them, but everything kept revolving in my head and stomach.

Bud's drawing. My back door.

June 22, 1944

I'm in Oxford and have helped Dr. McConnell proctor the final exam for the V-12 boys. I shall help him grade their papers.

The other girls are coming for Saturday and Sunday. June is as sweet as ever; I'm staying with Stewart.

June 23, 1944

These days seem like an empty shell. I just lie here and dream of you; I can forget the war and this immediate existence. My position in the war is beyond my poor power to control. I feel it is not right for me to remain a non-combatant. Ask your father what he thinks – he was in France during WW I. And now, here is a drawing of your back door.

June 24, 1944

I graded 100 V-12 exams; it took me 20 hours. We plan to meet the afternoon bus; Midge and Brose will be on it.

Mr. Fichter wants me to go to Columbus for two weeks while his secretary is on vacation. If there is a chance that you will be home on July 14, I shall *not* go. Mother thinks that I still need the rest.

June 24, 1944

These days with college friends will always be memorable, for they are really true friends.

I had an odd dream about you last night; it involved your *many* cousins. Did you say you have 40 cousins?

June 26, 1944

I had a wonderful time here in Oxford. We had a big picnic; we ate it on the university golf course. I know, but the grass was so soft and green. Besides we have already graduated, so what could they do to us? We bought sundaes at Folker's and ate them under the water tower. We could hear the music coming from the Huddle.

We moved beds around, and six of us slept in four beds. There were six of us with one mirror trying to put our hair up; there were six girls for two showers!

When the alarm went off at 7 am, I shut it off and set it for 8. Someone else shut it off at 8, and we finally rolled out at 9 am.

Congratulations on saving $200 in two months! But, what do you mean by saying that you won't have it long? You'd better have it and keep on saving it.

June 27, 1944

Letters seem so inadequate, but then most of the time they are very uplifting. At times when I should put my arms around you and tell you how very much I love you and how sorry I am that we are so far apart, letters are an inadequate example as a means of expression.

I have five days of leave coming to me. With travel time subtracted that would leave only 2 1/2 days at home. If you could come down, I might be able to stretch it to eight days with an added weekend pass. Do you realize how very little we have been together in the past several years?

June 27, 1944

This is what Daddy said to tell you about being in the States and not where the real action is: "Someone has to stay in this country to keep the wheels going, and you happen to be one who was so chosen. I was across 14 months out of 22 months in the Service. Where are the heroes – they're dead, some of them!! The others? What thanks do they get? None at all! I am treated the same exactly and sometimes worse than men who were never in the Service or who were in this country as I risked my neck."

Those were his ideas, and I think he can see the entire picture much better by looking back these 25 years than you seeing only the present. He's patriotic all right, you know that, but no one has ever done anything to show appreciation for his service.

I didn't see Marc when he was home, but today I received a very nice letter from him. You can read it for yourself. I wonder who told him about you?

June 30, 1944

Folker's sundaes!!! Well, you come right after ice cream as my favorite – only you won't melt. Are you offended? I'm sorry. I didn't mean it, but I *do* like ice cream!

July 2, 1944

You tell me exactly why I am so tired of writing letters – they are a poor substitute for being with you. If you decide that 2 1/2 days at home is better, then that's what to do. If you prefer to have me come there, just say the word, and I'll come. It's all up to you – start deciding! You haven't been home much since 1940. We had a grand time that summer; then I went off to college; the next year you went off to college. When you came home, you worked nights, and in the fall you joined the Marines. Since your furlough at Christmastime, we have seen each other only four days!

July 3, 1944

Do you remember the first time we heard "Indian Summer" on the Hit Parade? Just as that song represents the love call of early primitive Americans, so does it represent to me the birth of our love. Just close your eyes, and I'll be there beside you, just as you are here beside me.

I wonder why I never gave you a nickname? Maybe it is because Dorothea is such a pretty name.

July 4, 1944

It would be very inconsiderate of me toward my parents if I were to choose 2 1/2 days with them and with you as opposed to about eight days with you alone. I shall plan toward the short furlough.

July 4, 1944

I have been painting the woodwork in the living room. It hasn't rained here for more than a month, and the temperature is 100 degrees in the shade. I guess it's as hot as a firecracker!!

July 5, 1944

Bud, you're breaking my heart by putting ice cream ahead of me! How can you do this to me? It is so hot here that I am nearly melting – maybe I'm not so different from ice cream. We'll see how much you like ice cream – next time you go to the station to return to base, you can take an ice cream cone with you. When you're ready to leave and kiss me goodbye, you can just *lick your ice cream cone!*

A huge harvest moon is climbing up into the sky to remind me of the Carolina moon that darted in and out of the clouds at the beach in Morehead City.

July 7, 1944

I have been trying to discover information about my transfer to a Marine Bomber Unit. There is no information. I did not ask for a transfer. My transfer to a new squadron means that I will not make the Staff Sgt. rating for which I was scheduled.

July 8, 1944

Isn't it strange – you never called me by a nickname, and I never called you by your real name. No one can pronounce my last name (Fant) correctly, so I might as well change it. I shall change "Miss" to "Mrs." also.

July 9, 1944

Lick my *ice cream cone!* Indeed! I didn't mean it, honest. The moon you saw is the same one I saw the other night, bringing identical memories, but most of all I remember you and how much I disliked knowing you had to leave in the morning. I realized how much I would miss you. I'm missing you now, and it would appear that it will be ever so long before I see you again – unless I'm lucky.

July 9, 1944

I'm glad you have chosen to come home so your parents can enjoy your furlough, too. Mr. Fichter wants me to go to Columbus for two weeks while his secretary is on vacation. I could use the money; I haven't worked all summer. I told him a definite, "No." Mother is glad I'll be resting up for the time I begin teaching.

July 10, 1944

My first day in this new arrangement went smoothly; I seem to have renewed vigor. I need to stay busy so I won't be so lonesome for you.

YOU

My life is all I have to give
And my pleasures now are few;
But the happiest moments I ever spent
Were those I spent with you.

July 12, 1944

Thanks for the snapshot – the one you had taken with my picture. Mother and I are wallpapering, now that I have finished painting the woodwork.

It's too bad that your new rating didn't come in before Squadron 46 was abolished. Can't your new Squadron recommend you for the rating now? Would you be a mech at a base overseas?

July 13, 1944

I don't know anyone here at the line who could help me get a 71-hour pass. If I could, would you come down for just a weekend? Dawgonnit! Why doesn't this War end???

July 14, 1944

Mother and I have papered the ceiling, and I have paste from my shoulders to my fingers, in my hair, and under my chin. Your mother read me your long letter concerning your transfer. I assured her that you had not asked to be transferred.

Yes, Bud, you're right – we never have had an argument or a fight. (Maybe we've never been together long enough in the past four years.) Do you realize that we have seen each other only four days since last Christmas? We simply do not disagree; I hope we never shall. We can always just talk about it.

July 14, 1944

Do you realize that another paperhanger is probably most responsible for this War? You won't become another Hitler, will you?

All leaves and furloughs have been canceled as of today! We are going to Bocachiica, Florida. That is even farther away, so don't even think about coming down. I have the feeling that we are closer than we have ever been, for with each passing day we are both overcoming obstacles, even if they are only time alone.

July 16, 1944

You asked me if I'd come down for only a weekend. Of course, I would! At one time I would have said, "NO," because the trip is so hard, and the time is so short. Now I've changed my mind for no time is too short really, and a little bit is better than nothing at all.

July 16, 1944

I have had the most enjoyable day since I came into the Marine Corps – I have been daydreaming of our past, present, and future love. The dreams of you arouse within me feelings of placid wonderment. When I realized that I, too, shared in that review, I was very happy – so happy that I felt that if I opened my eyes, you would be here with me.

It will be months before I see you; I begin to dislike more and more the part I have to play in this War. I am not regretting my being here for the simple reason that I'm 100% American, and I believe in the preservation of our way of life.

PS. How about a date? When? I don't know, but save it, and I'll collect.

July 17, 1944

Friends tell me that it is obvious to them when you are in my mind and thoughts. My love for you is as obvious as the nose on my face!

July 17, 1944

There were 80 people from church here for a picnic yesterday; am I tired! Did you know Bob Skillman who joined with you in the Petzold Platoon? He was killed on Saipen Island in the Mariannas recently.

July 18, 1944

Everything is so dull here; it is quite a contrast from the artificial protection of college during this Wartime.

If you get a furlough, I'll be very happy to come wherever you are stationed. I'm not too tired; I've been resting all summer.

July 18, 1944

Now I know more details concerning my transfer: Bocachiica is in Key West, Florida. My squadron is VMB-622. V means heavier than air; MB means Marine Bomber. We shall leave Cherry Point before August 8. Now I understand

that I shall be transferred to Arkansas in four months. All leaves and furloughs have been canceled. We are busy servicing VMBs, and I have been promoted to Engineer Crew Chief in charge of 15 other engineers.

Bud's drawing. Airplane

July 20, 1944

I am very happy tonight for two reasons: your very interesting letter about your daydreams, and that I don't have to teach English. I'll teach business subjects and either math or geography. We use the geography book which Dr. McConnell wrote.

The War news is sounding better. Togo resigned, Yap was bombed, Russia is tearing along, Guam is being bombed, and there are advances in France and Italy. The Pacific War is going just as Dr. McConnell told us. The U.S. fleet should head for China and thus cut Japan off from the Philippines and other South Pacific Islands. Yap is very important, since it is so close to the Philippines.

What do you think about when you daydream about the future? I have concrete incidents to remember and enjoy when I recall the past, but I can only wonder about the future. The only thing of which I am sure is our love. Please hurry to collect on that date!

July 21, 1944

This situation is very dull and uninteresting, except when I am working on my plane. I daydream of you to escape all the regulations and mental strain of this routine.

July 21, 1944

Once JoAnn asked me what I was laughing about; I was thinking of something that happened, and I was smiling as if I were witnessing the real incident instead of only a memory of it.

I can't keep you in suspense any longer, so sit down so you can take the shock. Here's the surprise: The other day Mother told me there isn't any Santa Claus. That was a *terrible* shock to me, and I hated to tell you. That's my *surprise!*

July 24, 1944

I never did believe in Santa Claus; I could have put you wise long ago. Honestly, I am still waiting for the *real* surprise.

What do I dream of when I think of the future? I think about you and me. What can I do to be everything you would want me to be, and what could I do to make you happy? Next, I wonder about a future occupation. I wonder, when do I have the right to ask you something very, very important? I can sum it all up: a home, a family, a job, you and me in a life together.

July 25, 1944

It is still so hot; we received only a few drops of rain. It was enough to uncurl my hair. I remember when Bud McCollum uncurled my hair on the school bus when it rained after the track meet. Grrrr! I was absolutely furious with you for putting water on my hair! You were off to a very bad start with me!!

July 27, 1944

We need to keep our planes in flying shape, so the pilots can complete all their flying time and then go overseas.

July 27, 1944

Eleanor has invited me to visit her for four or five days. I shall accept her invitation since I can't go to Morehead City.

July 28, 1944

Your mother telephoned me for news of you, since you had not sent her a letter for a couple of weeks. She told me all the news of your family. Bill is back in civilization; he is farther and farther away from the battles.

July 28, 1944

At this very moment I feel very close to you even in this faraway place. While it is raining, and as the cool breeze passes over me, and as the rain drips from the trees after a clean shower, my mind wends its way home and to you. This subconscious mind is a refuge from the systematic work-a-day world here in the Service.

July 29, 1944

Each letter I write brings me one letter closer to the time when no more letters are necessary. It is almost dark now, so I must leave this porch swing and go inside. The stars are coming out. "Star light, star bright, first star I see tonight. I wish I may, I wish I might, have the wish I wish tonight." I wish you'd come home before September.

July 29, 1944

I'm sorry I play the part of a mean person in your dreams; you can rest assured that I am still the docile person that you know. I hope your dreams improve, because I have experienced two very vividly nice ones about you.

August 1, 1944

I have noticed a change in you from the "egotistical ambitious" person you once were, as you described yourself. Now you're thinking of the future as a mutually pleasant sharing of your life with someone you dearly love – meaning ME.

August 1, 1944

No, I haven't changed – just realized the very wonderful truth, that's all.

August 6, 1944

God is very wonderful for making love the predominate bond of mutual companionship. If life for me were to cease at this very moment, I could truthfully say that I have experienced a feeling of happiness that is ultimate in its true and live form.

August 7, 1944

Last night I dreamed we got married. They asked you to give the prayer at the wedding ceremony. You did a very remarkable job of saying a beautiful prayer, but I don't remember a word that you said. I could see us standing there.

August 8, 1944

I've been studying all evening; these large bombers are quite complex. I'm trying to learn as much as I can; I like being busy, for it keeps me from thinking about things which tend to make me homesick.

August 11, 1944

Our sacrifices are imperative to the outcome of this War. We are much the wiser for our experiences, not alone in worldly matters, but in the terms of a true blue love for one another.

True blue; me, you
That's the line
For just us two.

August 12, 1944

Now we are working even on Sundays; does this mean that we shall be going to Arkansas soon? I shall apply for a furlough just as soon as we arrive there. I am tired of Cherry Point and the food we have here. It has been five months since I saw you last Easter.

August 14, 1944

That was a confusing letter about your being weak and my being strong. And what confessions have you made and to whom? And why do you ask how my driving is coming along? I ride with Eleanor Ragon, the home ec teacher.

August 14, 1944

I know you remember last summer when you and I became engaged or rather reached an understanding of engagement. I want to be truly engaged so that everyone will know that first loves really do last. I love you, I miss you, and I need you.

August 15, 1944

I could write that book about all the wonders of "I love you." Yesterday I went on an oxygen hop. We took off at sea level and leveled off at 18,000 feet. We remained there for 15 minutes without oxygen. My nails turned blue and my eyes were blurry. Some of the fellows needed to have oxygen administered to them. After 15 minutes we put on the oxygen masks and climbed to 30,000 feet. All this is going on in a pressure chamber.

August 17, 1944

I did not write for a week because I thought you were on the way to Arkansas. I called your mother last night. She said she isn't a bit jealous when I get letters and she doesn't, just as long as she knows you are all right.

August 18, 1944

I realized that your letters ceased because you thought I was on my way to Arkansas. I am still here at Cherry Point!

Everything at home is changing so much. We have left so many things which we can never regain. Our only tangible hold on those things is our memories.

As to the confession to myself, I meant that I was glad that all the things *I had planned* were now discarded for something much dearer and nearer to me.

You, yourself, had told me you would learn to drive this summer.

August 19, 1944

Yes, Bud, I remember last summer when we decided that we would be married *someday.* You said we were "verbally engaged," for you had no ring. It seems such a long time ago; but then it seems that I have always loved you. I know that is not so. I was with you in school and didn't even know you.

August 19, 1944

Someday I'll let you write that book on "I Love You." I'll take all you say in shorthand and transcribe it.

August 19, 1944

I'm glad I like your parents so much, and that they like me; your mother and I talk very often on the telephone, and I visit them frequently.

August 23, 1944

You asked me about my blood pressure when I took the combat physical. It is 134, two points below what it was when I entered the Marine Corps.

When I'm thinking of you, I still have butterflies!

August 24, 1944

Does the crew chief ride along on bombing missions?

August 25, 1944

Tonight I heard the prediction of October 9 as the date the European War will end; the Japanese War is to be over by the end of 1945. I'm so tired of being away from you for such a long time. It doesn't seem fair to take years from young men's lives. I am angry when I think about it! I would be different if this were the end of all wars – there will be another, even worse. I'm supposed to be keeping up your morale.

A mouse just ran across the floor, and Brownie came to our rescue by devouring him!

August 26, 1944

Coop is a really swell fellow – he knows you. He hopes to someday find a girl like you. Isn't that a nice compliment? Today another fellow told me that he likes to mention you just to see my eyes light up.

August 29, 1944

The crew chief must fly four hours per month to receive flight pay. We will leave for Arkansas September 5; I'll have a new address.

I am very sorry to hear that George Schroer is another victim who has paid the price for our peace.

Please don't think too much of what we are being cheated; think of what we shall accomplish together and achieve in the future. I know that if I ever wish to see that future, which I now hold so dear, then all of us must work and hope for a complete and quick peace.

September 2, 1944

I am in Morehead City for the last time, watching the beautiful moon shimmering on the waves, and once again recalling those pleasant memories of your visit.

September 4, 1944

We are all packed to go; I am responsible for 15 fellows. The trip will take two or three long, dirty days – I hate to think of it.

I'll try to write on the train. I want to see you for a very, very definite reason.

September 6, 1944

I survived my first day of teaching at Ross High School. Busy??? Very! I have five different preparations each night. I like the "kids;" they are nice. They stand at their desks to recite – I've taught them that, at least.

September 6, 1944

Our train is a troop train, and as we pass everyone waves at us. The cinders are the worst part. They have an uncanny way of being just where I am.

I still am hunting and probing about my future employment. Whatever I choose there will always be the satisfaction of knowing that the most important part of my life is making you happy. You are a very, very definite reason.

September 7, 1944

We arrived in Newport, Arkansas; the trip wasn't too bad. There are 20 men to a barracks, and I am NCO (noncommissioned officer) in charge. There are two to a room, which is much better than 150. It is very quiet here, and I have a table on which to write. My first goal here is to obtain a furlough as soon as my enlistment year is up. I am anxious to see you.

September 10, 1944

Now is a good time for you to get used to living with only one instead of 149. When you come home to stay, I think you'll be living with only one – not even with the ten at your family home! If you are bored, perhaps we can do something about that to remedy the situation!

I can't wait any longer to tell you my surprise. I'm afraid someone has already spoiled it for me. I wanted to wait until you came home, but I can't wait. Bud, I have a car and know how to drive it! I bought it June 16 and in two weeks I passed my driving test. I told you I was not learning to drive, for by that time I was past the learning stage. I already knew how to drive, so I didn't lie to you! Miss Ragon and I take turns every two weeks driving to school. My car is a 1940 Chevy, two doors, black. It has a radio and a heater and red seat covers. I wanted to surprise you this summer, but you never came; I can't wait any longer to tell you my surprise. Did someone already tell you? Who taught me to drive? My little brother, Bobby. Yes, you may drive my car when you come home.

September 11, 1944

At times I have a feeling of hopelessness about ever having a chance to come home to see you. I love you very much, and I miss you.

September 12, 1944

Will you never cease to surprise me? I become thrilled more and more at your unlimited possibilities. For about two weeks I have had the feeling that you cut your hair – don't do that too often.

I think I could get five days before October, but then I wouldn't be able to get ten more until five months later; it's hard to tell where I might be by then. I'll wait until October 3 and get all I can – 15, if possible.

No one told me about your car. Your phony story about "there is no Santa Claus" caused me to wonder what the surprise really was.

I like your thought about living with one instead of 150.

September 12, 1944

They predict that the War with Japan will be over six months after the collapse of Germany.

September 13, 1944

In my weaker moments I find myself so far behind you. Not only did I fail to finish college, but now you have an automobile and can drive it. "Here, here, Mac; stop crying, or I'll throw myself a towel."

I think I may get a furlough at the end of the month. I don't know whether to spank you or kiss you, but I am rather inclined to believe it will be the latter.

September 15, 1944

Dorothea, start saving your gasoline coupons now, because we may have cause to use them before long. If everything goes as it should, I may be home in a few weeks.

September 17, 1944

Please do not surprise me when you come home. I need to know in advance, so I can do my work ahead of time.

September 17, 1944

I dream of you driving while I sit in comfort on your right. Say, are you a good one-armed driver? I'm so glad that you are just you and no one else. Thank you. Why? For coming into my life!

September 18, 1944

School will be dismissed on Friday, the 29th, for the Butler County Fair. I'll have a long weekend. I didn't cut my hair; a man's intuition just isn't accurate. I'm not way ahead of you; you're just not living a normal life in the Marines. You seem to think I just paid $850 in cash for the car. I'll be paying for it every month until school is out. I have a loan from the bank, not through an expensive loan company. Now you don't need a car – we have one. I'm not ahead of you; we're just even. I consider that the car is half yours, anyway. When you come home and don't like it, you can pick the next one.

September 19, 1944

Since Christmas of 1943 you have been home just four days at Easter. Tell that to your C.O. Tell him you'll have to spend your furlough grading papers for me if you don't come by the 29th!

September 20, 1944

My C.O. would never receive any requests in the declarative. They're always in the interrogative. Do you know what he would say? "Sgt. McCollum, how many men do we have in our squadron? 380, Sir. That's right, Sgt. Out of those 380, 350 would like to have the same request you have laid before me. Our purpose here is not to make our lives more convenient nor to arrange our Wartime program to fit in with those at home. It is almost an impossibility. As much as I am within sympathy of your case, I hardly think it fair to the rest of the squadron to grant your request and reject theirs. Good day, Sgt." That is my cue to exit, soooo Sgt. McCollum takes one step backward, does a snappy salute, about face, and walks out the door and SCOWLS!! Another victim of military discipline. Seriously, our C.O. is a swell fellow. I will probably leave here at 4:30 pm on the 27th, arrive in St. Louis and from there on, who knows.

September 20, 1944

What makes you think that I'll be doing the driving when you come home? You are already an experienced one-armed driver.

September 21, 1944

You're so sweet to use the pronoun "we" in reference to your car, but I really couldn't – not just yet. I am wholly happy that you have a car and can drive. Would you be able to meet me in Cincy when I come home?

September 22, 1944

I'm not counting on your coming home; I'm afraid I'll be disappointed. This is 1,000 times more fun than student teaching; I am enjoying teaching.

September 25, 1944

You're arriving home on Thursday – I'm so happy. I can't meet you in Cincy, because I'll be teaching all Thursday. Besides, I could never drive in Cincy traffic, and I don't know the way to the station. If you refuse to drive my car, I'll feel that you resent my having it. You picked a fine day to come home – my payday. We have a $15 raise, so now I'll receive $180 per month.

FURLOUGH – September 28 to October 8, 1944

September 29, 1944: ENGAGED TO BE MARRIED!! "Marriage is a commendable enterprise." (It is? Bud, such big words.) I have a 1/2 karat blue-white diamond ring!!

October 8, 1944

By this time, you are back at the base. The better we know each other, the more we are in love. My ring is just as shiny as ever, and I think it looks larger every time I look at it – the stone, I mean.

After the train pulled out, I could not go home. I went to your home instead. Then I went home and slept from noon until evening. You asked what I would like for my birthday. I'd like a cedar chest. According to tradition, we have to be married just as soon as I have the chest filled.

I wish you were right here now as I write this letter. I almost feel as if I could turn around and you'd be sitting there beside me – I just looked; you're not here. I must stop writing, for I'm making myself cry again, and you're not here to wipe away my tears.

October 8, 1944

Our goodbye was so fast and hurried that I hardly had time to realize I was leaving. I am very happy remembering our talks and hopes and many new memories. I realize that I had to leave *for this.* It isn't that I'm not willing to do my part, it is just that I'm tired of the whole thing. It was harder this time than ever before.

I made Staff Sergeant!

October 9, 1944

We worked for 14 hours today, and am I tired! I think the furlough didn't help to keep me in shape.

October 11, 1944

I'm rather glad that you miss me as much as I miss you, because that's where we stop taking each other for granted and realize how much we mean to each other. I shall *never* get over how happy I was on my furlough.

October 12, 1944

You left here on Saturday, and we heard nothing from you until Thursday. We were both worried about you. You wrote to me on Sunday, but didn't mail it until Tuesday, and it didn't come until today.

Congratulations on making Staff Sergeant. I've written a note to the *Journal* about our engagement.

October 13, 1944

All the girls are coming to Oxford for Homecoming. They know about my ring and are anxious to see it. It'll knock their eyes out!

October 11, 1944

You're all I've ever wanted – honest! I love you more and more as each day passes. My feeling is so wonderful and so positive that my furlough seems as though it is not yet ended. I seem to be waiting for you to come home from school, but you never come.

I enjoyed the day I went to school with you, hearing you teach, watching you, and everything you did is now a committed memory.

It is doubtful that any of us will attend the school I told you about, for it is to be closed this month. Perhaps I will be home for Christmas.

Now at this very minute we are miles and miles apart, but never so far apart that our love decreases. Distance may have made our love as strong and secure as the very friendship which houses it. It is nice to know someone as well as we know each other. Our understanding is mutual and our love everlasting. Our hopes and prayers are one and the same.

October 14, 1944

You're haunting me! I can't for the life of me get you off my mind, even for a short time. We're ENGAGED. Doesn't that sound wonderful? It does to me! I am so glad you will marry me I could almost shout loudly enough for the angels to hear me. Why must I feel like this when I am so far away?

I thought the air mail letter would reach you sooner, but that is not the case. Telegraph office is not open at 4:30 am.

I am a sentimentalist, really, and when people I love are suffering, I can't help but cry – no tears, no sobs, just aches. Mom is very dear to me; I love her very much, but, Dorothea, my love for you is so very, very much more forceful. When you were angry, I thought you were angry with me, and I discovered that you were angry at the way your *hair* looked.

I love you with all my heart; sweet dreams, and God Bless You.

P.S. I'm glad you like the ring.

October 14, 1944

We're all back in North Hall for our reunion. There are two beds for nine of us. June says to tell you she wants a ring just like mine. The girls are fighting over who is to be in my wedding. Cawein will play the organ. I told her to practice "The Marines' Hymn."

October 15, 1944

I am so far behind in answering letters from friends and family that I shall make this short and try to answer about two or three of the seven to whom I owe letters.

October 16, 1944

You said that when I lay my head in your lap, and you had your arms around me, I seemed to be *all yours.* Do you ever feel that I am not? Those two words are closer and more expressive to me than ever before. I am forever *all yours.*

October 18, 1944

I have little time during the day to let your spirit "haunt" me, but I think of you every time I look at my beautiful ring – which is quite often. The ring is prettier every day! All the girls were quite impressed. June tried it on, but it is much too large for her. I'll *never* quit wearing your ring. This is for keeps, for always, for eternity. I, too, am sometimes scared to think about the future if anything were to happen...but it won't...it just can't. Of one thing we can be sure – our love will continue, no matter what might happen. That's one thing that will never cease.

The last night you were home, I tried not to cry, but I wasn't very successful. I didn't want you to go home that last night, for I knew I might not see you again for a long time.

October 18, 1944

Our C.O. needed to go to the East Coast, so I flew back to Cherry Point with him. He took my plane, and I did not get air sick. I saw Coop and all the fellows.

I used to have a wonderful feeling, but it was nothing like the feeling I now have. It seems as though you are really here inside me, and I miss you more than ever. I want to be near you for always. Oh, I'm a lucky guy in a luckless world, but golly, how I love it. Remember all those goodnights we have whispered together.

October 20, 1944

I shall read part of your letter to my geography class. We're studying about the eastern mountains, the Piedmont, fall line, coastal plain, and ocean. Your trip back to Cherry Point gave you a view of all of this.

You haven't written home since your furlough; your mother thought that she had made you angry. Please write to your mom and dad!

October 21, 1944

The announcement of our engagement was in tonight's newspaper. I went to a football game and received many congratulations and good wishes. I want to be with you when they congratulate us.

October 22, 1944

I received my first pay since coming back to the base. I don't know what we would have done without your car *and* money.

I told my roommate of all the wonderful times I hold in my memory. All of them were not so cheerful, but they are certainly, to say the least, memorable. The Hi-Y party, the night I asked to kiss you, the day we decided to stop going together, how I really felt, how there was no room in my life for women, and how understanding and tolerant you were. I remember baseball games, night work, you at Cherry Point, and my furloughs. All of these thoughts were so vivid tonight; I doubt if I ever told anyone all of them with quite so much expression.

October 22, 1944

I received over 50 congratulations at church. Rev. Stoerker announced our engagement and referred to you as "a husky Marine." A man at church said, "What a rock!"

October 24, 1944

My mother holds a place in my heart right next to yours, but it is altogether different.

October 25, 1944

Your mother read me your letter; she was very glad to get it (at last). She liked what you wrote about you and me and *us*. Thanks for all the sweet things you told your mother.

THE WAR CAN'T LAST FOREVER!!!

October 27, 1944

Sometimes I just can't write what is in my heart. A letter may even spoil the wonderful feeling that I have. When I write I am even more conscious of your absence. It would be nice if we could see each other this Christmas – almost too much for which to hope. If I had Aladdin's lamp, I would wish that every couple in all this world could be as deeply and fondly in love as you and I. I miss you so!

October 27, 1944

They just played "I'll Walk Alone" on *Waltz Time*: "Till you're walking beside me, I'll walk alone. I'll always be near, wherever you are each night in every dream. If you call, I'll hear you, no matter how far. Just close your eyes and I'll be there." Isn't that right, Bud? I'm going to bed now, and I can see you when I close my eyes – you're with me.

I pray, too, that nothing will ever happen to change all our plans. A person needs something big and fine to hang onto in times like these.

October 30, 1944

Yesterday when we were in St. Louis I made you a 15-cent recording of my voice. I hope you get a big kick out of it; we laughed so much I'm not sure I got my 15-cents worth.

October 31, 1944

Sometimes I can remember things you've done or said so clearly that it seems they happened only yesterday. I can always remember about my ring – my hair was in pigtails, and you told me to close my eyes. When I opened them, you showed me the biggest diamond I had ever seen, and you put it on my finger. Then we watched the beautiful colors it reflects. Whatever made you think I wouldn't take the ring? I didn't even need to think about it, for my mind was made up long before September 29, 1944. How about remembering September 6, 1943?

November 1, 1944

Col. Bowen is being assigned to Hawaii. Today 15 men were assigned to Cherry Point to pull acceptance checks on our 15 new combat ships. It will take them about seven weeks to complete the job, and then things will move rather fast. Our planes will not go overseas until there are 175 hours on their

engines. That is about five weeks' flying time. So we won't be going overseas until after the first of the year – but who knows?

I keep thinking about that record. It was crazy. These fellows had me all mixed up, but my intentions were good.

I'm happy, because I know *our* tomorrow shall be a bright and shiny one – no clouds in the sky tonight.

November 1, 1944

THE WAR CAN'T LAST FOREVER. That's the only thing about which we can be certain – except our love.

November 3, 1944

I've been thinking about your ring – it isn't so big, really. But my sister said it's a little larger than the average girl gets. I didn't force anything on you – I wanted the feeling of giving and receiving to be mutual. Why, if you had been me, would you have been so positive?

November 4, 1944

Your record has arrived, but I have no Victrola on which to play it. I'll take it to school Monday and play it in the music room before school starts. You fellows have some interesting discussions. Do they value your opinions? I wouldn't want to be married to someone I didn't love or who didn't love me!

Chills went up and down my spine when I read about your possibly going overseas after the first of the year. I'm just plain scared when I think about it.

I'm waiting and waiting for "*our* bright and shiny tomorrow."

November 5, 1944

Today I saw a good movie. It was in close alignment with my feelings. When two people are in love and happily married, they sort of forget they're in love – it's just there, and the happy feeling derived from being in love is proof that never, either mentally or physically, do people forget. When two people become attracted to each other, they seem to acquire a new person within their old. When we are together, Dorothea, I have something that I don't have when I am away from you. It seems as if I am really not all here. Now I know why I miss you so much. When I am with you I become conscious of a power within me that isn't there when I'm away from you.

November 5, 1944

I received the $100 for our bank account. You'll catch up with my $200 soon.

November 6, 1944

I think the guys here do value my opinion. Last night a fellow came to my room and wanted to talk about religion. He was baptized as a Catholic, and now he wants to be a true Catholic.

Our orders have been recalled, and we are to go to the East Coast and get a new type of plane. Our squadron will be reformed and start all over again.

I'm really disgusted. I don't want to go back to Cherry Point for another Christmas. There is nothing I can do about it; I'm ready to throw in the towel and cease to care – but I am interested in planes and my work here. At Cherry Point it's crowded, the food is bad, and I don't like that type of winter. I am sorry and disgusted, but I know that I'll just keep on doing what they want, but I have to tell someone how I feel.

Dorothea, it is getting late, so I think I had better leave. *Dorothea,* let me go – I can't stay here all night. Goodnight.

November 6, 1944

I finally heard the record! I have listened a dozen times. All I have to do is listen again to hear you tell me that you love me. Next to my ring, I think the record is the nicest thing you ever gave me – and it cost only 15 cents. A friend of Ruth has loaned me her record player. My family has heard it several times. Mother said that Daddy listened twice when I was at work. She told him that he never said such nice things to her! When your mom comes home from helping Mart with her new home, I know she'll want to hear it. I'm glad you added the P.S. about your mom and dad.

Mart has brought your mom home; she, your mom, and several children came to hear the record. Your mom laughed about the part of not being able to take you to the zoo for fear they'd keep you! My mother liked the part about staying married even after we go to Heaven. You asked about my ring – it's beautiful but lonesome. It needs a plain gold wedding band beside it for company! The record is the next best thing to a furlough. It is even better than a phone call, because I can hear it over and over again. You said, "Loving you, Dorothea, is like living in another world." I get chills when I hear you say my name!

I hope you can come home for Christmas to help me decorate the tree. Won't we have fun decorating one for our children *someday?* I deposited your $100.

November 9, 1944

When we're married, our love won't be expressed in letters or X's and O's, but in every act we do; it'll be a part of our lives even more than now. I know what you mean when you say you're just not all there when I am not with you. I'm feeling the same way; I am really someone different when you are here.

I've played the record so much I have memorized it. I like what you said; it's very beautiful. I like to remember the ending, "Bye, now. Love ever and ever, Me."

November 11, 1944

I've been hoping and praying that you will not be going overseas, and it seems that my prayers are answered. Keep doing what they tell you to do, and one of these days they'll tell you to go home!

What do you mean by saying, "I can't stay here all night"? You do, *almost*. You're here 3/4ths of the night, but *I like it*. Someday, not so far distant, I won't make you go home – not ever. We'll be in our own home *always* together.

November 12, 1944

I never dreamed the record would mean so much to you. Things are very confusing here on the base.

November 13, 1944

There are two coal stoves at our end of the barracks. We can make fudge, grilled cheese sandwiches, hot chocolate, bacon and eggs, etc. We rival your college spreads. I might send you a couple pieces of fudge made in my mess gear. We can get sugar, cocoa, cheese, bread, and other ingredients from the mess hall.

Dorothea, I don't believe you ever talked so much about anything I gave you, except your ring, as much as you have about the record. I'm glad you liked it.

November 14, 1944

Now we don't know what we're doing. Our C.O. went to Washington as soon as he heard about the change in our orders. He was successful in keeping our original plan to go overseas. I'm sorry for your sake and for Mom's, but it will relieve my guilt. Man's natural heritage is to protect those things he loves. Right now I don't have that protective feeling. Sometime soon I shall realize the fulfillment of my most cherished dream – a lifetime with you. That thought keeps me happy, and it won't make any difference where I am. With each letter I write, each time I see you, I've grown to love you more and more. I've learned not to count on rumors.

I had another typhoid shot, and as usual I'm becoming woozy. I may or may not be saying all those nice things 20 years from now, but if I remain, as my dad has, I know that we will be much happier and more in love than now.

November 14, 1944

Your mother called me. She's worried that you might be going overseas. What can I tell her to relieve her mind?

November 17, 1944

The way things stand now, I won't be going overseas for a long time.

November 17, 1944

Your mother has invited me for Thanksgiving dinner. Aunt Emma has invited me, too. Her son, Don, is home, and I want to see him. I suppose he is my favorite cousin.

November 19, 1944

I just returned from a movie which reminded me of us in so many ways. I can see you looking up at me and me looking down at you, thinking how very, very lucky I am. There is an understanding of love for which we are both grateful. In appreciation, I just need to take you in my arms and kiss you.

FURLOUGH – November 19 to 23, 1944

November 23, 1944

I had Thanksgiving dinner with your family. Then I had another at home with my family. The movie sounds good; I'd like to see it. I, too, have that wonderful feeling when we are standing so close, and I'm looking up at you. I feel exactly the same as you, and it is then that your kiss seems so special.

November 26, 1944

That was such a nice little leave; I haven't fully recuperated. I had a wonderful time. I'm hoping to come home again for Christmas.

November 27, 1944

I am 22 years old today – thanks for the cedar chest. I, too, am not quite rested up from your leave. This is the happiest birthday I have ever had!

November 30, 1944

Today I am in Georgia; our plane hit a tree top, and I need to pick up a wing.

December 4, 1944

I have a $1 Christmas present from the Grange. Thank them for me when you see them. Thanks for the renewal of my subscription to *Reader's Digest*.

December 5, 1944

It is rainy today, and we don't have to work. I miss you more when I don't have to work. I'd like to be home for Christmas. I am looking forward to that day with patient anxiousness.

December 6, 1944

Tomorrow, Dec. 7, will find the USA in her third year of active War against Japan. Things today look much more hopeful than they did at that time, but such a hope has not been gained without a very high price. I am thankful that I am still able to enjoy those things in life which truly make it beautiful. All of my memories, since I came into the Service, are not unpleasant. Quite the contrary. It seems my life began on June 25, 1943, when you became a really and truly living and pleasant part of me. Then there was my furlough in October, 1943, and your visit to North Carolina in September, 1943. I'll never forget the wonderful time we had in that simple little city – Morehead City.

There were a few disappointments – I flunked a flight physical, and you had scarlet fever. I did not receive a letter until the middle of January, 1944. I came home for three or four days at Easter and went to church with you in my dress blues. You began to introduce your cousins – there were so many of them that I had a nightmare.

I didn't see you again until the end of September. What a grand furlough, and *all* because of you. I remember very plainly giving you your ring on September 29, 1944. A week and a half ago I was home again.

I love you, my dear, and only that fact has enabled me to remain as happy as I have been since entering the Service.

December 8, 1944

We are so far apart in miles, yet so close in our love for each other. Our life pattern has a common interest, and there is a single objective – the day we shall no longer be apart. I'd rather lie here in my bunk and think of us than go out on liberty for the weekend. Remember, I'm always thinking of you and loving you with all there is of me to love.

December 8, 1944

I haven't written for a week, because I have been ill. After the cold was better, I had chills and fever for a week and missed school for a week, also. The doctor said I had yellow jaundice just like JoAnn and Bob had. I look like a Jap – yellow eyes and all. I was starving, but food would not stay down. I'm better now. My illness was not your fault.

December 10, 1944

Some of our fellows are being transferred back to the Point. I have my fingers crossed. I don't want to go back there – boo hoo! I have the craziest premonition that something is about to happen.

I am becoming more and more anxious to be near you as Christmas Eve draws near.

December 10, 1944

I am glad you are feeling better; I was worried and anxious. You were never ill until after you had scarlet fever.

How can I stop telling you what my heart keeps repeating? I know only that my present want of you is very strong; it hardly seems to be so close and yet so far away. It is like one of those dreams in which you keep reaching for something you cannot quite grasp. I know that *someday, somehow* we shall be much happier and *together.*

December 11, 1944

I don't think it is right for two to be married and then not to be able to live together. Perhaps being together for just a short time is better than not at all, but I hope we'll *never* have to be separated after we are married.

Your train ticket home is all the present I need for Christmas. Just save your money and come home. I keep remembering that you said, "I wish it were 1946, and we were going home – to our own home together." I see such a nice picture in my mind when I remember.

OH, I WISH THE WAR WOULD BE OVER SOON!

December 13, 1944

You're always right here in my room. You seem so real that I want to reach out and grab you. I love you with all my heart, and no distance, no incident, not even the War can deny me that wonderful feeling.

December 13, 1944

Staff Sergeant's mother has to call his girlfriend to have a little news of him.

You'd think he could send a little note to tell her his heart is big enough to hold all of his love for a girl and for *her, too!* Next time you intend to write to that girl, send a note to Staff Sergeant's mother instead!

December 15, 1944

I am not tired of having you tell me what your heart says. I always look for that place in your letter where you tell me how much you miss me, love me, and want to be with me.

My ring is especially bright and shiny tonight – a constant reminder of you and our love. I really don't need a ring to remind me, though, for the thought never seems to leave the center of my brain.

December 17, 1944

Thanks for reminding me to write home if only to say, "Feeling fine; all OK." Do you know what I've been doing today? I've been making candy for the fellows – chocolate fudge, peanut butter fudge, taffy, and sea foam. Not a failure in the bunch!

The nose wheel on my plane developed a structural failure in flight and ruined the auxiliary landing gear door. This can be disastrous, but the pilot returned safely.

A week from now I may be home. Maybe?

December 18, 1944

Christmas Eve is a week from tonight. I'm afraid to believe that "Maybe?" It has been only a month since you were here – November 19 to the 23rd.

December 18, 1944

I have a pass from *December 18 to the 26th.* I want nothing for Christmas – only you.

Christmas, 1944

I am waiting for you to come, and I wish you'd hurry. Thanks for the pin and bracelet – I like them.

December 26, 1944

I loved every minute of your furlough. Your grin – that's one of your nicest characteristics! Somehow since you were home I have a feeling inside that it won't be much longer before you'll be home to stay. Then we can plan our own lives without any interference from Uncle Sam.

December 28, 1944

It will be quite some time before I forget even a small part of that Christmas leave. I only know now more than ever before that together we shall be ever and ever so happy. I love you, my darling.

December 28, 1944

I had to buy new brakes for my car. The cost was $16.33.

December 29, 1944

You are the most important and wonderful concern in my future. I am not here – at least not all of me.

December 29, 1944

I like collecting things for my cedar chest. We'll have a very nice home – everything nice and new and shiny like my ring. Do you think we shall be able to have a brand new house? Maybe I'd better not want too much, but I hope all our dreams do come true. I like talking to you about everything. Could you tell how happy I was? Sometimes it isn't necessary to say anything, because we both are thinking the same thing.

You know, we should have very happy children. Why would I say that? Well, their father and mother will be so much in love and happy that they won't be able to be anything but!

I'll be very happy when I no longer need to write "Goodnight," but we'll be home, and I can just whisper it in your ear.

December 30, 1944

I wish the very best for you in the coming new year. I want you to be happy, and I do pray you won't be ill any more. My love shall be with you all through the New Year, and I pray that soon we shall realize our fondest hope in 1945. Happy New Year!

December 31, 1944

We all enjoyed the delicious box of cookies, chocolate covered cherries, date bars, and the fruit cake. Oh, I can't forget the cupcakes. Everything was great, and I shared it with the fellows.

I just returned from a trip to Mobile, Alabama. I really enjoyed the trip: the Wright brothers did a great thing when they flew 103 feet in 1903 at Kittyhawk, North Carolina.

Love ever, and ever, and ever and kisses.

Bud.

Part Three
1945-1946

"You are all I ever wanted. Things like that are for storybooks and movies – but we are fortunate to be living just such a life."

After I graduated from Miami in June, 1944, I was hired as a business teacher at Ross Township School. My salary was $1500 per year, for which I taught Typing I and II, Shorthand I and II, bookkeeping, 7th grade geography, and girls' physical education from 7th to 12th grades. I supervised a study hall, at which time I was also librarian, kept the school activity books, was a class sponsor, school newspaper advisor, senior class annual advisor, and was in charge of bookstore supplies for the faculty. I liked being busy – the War was still going strong – so time passed quickly. I taught at Ross for three years before and two years after my marriage.

I purchased a 1940 Chevrolet for $850, but did not yet know how to drive. Bob teased until he talked me into starting it, going backward and forward, and finally going around and around the barn lot. When my dad came home, I was ready to hit the road! We drove to Symmes Corner and then down High Street. That was the end of my driver training instruction.

The war was finally over – Germany surrendered in May of 1945, and President Truman dropped the Atomic Bomb on Japan in August of that year. Servicemen began to trickle home, most intent on taking advantage of the G.I. Bill of Rights for help with college.

January 1, 1945
Dear Bud,

HAPPY NEW YEAR!! Your Christmas furlough was great, even though it was too short. Did you ever stop to think how different our lives will be after we are married? I feel like a different person when you are here. Our entire life will be different – there will be no mother and father to take care of everything, to be responsible. There will be no bugle to tell you to get up, eat, sleep, etc. We think that we know each other very well; but we'll need to become used to each other. I'm not used to having a crazy guy entertain me with Abbott and Costello jokes, lose my car keys in his hat, shine his shoes for hours at a time, tease me, laugh *with* me and *at* me, and best of all love me 24 hours a day every day!! Will 1945 be the year we begin our life together?

January 3, 1945

I do want a nice new home, but it will be only a house until we move all that we now have in our minds and hearts into it. I never want to disappoint you; my prayer tonight is for strength to always keep you happy.

January 3, 1945

Thanks for the beautiful Marine earrings! I hope I shall no longer wear any Marine jewelry in 1945. I'm expecting this new year to be a really *good* and *new* year. When you were home, there was no reason for dreams, because we had the real thing.

January 4, 1945

It is easy to recall a memory, but it is much nicer to experience the feeling that accompanied that memory. I'm glad to know that my little brother Bill will be home from the South Pacific soon. Now as I write to you, I just want to relax and enjoy loving you placidly.

January 4, 1945

This letter should arrive on your birthday; now you are 23. Our birthdays seem to be coming so fast; we've been writing letters for so many years. It seems as if only yesterday that you were 21.

Your mother is hoping that Bill and Gay will be home at the same time. Gay will have five to ten days beginning January 6. Your mother wonders if you could receive a Red Cross furlough so all three could be home at the same time.

January 6, 1945

My plane flew to Memphis, and I have liberty. We ate fried chicken and each ate two dozen fried oysters.

January 6, 1945

I did not write last night – I have been playing *butcher!* Daddy butchered a steer, hung it between the barn doors, and the temperature rose to the 70° mark. Two hind quarters were still hanging outside to cure. With the temperature so high, we had to hurry and can all the meat before it spoiled. So, I, yes, I said *I* cut up both hind quarters into dozens of all kinds of steaks. Those quarters were really big; you should have seen me struggling with those legs. Mother gave me a knife and a booklet to guide me as I cut up round steaks, porterhouse steaks, sirloin steaks, "T" bone steaks, and club steaks. We took out some time to eat steak, and then Mother boned the meat and canned it in her big pressure cooker. Mother was up until 4 am canning the meat. The scraps were made into hamburger.

The brake drums have to be made smooth; it cost $1 per wheel. Every week that car demands more of my money.

Our bank account shows a balance of $572.16.

January 8, 1945

Gay arrived Saturday, and Bill came on Sunday morning. He is so grown-up and so handsome. Wow! He is so polite and refined that I can't believe he is the same boy who joined the Marines with you. He is exhausted and doesn't know how to act or what to do. He seems lost and nervous. Your mother asks too many questions; everyone else doesn't. He was on Guadalcanal before a coast guard cutter brought him home.

FURLOUGH January 8–18.

January 16, 1945

It was so nice to be home when Galen, Bill, and Leiser were there. We did have a swell time seeing them together, didn't we?

I can never stop being thankful for all the happiness you have given me. You cried so hard when I left; I have never seen you cry as you did this last time. I feel so inadequate when I am unable to say anything that will assure you of our future. Dorothea, your faith in God is certainly strong enough to believe that He can preserve our future happiness.

I have been told that I am now eligible for flight training. It would add another two years to my Service time. No, thanks. But if they insist, I will have no choice.

Fifteen fellows are leaving Monday for the West Coast. All are mechs; four crew chiefs. I am not one of them this time.

I miss our talks; they're nice, aren't they?

January 16, 1945

I had lots of school work, but I am all caught up after your furlough. This work takes my mind off your having to leave again. I just couldn't help crying so much when you left this time. We were so happy when you were home; I never felt so bad at any time before. Now here we are – writing letters again.

Bud, after we're married, let's set aside some time each evening when we can talk about what happened that day and plan for the days to come.

January 18, 1945

I will send you $50 for our banking account. I am taking a correspondence course from the Marine Institute. I am enjoying your *Lincoln Library* Information.

January 19, 1945

I just read your sweet letter, and I am on the verge of tears again. I never felt quite like this before, and I don't know exactly why. I know it hurts you when I cry, but now your letter gives me something to remember. If anything should ever happen, all our plans and dreams would only mock me.

I'm all right; school is good for me. I'm so busy all day long that I have little time to think.

January 19, 1945

Today it was cold; I washed my car anyway. I also washed my hair, and now it is very soft and fluffy the way you like it.

I added a pair of pillow slips I had made in the 7th grade to our cedar chest.

January 21, 1945

Today I received your first letter since I came back, and even though it does not nearly compare to talking to you, it was very welcome.

We have been going together for more than five years. Ours was a *new* love that grew and developed, as our feelings and ideas found a similarity, into a wholesome and wonderful love in which we have found more happiness than either of us had ever before hoped.

January 22, 1945

Our short lives together have been so light and happy and clean; we have no regrets, no desire to stray from our happy little world. To be able to remember all those happy moments is a gift for which I shall ever be grateful. I look at your picture, and you're almost here – almost.

January 24, 1945

It would be nice if we could have $1200 in the bank by next Christmas. I have no more car payments – only repairs!

January 25, 1945

I love you and miss you; never did I have a feeling such as I have now. I can't get over not having you with me. You and that furlough are another life.

We fly to Montana tomorrow. We refuel in Rapid City and then fly to Billings, Montana; then on to Denver. I am snowbound without any money.

January 28, 1945

What in the world are you doing in Colorado? I knew you didn't have enough money when you returned from your furlough. I'll be glad when you are back in Arkansas.

I spent my last shoe stamp on a pair of black pumps. I'm figuring my income taxes. Since September they have taken $100 from my salary, but I may have most refunded.

January 29, 1945

We left Newport at 4 am and at 10 am we had flown over a great deal of the Black Hills of South Dakota. We sat down (landed) in Rapid City, where the wind was blowing at 40 miles per hour. After refueling, we got out of there in a hurry. For two hours we flew over the Bad Lands of Montana and landed in Billings. We stayed there for six hours. We took off at 7 am, and after three hours of blind flying, we reached Buckley Field in Denver. We are snowbound, and I have no money. How long we are here will depend on the weather. I miss you, and when I am far away and alone, I realize how very much I love you.

January 29, 1945

The War is going well in Europe, but my schedule in the Service is uncertain. Our squad will be split up – we are pushed around like pawns on a chess board. When things are rushed and complicated, I become lost in a chaos of mental confusion.

I have this lyric to remind me:

Sittin' and wishin'
Won't change your Fate.
The Lord provides the fishin'
But you have to dig the bait.

January 29, 1945

I'm too lazy to do any school work; I just don't feel right. I plan to see the doctor tomorrow, because I feel almost the way I did last spring – that darn scarlet fever! One of our teachers had scarlet fever about the same time as I. She quit teaching and is in the hospital. I wish he'd give me a prescription for YOU.

January 30, 1945

I'm thinking of a summer job at the business college.

I've cleaned my diamond ring – it is so big and beautiful. Bud, do you realize how surprised I was when I saw how large my diamond ring was? I had never *ever* hoped for a ring like that – I could hardly believe my eyes! You are so very nice to me.

I have a couple of problems for you to think about. I am in charge of a March assembly program. Think about a theme and what we could present for an assembly. The second item for your thought concerns our Jr.-Sr. prom. We need to plan a menu for refreshments, hire an orchestra, and decorate the gym. We need a theme for the prom.

February 1, 1945

I'm sorry you aren't feeling well; be sure to see the doctor and take care of yourself.

At least something has happened to our squadron, but we don't know the final results. We have been decommissioned; no more flying.

February 1, 1945

I'm glad you're back in Arkansas – now please stay there. I was just sure you'd crash into one of the Rocky Mountains.

The temperature dropped to zero, and my car froze up. I seem to spend my pay check for gas, and oil, brakes, and brake drums. Daddy helped me with the frozen car, and now I have plenty of antifreeze.

I've invited your brother to go places with me (games at school, etc.) but he is too busy every night. He doesn't need me to entertain him. Girls, girls, girls have entertained him!

February 1, 1945

Whenever I recall a pleasant incident in our past, it is as if I were experiencing it for the first time. You like to have me talk to you and tell you what I'm thinking. Well, these fellows do too. Today I was telling them about our last Saturday night together. It is so vivid in my mind that it is like reading it from a book. When I pause to laugh, remembering your expression, it only tends to increase my listeners' curiosity.

Our memories, hopes, and convictions are so mutually a part of both of us that sharing them in letters tends more and more to chop *our niche* in the future. We don't want a large place in tomorrow – only an adequate place in which we can humbly and devotedly share our love.

I love you so much, it doesn't seem quite enough just to say, "Goodnight, I love you."

February 4, 1945

It is icy and very cold. Yes, I'm being careful. The Cincinnati buses aren't even running! There is a great fuel shortage in Ohio, and all public buildings (including schools) were closed from Friday until Tuesday. This rule may be enforced until April. The theater is closed, and even some war plants have been forced to close. There is no coal anywhere in Ohio.

February 8, 1945

I have not been transferred – we will be split up. There are 150 B-25s coming down here, and we are doomed to preserve them. Then I will be transferred alphabetically. I WAS NOT PICKED to be transferred. I am now attached to SMS 1P which means Service Marine Squadron 1st Provisional. My pay will be cut $40, as I will not have flight pay.

I can't think of anything as a theme for your assembly program or prom. It would be nice if I were able to attend your prom.

A lasting happiness with all my love and you – that is my prayer tonight.

February 8, 1945

Now I've lost my voice – my students are delighted.

February 11, 1945

When I arrived in Oxford to see the doctor I was told all appointments were canceled, so I saw Dr. Leyrer. He gave me some medicine that worked very promptly. I go back in a week. I'm feeling much better.

February 11, 1945

You rate two letters in one day. We're (the girls) invited to Martha's home for the weekend of March 3. If you should be coming home, I'll cancel.

I'm upset about the girl Bill is dating – after one week, she thinks she's in love with him. GRRRRR. He can't seem to discourage her. She bothers your mother with tales that Bill is mean to her. I don't like her!! I don't want her for a sister-in-law!!

February 12, 1945

I think all the prayers for you must be influencing the Marine Corps. I don't care how much they decrease your pay as long as you are not going overseas.

The prom will be in April; maybe you could get a 71-hour pass???

Now the fan belt or something is squeaking, and I think something is wrong with the water pump. Where is it?

February 12, 1945

My plane is supposed to leave for Cherry Point tomorrow – I hate to see her go. When a squadron is broken up, you never feel you are decommissioned until your plane taxies down the runway for a farewell takeoff. Today four of them buzzed the field at 300 mph about 20' off the ground and wagged their wings to say goodbye. My position is very uncertain.

February 19, 1945

Your letters are always just what I need; they mean so much to me.

Someday when we have nothing to do, we'll read our letters and remember how our love had to be spread over so many pages. I love you so much – it makes me want more and more to be a good husband.

I flew with Col. Walsh and Capt. McGee back to Cherry Point. Coop, Koehler, and I went to a movie. It was great to see them again! The next day we flew back, but had to land at Walnut Ridge because of bad weather. The pilot and co-pilot went back to Newport, but I stayed with the plane, slept in the brig, and the next day Capt. McGee came for me in our plane. Tomorrow I report for duty with Lt. Somebody. I am now Facility Personnel with the 9th wing. Someone needs to straighten out this mess!

February 20, 1945

I never have time to do all I want to do. I have not worked any of the math problems for three weeks. Days are short, and weeks are long.

February 22, 1945

The time between now and the day I am discharged is forgotten as far as I'm concerned. That sounds strange, but it is true. I don't care what happens. I only hope whatever it is will be soon. The terrible feeling is much similar to that which I had several years ago. It scares me, and I don't like it.

February 23, 1945

Dr. Stafford can't figure out what's wrong with me, so he wants me to go to the hospital for the weekend for some tests. What is making me so pepless and tired? The scarlet fever may be the cause. Don't worry about me – the doctor says it is nothing serious.

That spring in the car wheel came loose again and has started to grind – one more thing wrong with the car.

February 25, 1945

My days are missing the best part of my life. My days are not full and wholesome. I do not like my job. We have 213 planes, a quarter of a million dollars each, to be *put out of commission* (preserved for storage). That's about $53,000,000 sitting here, slowly going to waste!! It is raining again, and it is warm, but I feel empty without you. I hear the ticking of the clock as it constantly reminds me of time. Time is passing, and I am standing still. There is nothing I can do about it. I was just home, and now I have come back here. This is the generation devoted to ending this War, but is it right for us to wait for the end of the War to be married? No! No! But shall we keep our dream of waiting?

February 26, 1945

After a grueling day at school, I am sitting at the garage waiting for someone to fix that spring in the wheel.

The doctor said all my test results were very good. He thinks I just worry about too many little things. Now I'm worrying because you're so dissatisfied with your new assignment. I'm worrying about Aunt Lil because Uncle Russell has asked for a divorce. I can do nothing about these things, but I still worry.

February 28, 1945

Between me and the car, I'm spending all my money on "repairs." The weekend in the hospital cost $22, including all of the tests. I paid $6 for prescriptions. If I have no money, I'll be even more nervous!

I don't know what to say to you regarding when we should be married. It goes over and over in my mind. Yes, No, Yes, Maybe?? I think we'd be happy either way – married now or after the end of the War?? I am more confused with each word I write.

March 1, 1945

You have a right to be concerned about everything, but you need to adopt a "mental file" according to importance. Place the unimportant in the rear of the file, and think only about those things which are necessary. Put that grueling day and the car at the rear of the file.

I'm sorry I grumbled about my new assignment.

March 3, 1945

All of us "roommates" are going to Martha's in Eaton for another reunion. Jim and Eleanor are married. Pity poor Jim with five schoolteachers and two other girls – he wants some help from you! They seem very happy, but are together only on weekends. They show me the other side of marriage.

Martha and I talked until dawn in her big bed in their very large home. It was almost like talking to you – she is so calm and collected! She had an answer for every argument I put up; she thinks I should just say, "Take me with you and don't make me think about anything. Take all the responsibility, because I am so tired of thinking, planning, and caring for details and being confused." What a wonderful, wise roommate – but I didn't do it.

March 5, 1945

The doctor says that all my tests are perfect. He thinks that all I need is *you.*

March 6, 1945

Our base team was invited to Little Rock for an AAU basketball tournament. I haven't practiced with these fellows, so I didn't play very much.

I'm looking forward to my next furlough. I need to talk to you. When I'm with you, I'm very happy, and I like it. When I am playing baseball or basketball I have a feeling of personal satisfaction that relaxes all of me – a temporary relief from all the artificial things in the world.

The doctor is right – you need a mechanic for the *car* and ME for *YOU.* I can take care of you both!

Don't worry about Bill. If he is in love, he can't help it, just as you couldn't help it when your mother tried to tell you I didn't like girls.

March 7, 1945

Bill is supposed to go overseas again. He plans to give *that Doris* a ring before he goes. She is going to Parris Island to see him. I DON'T LIKE IT!

We're having great floods around Ohio. Our fields are completely covered with water, and there is water behind the barn. The Ohio River is up to 70' in Cincinnati.

March 8, 1945

Poor Jim – what a blessed plight! Martha is right. This indecision makes you nervous. I will be happy to take all responsibility as soon as I am prepared.

March 10, 1945

The senior girls in my health class want to know how you feel when you are in love. They admire my ring and peep out the window to see if you have come at 3:30 to take me home. I have tried to tell them, but I know you could write an essay on the subject for them. Will you? I tried to put it into words, but before I finished some of the girls were looking rather tearful, as was their teacher.

I'm beginning to hate writing letters, and now in typing class I am teaching *letter* writing – woe is me.

I can't help remembering that Millie had only *one dish towel* – that made quite an impression on me. I shall not live like that! Only *one dish towel* is symbolic of marriage during wartime.

March 11, 1945

I am waiting and waiting – never knowing what I will be doing next or where I will be doing it. Preserving bombers seems like a big money-wasting scheme to me.

March 13, 1945

And here is my essay for your girls: When I told you we were no longer "going steady," you kissed me goodbye. One hot tear fell on my cheek. It warmed my heart, and I was a *goner.* I couldn't eat, couldn't sleep, I walked on air, I was happy as a lark, and my stomach was full of butterflies. Everything you did interested me. I missed you and wanted to be near you. That was in 1941. It was 1943 before I admitted to you the truth. Love is a bond of friendship which God alone gave to two people.

March 16, 1945

When I think of all the nice memories, it makes things a lot more pleasant and easier here in so many ways.

March 18, 1945

Dr. Stafford sounded just like Martha today. "There is nothing wrong with you; our tests prove it. When the War is over, he'll come home!"

Lately I've been dreaming about you. There was no story, just happiness. The last two dreams made me as happy as if you were home on furlough. It has been two months since you were home. I hope you can come for the junior prom.

Martha is so calm and quiet. I wish someone would sit me down and shut me up when I am buzzing around, being noisy, and talking too much!

March 20, 1945

It would be fun if I could be home for your dance on May 11, but who knows what will happen by that time. I hope I can arrange it, for *hope* can be a very effective morale builder.

March 20, 1945

Today I just ignored many of the things that would have ordinarily made me nervous. One boy came in full of mud; I just let him sit there, mud and all. I skipped a few other things, including a job Mr. Finkbine told me to do.

March 21, 1945

I am thrilled when I remember the night I gave you your diamond ring.

March 25, 1945

After the movie the single guy walked down one path, and the married couples walked down another. It is my hope and prayer we shall walk that second path hand-in-hand, soul in soul, heart in heart, and mind in mind *someday.*

Easter, 1945

Thanks for the gardenia. They turn brown, but always smell sweet even then. All of the girls took a whiff.

March 29, 1945

No amount of your pleading with the Marine Corps would have any influence on my receiving a 71-hour pass for your prom. I can't even ask until the Monday before the weekend.

March 30, 1945

It's that car again. A flat tire cost me $3. Now it needs a grease job. I will give you this car!

April 1, 1945

I miss you most of all on days that correspond to other happy days. We do not know when this War will end.

April 2, 1945

I still weigh 115 pounds. I am sending cookies, but I had them packed before your letter came asking for more. Your mother gave me ten lbs. of sugar.

Now nothing happens when I press the brake pedal – a leak in brake fluid?

April 7, 1945

It's that car again; now the battery is dead. I received your money order for $100. I will put it in the bank.

April 9, 1945

My new contract will be for $180 per month – $1620 per year. I'll teach business law instead of bookkeeping and geography. I shall be senior class advisor. Instead of dreaming of you, I am dreaming of teaching and all those kids.

April 9, 1945

Ho, hum. Another monotonous week of work ahead. I am sending all my love, with all my heart, for all my life.

April 11, 1945

Mother dreamed you came home for 15 days.

April 12, 1945

It isn't any fun taking care of myself. It would be fun having us back in college with so many other returning couples.

April 14, 1945

I am playing baseball – pitching. I attended a memorial service for President Roosevelt. God must have a very good reason for taking him at this crucial time. Roosevelt ended all his speeches with, "To the honor of America and God."

I think it is very uncertain that I can come to your prom.

April 16, 1945

Thanks for the Easter box. You may spend the $100 if you wish or put it in the bank. I have not spent much time on the math course. I have been thinking about college and some other things.

Bud's faculty yearbook portrait in 1950.

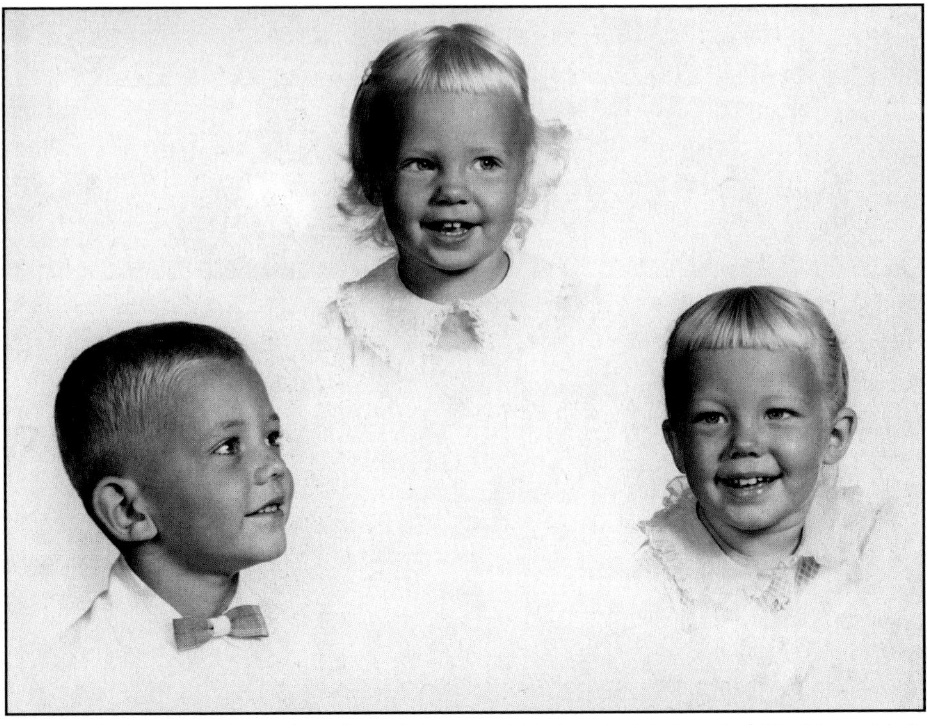

Buddy (left), born in 1949. Melanie (center), born in 1953. Pam (right), born in 1952. Now, with the benefit of hindsight, I sometimes wish we'd had more children!

The five of us in 1955.

First-string Taft High School basketball players in 1962, the year they won Ohio's State Championship. Note that Bud is standing behind them on the right. He always preferred that his teams should bask in the glory – not him.

A locker room celebration on February 7, 1976, of Bud's 400th basketball victory. Taft High School beat Talawanda, 78-49.

Above and below: The 400th victory celebration.

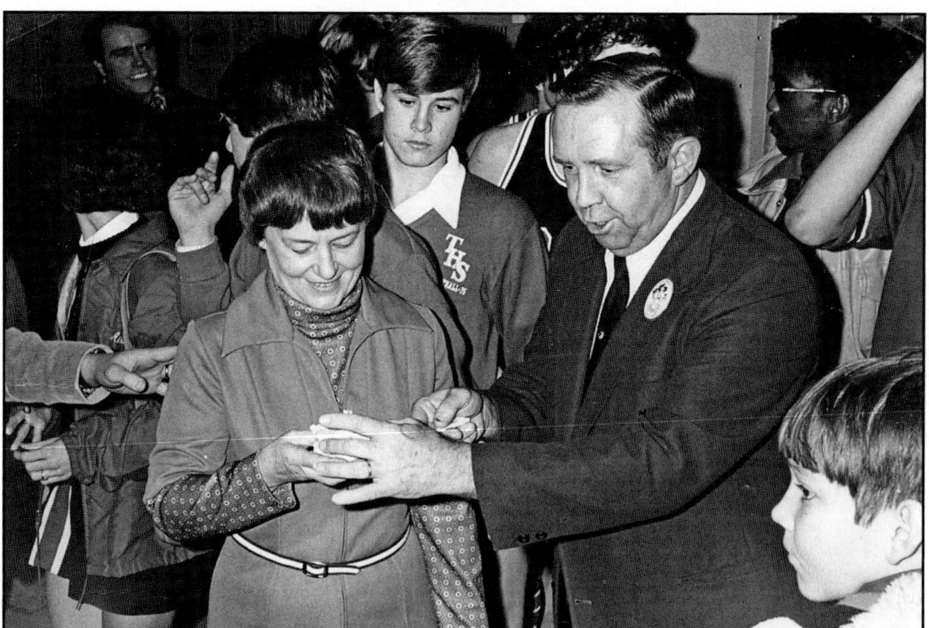

McCollum Taft's top teacher for '79-80

Marvin McCollum has been named Taft's Top Teacher for 1979-80 at Taft High School.

McCollum teaches world history, psychology and is head caoch of Taft's basketball team, a position he has held for 21 years.

He received his bachelor and master degrees from Miami University and also holds an associate degree in secondary administration.

McCollum has 32 years of teaching experience and is a member of the National Education Association, the Ohio Education Association and the Hamilton Classroom Teachers Association.

He has been a member of the Ohio State Achievement Committee for social studies for six years and also served as president and director of the Ohio High School Basketball Coaches Administration.

The award makes McCollum eligible for the Teacher of the Year award to be made later this year for the Hamilton City School District.

Selection of McCollum was made by a committee of Taft administrators, teachers, students and parents after reviewing nominations made by parents, former students and students currently enrolled at Taft.

Taft High School's Marvin McCollum, *named the school's outstanding teacher for the current school year, speaks here to Taft teachers who gathered for a reception at the school.* **Journal-News** *photo by John Janco.*

Being named Taft's Top Teacher was always the honor which Bud cherished most.

On a post-retirement vacation in Minnesota in 1983.

Two extremely successful teaching careers.

Bud in his element—coaching basketball. That's Buddy in the background.

A moment of reflection in 1982.

Our last formal portrait taken together in 1990. Bud would pass away in 1991.

April 26, 1945

We are going to Brose's May 4th for the weekend. Eleanor may go if Jim may go fishing. I signed my contract for $180 per month, less $30 for taxes.

April 26, 1945

I enjoy pitching; I read all I can about the techniques. Pitching is actually a study in physics (levers). It requires a great coordination of muscles and mind, probably more than any other sport.

I really hope to be home for your prom on May 11. I am afraid something will happen to ruin my plans.

The men working under me are working so hard. It's difficult to realize that many receive only $15 per month with bonds and allotments taken out.

I'm ever so thankful you're *you*. I like you, honest!

April 27, 1945

Dr. Stafford asked when you'd be coming home on furlough. When I told him you might be here for the prom at school; he said I wouldn't need him much longer. I have some iron pills; I am *nearly* 100% OK. According to him, seeing you will erase the "nearly."

April 28, 1945

Don't worry about Bill. He sent Doris home because she is not his type!

I am still hoping to be able to dance with you at your prom.

April 30, 1945

I hurt my knee at baseball practice today. I can hardly walk. I hope it is better by tomorrow. I may not be able to come to your prom.

You are so much a part of me that I am just not here.

May 4, 1945

Everything seemed to go wrong today at school. The mimeograph machine didn't work, and I almost slapped a couple of girls.

How is your knee? Mother said to tell you to wear your dress blues. I don't care what you wear – you'll look good to me. Send me a telegram so I'll know *if* and *when* you can come.

We had a grand time at Brose's; we always do whenever we can get together.

May 9, 1945

I called you on the phone. Guess what – I was planning to wear my blues. I hope they lift these restrictions. If they do, we shall leave on Thursday with a 71- hour pass.

71-hour pass.

May 14, 1945

That was a beautiful prom; I'm glad I made it.

May 14, 1945

Home and gone again – you told me not to worry about anything. As long as I can remember, I have had to do things which require responsibility. Elementary teachers gave me extra things to do, and even Mr. Finkbine gives me extra things to do, because he knows I can do them. Sometimes I wish I were a moron for a while, and no one would make me do anything, because I couldn't do it right. I am tired of all this responsibility. When you came home and held me in your arms, all the responsibility left me. I felt as if I were in Heaven. I felt so secure and protected. After all the work at school, I can finally relax. Why do I keep saying, "No"?

May 15, 1945

That was the best prom ever! Do we still want to be married *after* the War is over? Please tell me exactly how you feel. We could change our minds?

May 15, 1945

I'm very happy today, even though you are gone. We're busy tearing down all the beautiful decorations; these kids are such good help, and I like them – every one of them.

I'm remembering your telegram telling me not to worry about anything. I'm trying.

May 16, 1945

Your leave went by so fast. I hope our life together doesn't fly by as quickly as your leave did. If it does, one lifetime won't be enough. *Forever* would be much better.

May 16, 1945

That last leave seemed unfinished; I feel as though I have awakened in the middle of a dream. Does it seem strange to you, too?

I left some things at home. Will you call Mom and send them to me? I especially need my keys.

My goal doesn't have to be more love, more happiness, or anything nicer, for these things just seems to grow each time we are together.

May 17, 1945

Time goes fast when we look back, but very slowly when we look forward. I have a feeling that life will be too short, but I just know that God lets a love and companionship like ours go on and on forever.

May 19, 1945

I'll deposit the $40 when I cash my check. I talked to your mother, and the keys are on the way. Everything is "wild" at school as they anticipate summer vacation. When one student acts up, it ruins the entire day for a teacher. All is almost as noisy at home as at school. Bob toots his horn, JoAnn is singing, and Ruth talks, talks, talks, talks every minute.

May 20, 1945

Every time you come home we are more and more and more in love.

May 20, 1945

As I begin to write this letter, Bing Crosby begins to sing, "I Remember You." Isn't that a coincidence?

When my life is through
And the angels ask me to recall
The most thrilling of them all,
I'll tell them, I remember you.

They tell me I cannot have another furlough before September.

May 20, 1945

No matter what the situation, remember one thing above *all others*; you must have faith in our love. My knee is much better.

May 21, 1945

Two nights were very short – it was dawn before I went home. A 71-hour pass is not nearly enough! If you can learn to drive a car, you can certainly learn to be my wife. Why are you so skeptical? I know what I want. I committed myself, and now I have only hope. I have no vocation.

May 23, 1945

School is out – no more teaching, no more exams, no more papers to grade. It's that car again. Now I need a new tail pipe and muffler – $8.50!! All the kids in your family passed – they wanted me to see all their report cards. Your mother thinks I should go to Arkansas to work this summer. If it were she, she'd go. She thinks I should go and marry you, but I replied, "I don't want to." How I have confused your mother!! But I do want to, and now I am more than ever CONFUSED.

May 25, 1945

Gay and I had a grand time while Sis had two more days of exams. He is so much like you in so many ways. He loves me 1%, but if I were to become his sister-in-law, he'd raise it to 2%. Even Gay asked why I did not go to Arkansas for the summer – "I want to, but I don't want to." Your whole family is questioning me. My answer didn't make sense to them, but Gay understood. All your siblings are mixed up too – they call Gay "Bud". You have always been successful in whatever you have done, and I know you will be successful in your life's work.

Last year I didn't have a car, couldn't drive, and had no money. This year I have a car, have learned to drive, and have only one more payment on the car. I know we can do whatever we have planned with God's help!

May 30, 1945

We are back to writing letters – I'm so tired of it. I dreamed of freight trains and pigeons. It will be so expensive to build a house after the War. We may need to wait a little while for that house.

I'm so glad that Bill sent Doris home!

June 1, 1945

Each time I see you my love seems to grow, although I don't see how it can. You said many things which seem to have chased a few of my worries.

June 1, 1945

I HATE THE WAR!!! I love you more and more each time you come home – I think I'm repeating myself!

June 3, 1945

I have just finished reading *Marriage Is Serious Business* by Dr. Ray from New York City. We are OK on every point he makes. We already know that life will not be a "bed of roses," but when that time comes, we shall be prepared for it.

We should plan your eight-day furlough. If we don't, we might be bored or even end up married!

June 4, 1945

I know now that someday we shall be sorry we have waited. I think our reason for waiting is just an excuse. Today I sprained my ankle badly – I am confined to my bed.

June 4, 1945

After we are married, there are so many ways in which we shall appreciate each other. I had to smile when you wrote that you were washing my shirt. Why? Oh, I don't know. I guess it sounded so much as if we are already married – an echo of tomorrow.

June 6, 1945

Today I mailed your blue pants, belt, and white hat cover. How did you sprain your ankle?

I am afraid, too, that we shall be sorry that we have waited to be married. I do know that I would do *anything* you really wanted me to do.

June 6, 1945

Remember when I told you it was wonderful to love someone, but it was much more wonderful to like someone you loved. I think I've known that for a long time.

June 8, 1945

We played baseball at Ft. Smith. When our plane didn't come after us, we stayed all night. There are quite a few German prisoners here, and I talked with a few of them. They were not bitter, and they took their jobs seriously. There were no guards. One man I spoke with was from Munich – the seat of Nazi growth. He was taken prisoner in North Africa. He was quite good-looking with an accent attached to English. They were on the honor system, looking forward to the day they could go home. Some were enjoying it here.

June 9, 1945

While I was playing ball at Stuttgart army base, Zim picked up my mail – what a good friend he is.

Why do I agree with your "NO" when it comes to marriage now – not waiting for the War to end?

June 9, 1945

I am bored and ready for school to begin again. I really do like teaching. I have found no summer job. All you want is my love, trust, faith, and patience. All I want is *you,* my Bud! I want to live with you, for you to be my companion and friend, my husband, and father of my (our) children – that's all.

I HATE THE WAR!

June 11, 1945

My work here seems only secondary. I am not too interested in it. I am dreaming about us, and I am happy today, Mrs. McCollum – I never said that before. It sounds good to me. The nicest thing anyone ever told me was in your letter telling me all you ever wanted.

Our baseball coach is shipping out, and the team voted to have me be their coach. The more that an opportunity like this comes to me, the more I want to be a coach. I have lots of ideas to improve our team. We play a night game in Tulsa with a banquet to follow. I am hoping for a win.

June 13, 1945

This War had better end soon. I have reached a point where I am lost without you.

June 14, 1945

When we are married, you will come home, hold me in your arms and ask, "What are we having for supper?" And I shall tell you, "Nothing. I told you I can't cook!"

June 15, 1945

And now you're *coaching* the baseball team! I think it would be great if after the War you finish college and become a coach – you'd like that!

June 17, 1945

Why is it so important that you know my height, weight, etc.? I'd like to know just what kind of discussion you had. Are you Marines trying to compare girlfriends? You have me down right – 5'4", about 120 lbs. I am 24" around the waist – Scarlett O'Hara was only 17 1/2". Does this information meet with your approval?

June 20, 1945

The baseball game in Tulsa was rained out. The score was 0 to 0 in our

favor. Being a coach would be fun, but four years of college would take a lot away from us. I'd want you to be with me, but it takes money to go to school and eat and sleep. I'm not sure it would be best.

I have asked for a furlough between August 24 and September 2. Is it a date? I'll do my best to not stand you up and to be on time for *once*.

June 27, 1945

I am trying to decide if I should or should not go back to college when the War is over. There are times when I am sure the answer is "No," and then there are times when I am sure the only answer is "Yes."

June 27, 1945

I was wrong to think you were not interested in a baseball game. I remember your being one of the foremost rooters our high school ever had. I have always been a sports enthusiast.

June 28, 1945

In 3 1/2 months I will have been in the Marines for three long, dull, precious years. It seems like a long time, and I am tired of it all. A furlough is our only diversion. We live with restrictions, limitations, never acting as we would want, but as they want. Life is so routine and boring. You can't do this; you can't do that. You're always walking a fine line, being careful not to break any rules; and if you do, trying not to get caught! I'm sick of it all.

I want to come home and begin *my* life. I miss being happy with you and loving you. I am thankful that God gave us memories and will power. I am also thankful that we are able to recognize that there are things larger than we are. But why is there greed, hatred, and cruelty in this world? I miss you so much, and it seems so unfair. I am not as morbid as I sound, but sometimes...

June 28, 1945

I visited your home today – talking and talking with all of them, and then Asenath fell asleep in my lap. (It seems as if your family has a weakness for that!) I enjoyed a delicious chicken dinner with your family; I think I miss you most of all when I am there.

Jean's husband has been sent from India to the South Pacific. Your dad had the house painted. Your mom has a new living room couch and has had the dining room wallpapered. June has a boyfriend, and Junior has the whooping cough. Your mother flopped backward in the lawn chair on the hill. She wasn't hurt, but it was a comical sight.

July 2, 1945

The War can't last forever. Think about the good part of your life and the part that is yet to come. Now that car has stopped completely – needs a new spark plug. I think it needs an aircraft engineer.

July 2, 1945

There is one thing I want you to know. I've loved you since Heaven knows when – there, I've said it again. (Is that an original or part of a song?)

July 4, 1945

We played Muskegon, Oklahoma, last night and won 6-1. Before I became coach, our record was three wins and nine losses. Now our record is five wins against two losses. The team is developing into a better team each day and seems to play with new vigor.

We are de-preserving these planes which we preserved! A test hop was successful. Today we are sending ten or fifteen to Elizabeth City, North Carolina, for modification. They are putting rocket tubes on them. The days just lull by. Oh, if only... I dream about the day when we shall be together forever.

July 5, 1945

"Semper Fidelis" – That's the Marine Corps motto. Mom and Dad will be very happy if we get married – they have become very attached to you. They, too, have waited so long to have you as a part of the family. Thanks for the detailed description of all that is going on at home. Your letter makes me feel that I am almost there.

July 6, 1945

I feel ashamed at not having been overseas. I have not done my part. There are 350 of us here with the most important job of any Marine aviator. We have the highest rating – non-expendable. We are frozen. I should go overseas – thus I am ashamed and disgusted. If they were to tell me that I could get out of the Service tomorrow, I would say that I want to stick it out until the end of the War. My *Marine* morale does not need any uplifting – just *my* morale.

July 7, 1945

You can't possibly know how very good I feel when you visit home, and then tell me about it.

Tomorrow we must drive 400 miles to a ball game. I'll play as though you are right there watching me.

July 8, 1945

No, Jim isn't a model husband – he's just very nice, tall, dark, and handsome. He kindly tolerates us girls, and Eleanor loves him. He wants to tell you what a *terrible* life you'll have when we are married.

I, above all others, am aware of how many precious years you've spent for Uncle Sam. It hasn't been all bad. Someday we'll be able to see the good from it. Everything works out for the good. Think about the best part of your life that is yet to come.

The other day my car chugged so dreadfully; I thought it was *finished.* All it needed was a new spark plug.

I had a horrible dream last night. The Japs were torturing me and sliced my arm! I'll be glad when you are here on furlough, because I'll never think of things that bother me. I always feel so safe and protected when I am with you.

July 9, 1945

The longer I know you, the less I find that I know about you. I really enjoyed your letter; you said so many nice things.

I believe that there is something good in everyone. It is pleasing, very pleasing, to know that in all this world I love someone and am loved by someone in a sincere, friendly, devoted, *and* understanding way that seems to *almost* complete everything for which I have ever hoped.

July 9, 1945

I would be so happy if I could watch you play ball again and be so very proud of your ability. On Sundays you played on Garrett's team with Gay and Bob. I enjoyed those games, but it would have been better if I had understood exactly how you felt about me. I was afraid to hope you loved me – I was sure you didn't and *never* would. You had me so mixed up – *saying* one thing and *conveying* another with your actions – those sweet, soft kisses. I'd have believed you almost disliked me a great deal if you'd have stopped kissing me. Every time you kissed me or held me close, I was *almost positive* you were in love with me. Now I know that that last feeling was correct – if I had only known then. You had me all mixed up! Isn't it nice to remember?

July 11, 1945

I am sorry that Gay is not treated well by Sis. He plans to go back a couple days early from his furlough. He sees in you acts of devotion which he would like to see in Sis. It is nice to be able to write to you about baseball, and know that our love is secure.

July 13, 1945

I wish I had been more truthful with my feelings. You did not understand why I acted so mean to you. I felt sorry.

July 12, 1945

Now *that car* needs a $10 water pump. I am so tired of this responsibility – I want to hand it all over to you.

July 15, 1945

Today we lost two games. My pitching record is 2-2, but I struck out 12 men. I can close my eyes and see you.

July 15, 1945

I went to a movie while the car was in the garage. I now have a new water pump, a clean radiator, new hoses, and clean spark plugs. I have a $70 refund on my taxes. *Someday* seems a long way off, and it never gets any closer.

July 16, 1945

I will be glad to take care of the car for you and to have you hand over all your other responsibilities to me. I will teach you how not to worry about every material thing.

July 18, 1945

The car is good now. You said you would teach me not to worry about such things – you are exactly what I need!

I went barefooted, and a bee stung me.

July 20, 1945

I am listening to "Hit Parade" on my radio; are you listening too? A bee did sting me, and I have to laugh, thinking about it. We had a bee hive and Dad was too busy to steal the honey, so I told Mom I'd get the honey for her. I talked Earl Link into helping me, and we started our trek with complete confidence. We were rigged to do the job. I took off the top of the hive, and

there amid the buzzing thousands of bees was our treasure. Earl had the smoker (supposed to make them calm) and I had a knife and a pan in which to place the honey from the racks. Bee nets, which protect the face, are placed over hats with brims to support the nets, and they tie around the neck with a draw string.

When Earl was bending over the hive, his net left an opening between the brim and the net. The bees got inside his net, and he did not notice them. This made them very angry, because the netting had crushed several. The chase was on!! I was running as I had never run before, and despite my yelling for Earl to stop following me as all the bees chased him, he stayed close to my heels. You should have heard us! Every time a bee stung me, I would let out a yelp, and Earl was crying out three times as much as I. Not only were we yelling in full flight, but I was busy removing some bee-laden clothing. I got off with only a few stings, but Earl had to go to the doctor and was very sick for several days. He had twenty stings on his face alone.

Even now to this day, Earl will not eat honey, not even when it comes from a jar. Now I can find humor in that hectic day. Oh, by the way – I got the honey for Mom.

July 20, 1945

We have had three busy days – one of our ships could not get his landing gear down and after two hours, he made a belly-landing in the emergency way. The plane weighs 30,000 pounds.

We played ball against the Fourth Ferrying Command. I played second base and had two triples and a single and drove in seven runs. Then we drove 164 miles to play Stuttgart Army base – but we lost. We blew out two new tires. I am still counting on an eight-day furlough – but I am never sure.

July 22, 1945

Your brother Bill and Bill McDulin are both at P.I. Bill is fitting shoes on new recruits. McDulin is being sent to warrant officer's school in Fla.

July 23, 1945

I'm counting on those eight days in August. The doctor says I need more iron in my blood – pink and green pills. He just keeps asking about you, saying that you are all I need. Once he said that my trouble is that I am too young! (Whatever he means by that.)

July 24, 1945

Just being near you, talking, listening, and seeing you can make any furlough as beautiful and wonderful as any fellow could have the right to expect.

July 25, 1945

My buddies, Chester and Eggie, are arguing with me about you. They threaten me if I don't get married on this furlough! But they are both 28 and not married! Now my work schedule has me up at 5 am.

July 26, 1945

The news of War sounds better every day! President Truman has made a proclamation from Potsdam telling the Japs what we mean by unconditional surrender. Do you realize what it will mean to us if the War is over soon? I get goose pimples just thinking about it. We didn't celebrate on V-E Day, but just wait until V-J Day!! (I think V-E Day was last spring?)

July 27, 1945

I'm wasting so much time just waiting, waiting, waiting for *someday.*

July 29, 1945

Medicine reaches its highest degree of development during Wartime.

Dorothea, it is nice to hope that the War will be over soon, but today I heard on the radio that Japan has rejected our peace offer, so I guess it will be a few more months before they say "uncle." On the radio they are singing "You Belong to My Heart," and I want you near me *now! You are all I ever wanted.* Things like that are for storybooks and movies – but we are fortunate to be living just such a life.

July 31, 1945

Today I heard on the radio that the Japs may have to give up by the end of the year because of the food shortage. We've sunk so much of their shipping that they might consider the Potsdam ultimatum. They'll regret it in the months to come.

You want to know my reason as to why I am not there with you – I believe that when two people are married they should be together – not only on furloughs, but *always.* You do not want me to live in Arkansas on a Marine base under Wartime conditions. That's not what we have planned! We don't want life to be regulated by the Marine Corps. If our love was all that counted, I'd *definitely* be there! But if the War lasts *much longer,* we'll change our plans.

July 31, 1945

In 24 more days I shall have a furlough – but I have a premonition

that I won't get it. When I think of coming home I get that empty feeling inside – almost like butterflies again.

August 1, 1945

My schedule for teaching will be easier this year – I'll even have a free period. I am anxious for school to start.

August 2, 1945

When the War ends, I shall have to make a few decisions. Shall I go to college, shall I choose an occupation to my liking and then work toward bettering myself, shall I just let nature take its course? Shall I take a conservative or radical view of the offerings of this old world??

The deciding factor and the one which is most considerate is that I shall not disappoint *you*, and thus lose faith in myself. I love you very much, and I want you to be happy in your love for me. But sometimes circumstances cause people to be very unhappy. Going back to college would be the easiest way, but would that be fair to you?

August 2, 1945

Four of us played golf today. We put on old clothes and old tennis shoes, and it almost seemed we were not in the Marine Corps for an afternoon. I received the enlarged snapshot. It makes me feel good to see me just sitting there with you – to know that the love we feel is so wonderful. Our love is not something that just happened – it's a wonderful union of understanding and happiness that we found in each other. I like you for being *you*.

August 5, 1945

Things are not going well for Woots and Bob – worse than ever. Bob is telling people that they shall get a divorce, she beats him (?), and now she wants to take away his car. He wasn't home when I stopped by. Woots put on a big front – everything is just fine. Today is their wedding anniversary; she might not go back to him. The Sauerbecks' back porch is piled high with pots and pans, clothing, and all their possessions. She'll cover up and put on a big front for a long time.

August 7, 1945

Mother and Bob left this morning for Piqua and the church camp, and I am in charge. Already my hands are red from washing dishes three times a day. How about an automatic dishwasher?

There are only 17 days until August 24; you haven't been home since last May.

Daddy gave me gasoline stamps for 12 gallons, so I can save my 30 gallons for when you're here.

August 7, 1945

The release of the news of the atomic bomb has everyone around here in an optimistic mood, while at the same time there is foreboding or cautious and dubious attitude as to the control of such a powerful instrument. Science can tax our powers of comprehension. There are a few possibilities involving the use of energy. I hope Japan realizes the destructiveness of this atom bomb and sends a favorable reply to our proclamation.

Gee, won't it be wonderful when this is all over, and we can begin our lives without any wartime restrictions. I'm not so sure that I'm not ready at this very moment to get married. When two people are wholly and sincerely in love, *nothing* should keep them apart; yet my love tells me to be patient and conservative lest I do something that would hurt or disappoint you. Why should we give so much of our lives to individual reasons which we both dislike? When I am asked why I keep waiting, I give a simple and pointless answer, "I don't know." Nothing bothers me more than this. I want to come home and talk to you. I am enclosing a money order for our bank account. Someone stole my watch. Tomorrow three of us will go to Eagle Mt. Lake for a baseball game – why do they want us?

August 8, 1945

Your mother bought a new electric stove, and my mother is buying her old one. Woots and Bob came down – he has a 1943 Buick Super. It makes my old Chevy look sick, but at least it's paid for! For two hours I had to listen to him bragging. He talked about himself continuously. It made me sick to hear him "blow." The new car is in *his* name, so when they get a divorce it will be his!

August 8, 1945

I feel elated now that Russia has declared war on Japan. Maybe the War will be over by the time you get this letter. How much longer will they keep us in the Service? We are so important to each other – I want to talk to you about it when I come home. When Dad and I used to work together, he told me that if something isn't worth doing well, it isn't worth doing at all. I never want to forget all the things Dad taught me.

August 9, 1945

My family has survived on my cooking. I used up all of our meat, so I don't know what I'll fix tomorrow. When I think about the War's ending, I just feel funny (no, strange) all over. The end of the War will close one chapter of our lives, and begin another. That's wonderful, and I want it too. But the new chapter of our lives "sorta" scares me – I guess it's because of the unknown. I've been dreaming of addressing all those wedding invitations.

August 10, 1945

The surrender has not been accepted! After a week of housework my nails are all broken and ugly; I'll be glad when Mother returns. I cleaned the whole house, fixed all the meals, skimmed the milk, and a dozen other things. And then I fixed your scrapbook up to date. Will they keep you for six months after the peace? Adjusting to peace will be as difficult as it was adjusting to war. Within 24 hours after the surrender, gas will no longer be rationed.

I nearly jumped out of my skin the other day. The phone rang, and I heard, "Dorothea." I thought it was you, but it was your dad speaking my name in your soft way. He was just checking to be sure the stove had arrived OK. Jean is on vacation, and she and your mother took all the kids to the zoo. They watched the kids, and the kids watched the monkeys.

August 11, 1945

The peace news gets better and better, and I fall asleep thinking of us and our lives after we're married. It's that car again. Now it needs a new battery. I get it and the muffler tomorrow. The city is making plans for the V-J celebration.

August 12, 1945

We shall have to negotiate the washing dishes problem – my sisters always did that.

WHOOPEE!!!! Japan has just accepted our peace terms at 9:33 pm. Shucks, they have been told to hold the flash – 9:36 pm. I love you and respect you in every way possible. *Love is an element of the soul* and all those parts of your personality that make you, you.

August 12, 1945

We heard both flashes, too. We're trying to wait up for more news. The bells and whistles began to ring, and then they stopped abruptly after the second flash. Can we go to visit Eleanor and Jim when you are home? All the girls will be there too.

August 14, 1945

Less than an hour ago, I heard the news!!!

THE WAR IS OVER.

We're going to town to join in the celebration. It's raining, everything is closed, and the people are going crazy! Now we can begin to live.

August 15, 1945

THIS IS OUR DAY – V-J Day!!!! We were playing golf when the groundskeeper came running to tell us the news. My first reaction was an avalanche of goose pimples which smothered my desire to yell and knock that golf ball from here to Japan. None of us said much, but our minds were not on golf! Finally about halfway down the fairway I did yell – so loud that it could have been heard back in Newport. I finished the golf game in a maze of happiness. My immediate thoughts were of us. I haven't celebrated, unless you want to call mental exuberance celebrating. It seems that I shall be in the Marines for several more months – or even possibly for another year. The new chapter in our lives scares me, too, but that may not be the correct term to use. I save further explanation for the furlough.

August 15, 1945

Fill 'er up! – no more gasoline rationing! I won't need those "A" stamps. Can you bring your blue trousers? I'm tired of all that khaki. Jean said she dreamed we were married on your furlough date. Again your mother asked me, and I guess I disappointed her again. When I hear about Bill and Millie it causes me to stop and think. Kak told me he is to receive a bicycle this week. His hair is white just like Bill's.

August 17, 1945

I would prefer an essential duty so the time would pass more quickly – we are all frozen here. If I have to stay in here another year, I shall without question, but that won't keep me from being resentful. You know what I want? You, but after that, homemade ice cream.

August 19, 1945

Bill should be home when you are here. Another flat tire.

August 20, 1945

I read your last letter twice. The Squadron Office wants to check on those five days of furlough last year. I spoke with the office "pinky" and he sent me to the 1st Sgt., and a guy from pay master involved himself, and they decided on a three-day furlough. I gave reason and reason why I needed more than three days, and finally the 1st Sgt. figured a way for me to have eight days.

August 21, 1945

I'm working at school this week, helping Mr. Finkbine get ready for school's starting. Bill is home. I am going to apply for a new tire. There are 19 big cracks in the side wall. A boot would be so large that the entire tire would be just a boot. I have a new jack, so if a tire wants to go flat, I'll just change it. No tire can scare me anymore!

And now someone else wants to quiz me as to why I am not being married when you come home in a few days. Why are they all so nosy and curious? I can't explain to them.

August 22, 1945

Today I received a sad letter from Bill McDulin. It is a tragic story, but not completely a surprise. I sensed it when I first knew them. The disappointing thing is that Millie told him that she never loved him – just like your Uncle Russell.

I'll be home Sunday. You'd think we'd get used to those *hellos* and *goodbyes*, but each time I am more anxious and excited.

FURLOUGH August 24 – September 2

September 4, 1945

I am teaching Ruth Ellen at her home from 4 p.m. to 5 p.m. each day – that makes for a long day. I receive $1 per hour. I know not what to do in a free period – never had one before. School is quiet, and I am much more relaxed than during my first year. When I think about June, I wish I were in Arkansas right now, but perhaps it is better this way; I said "perhaps."

September 4, 1945

Now I know exactly what I want; you gave me a feeling of confidence in the future, and never have I felt so sure of us. We're not really bad off; I've never loved you more than at this very moment. That last day we spent together was the happiest day of my life. What we have and share is really all I ever wanted. I have September 29 marked on my calendar – that was an important day for me (us), and I shall never forget it.

September 5, 1945

Every day that you were home was different and nice, but the last day was better than all the others put together! You should be able to prove your point the next time you have a discussion with your "buddies." I dreamed I was in school last night – in school all day and all night! Too much. I'd rather dream of you.

September 5, 1945

I think I may be home on the 29th. We had a discussion about weddings – one fellow had just been married. It sounds so complicated – so much to do and remember. My mind is whirling and buzzing so fast when I remember my last time home.

September 6, 1945

Our love is wonderful, and we can want nothing more than to share it with each other.

September 6, 1945

We were both so happy, for we would be living as we would want to live after we are married, with a few exceptions, of course. Those things are close to my heart and firmly embedded in my memory. I am wondering if I (or we) can wait until June – I hope I am discharged before then. There is still the possibility that I may go overseas. I agree, we are too much in love to stay like this for many more months!

September 7, 1945

I know what you can do during your free period – relax, read, write, talk, sleep – anything to divert your mind from your work.

I have an opportunity for a good civil service job – $1.50 per hour. I may be tempted to try it. But I might be sent anywhere in the U.S. to an R & R shop. I'm only wondering, so don't get excited. I am a realist. The plan that has made me most happy is the one you suggested – college and coaching. But would we be happy with you working, and our not having any children for quite a long time? I need to hold you in my arms and kiss you and talk to you about this.

September 7, 1945

I received the money today; I shall deposit it. The newspaper clipping about Bill and Millie is enclosed. Don't worry about our wedding – it will not be complicated at all. Just take my hand and say "I do." You've waited so long; I won't make you wait a minute longer. Sometimes though, we don't know what might happen.

A 71-hour leave.

September 10, 1945

I hope you can meet me in Cincy. That would give us a few extra hours. When we first see each other there is an immediate outburst of attraction, and I cease being *Sgt.* and become *Bud,* and the world is ours until we again have to say goodbye!

September 10, 1945

I HATE THE WAR!!! IT'S OVER – LET THESE BOYS COME HOME!!!

I talked with Mr. Bogan – he wanted to see my ring. He was most interested in your plans – he thinks you'd be a very good coach. Coaches are the highest paid of all in the teaching profession, and they are needed now! Teaching is a secure job, and he thinks you'd be very happy – enjoying your work is very important. I wish you could have talked with him – he knows both of us very well. We don't want to live away from our families and friends. You'll have to work a long, long time earning us a living. The civil service job would let us begin our plans much sooner. But, there's always that "but," don't decide by that reason only. I'd be happy if you were in college, and I don't mind working, because teaching is not like a job – not like any office jobs I have ever had.

I too, am not happy about starting a family for such a long time, but (there's that "but" again) we've been together for such a short time during these years that I'd like to have you all to myself for a little while. You will be such a good father, and I'll be happy to share you with them.

Back to the subject – our Ross Commencement speaker pointed out that we have many trained in mechanical skills, but what the world needs is people skilled in helping others – the personal skills of a teacher and coach. I thought of you.

September 11, 1945

A college degree should stand for an accomplishment for an immediate individual purpose. We can want nothing more than to share our love forever, and we shall do just that.

September 11, 1945

My cousin Ray is coming home and will be married in a couple weeks. He had 125 points and ten battle stars. Maybe you'll be home for the wedding. When I think of June it seems so close it almost frightens me, and at other times it seems so far away – *much* too far away. In the midst of these wonderful thoughts of a June wedding, the study hall bell rang and brought me back to reality. Aunt Emma talked with Mrs. McDulin (they live just across the alley); she tells her that the guy Millie prefers to Bill is running around with someone else while she is here. "Poor Millie." I hope I don't see her – what could I say?

September 13, 1945

Three of us have been invited to the home of our supply sergeant for dinner tonight. Sgt. Yum.

I was happy to fix your car – I like doing things for you. I get a great deal of pleasure in just watching you perform those acts common in everyday life – like fixing my breakfast.

September 13, 1945

I hope to have a new tire by the 29th when you come home. I am going to see the ration board today – maybe they will approve two new tires. I don't want to take you away from your family when you are home.

September 15, 1945

A hurricane is coming to Florida, and their planes are all coming here for protection. They will soon be calling me to help. It should be a lot of satisfaction to know that Ruth Ellen is doing so well back at school. Mr. Bogan is right – I'm pretty sure that coaching is what I really want to do as my life's vocation. It fits with what I am qualified to learn. You wrote all the things I wanted to hear; I value your opinion so highly!

An article in the *Reader's Digest* points out the fact that we are headed for an educational *collapse* unless students are encouraged to choose an educational vocation. I am glad the seniors choose you as their class advisor – and you wanted to be chosen. It shows their respect for you not only as their teacher, but as a person.

September 17, 1945

I have been happy in my life, in fact, most of it has been fun, even though there's a serious side; the nicest part, the happiest phase is the one I experience

loving you as I do. I feel that there is happiness awaiting me that is far more wonderful than the nice happy feeling I now know.

September 18, 1945

Your little nephew is walking now – he's a little wobbly, but he makes it. We made more ice cream when Aunt Lil came down. Poor thing – she can talk of nothing else. I'm glad to know how your parents feel about us – I didn't take you away from them. They understand very well because they are so very much in love too.

September 18, 1945

I'm lonesome, but just telling you makes me feel a little better. I'll bring Mom a new head scarf and Mart's jewelry.

September 21, 1945

Tomorrow I am going to have the clutch checked on that car. Something's not right. The seniors are choosing announcements, class photos, caps and gowns, parts for the annual play, and planning the senior dance. I will have earned $80 instructing Ruth Ellen at home. I attended a shower for Ray's wife-to-be. He's happy to be a civilian after three years in the South Pacific. The wedding is October 4, and he'll be wearing his uniform. She is a lovely girl – I like her.

September 21, 1945

I always like meeting and seeing you after I have been away – it's like hearing "The Star Spangled Banner" at the proper time.

September 23, 1945

I saw Sis; she is hoping they will send Gay home for good. The Army is discharging men with two years of service. Yesterday three more people asked me when we were going to be married – including Millie. I didn't mention the divorce. She has two diamonds on her finger and is wearing Bill's Marine earrings. Millie said to tell you she loves you for the telephone call and for coming to see her.

September 24, 1945

No one has ever been more considerate of my welfare than you. I feel humbly grateful. The most considerate of you and the hardest to carry out was *not* volunteering to go overseas. I was so tempted until I thought of my promise to you and its effect on Mom. I never volunteered.

September 25, 1945

My papers for a furlough are typed and ready to go through the official channels. Now I must be patient that everything is OK. I should arrive in Cincy on Friday morning. I'm not counting on a discharge before June, perhaps sooner – if I don't have to go overseas.

FURLOUGH September 25 – October 2

October 1, 1945

Two Marines watched me say goodbye to you, and they were definitely impressed. I didn't know if they wanted me to tell them goodbye or – they just smiled sweetly. Already I'm checking my schedule to plan another leave for you. I have a holiday October 26, Thanksgiving November 22 and 23, and Christmas December 21 to January 2. April 19 is Good Friday. My ring is extra shiny as if it knows it is one year old.

October 1, 1945

I am even more happy than I was a year ago.

October 2, 1945

I know what and wherein lies my happiness, and I must be sure that what I am doing makes you happy too.

October 3 , 1945

I am remembering and reliving each part of my leave. Remembering draws me home.

October 5, 1945

Another anniversary, but not as pleasant as September 29. I am glad it is now and not three years ago. Each time you come home, I love you even more than before.

I need another chaperone for the class hayride. Leiser would help me, but he has plans for that night. He is your best friend back here. He has already been discharged. My cousin was married last night – a simple, beautiful wedding.

October 6, 1945

I am very much in love with you and miss you with all my heart.

October 7, 1945

I remember now how little I came to see you a long time ago, and how I felt the night you wouldn't let me kiss you. I have never shared my life with anyone in any way, but when I told you, "I love you," I've been sharing it with you, and I LIKE IT.

October 8, 1945

I know we'll agree on most things – I'll just hold you in my arms and we'll talk, heart to heart. My credits from Wake Forest are almost nil – I want to start over. I didn't study; I was so tired from sports that I just didn't feel like it. I am now determined and confident.

October 9, 1945

We're so busy at school with pictures, the Annual, measuring for caps and gowns, etc. So many of the boys have been discharged. I am happy to read in your letter, "Once I get home, I shall never leave again *unless* you are with me."

October 10, 1945

I'm trying to get a leave beginning on Saturday instead of Friday – I'm so tired of trying to plan and hearing "maybe."

October 10, 1945

Tomorrow night is our hayride. I'll be glad when that is over – taking all those kids is quite a responsibility.

October 14, 1945

I wish with all my heart that I can come home soon *to stay.*

October 17, 1945

Your folks left for Georgia this morning. Ruth is staying with me. On

Saturday all the girls are meeting in Oxford again; even my roommate can come. Gay wants Sis to come to California for Christmas, and she wants to go, but Gay is afraid for her to travel so far alone.

October 18, 1945

Bill McDulin and Johnny Woedl are home on leave. Bill expects to be discharged between January and March. It really makes no difference to me what you decide about college. Don't go to college if it is against your real feelings. If just thinking about it makes you unhappy, you shouldn't go. You are not old, tired, and worn out – just come home, and we'll take care of all that!

October 22, 1945

What a time all you girls must have. We have some fun too. We caught Tony in the bathtub and poured cold water all over him – you should have heard him yell! My pass has been made out – now if Capt. Burr and Capt. Zoda sign it, I'll see you next Friday. Bill and Johnny are both home.

71-HOUR PASS

October 29, 1945

A 71-hour pass was not very long – here Friday, Saturday, and leaving on Sunday. Back at the base and the Marine Corps on Monday.

October 29, 1945

That car again. Now there's a leak in the hydraulic system – between $5 and $8. New cars are on display – I shall take a look. I don't know who is eligible to buy the new cars – I am probably not.

October 31, 1945

Do you mean that you will have a furlough November 20 to December 5 or 6? When you're missing me, try to imagine this time next year.

November 1, 1945

I'll help you address those Christmas cards. We couldn't survive those days we just spent. Our work here is almost complete – the base will close – I will be reassigned. I'll take a furlough whenever I can get it.

November 1, 1945

We're so busy at school; we are planning a Thanksgiving dance. I am daydreaming about us even more and more. It will be difficult finding a place to live.

November 6, 1945

We have only five planes left; one of them is assigned to me for a "plane check." Everything has changed – now my furlough starts November 12 and ends the 30th. Any time at all is wonderful! I'm glad you talked with Dean Ashbaugh. He gives us encouragement. A new black dress for the dance – I don't care what you wear; I may not even notice – no-o-o, not much.

November 6, 1945

You'll be here for our dance – it'll be so nice to be dancing in your arms!

FURLOUGH November 12 – November 30

November 29, 1945

I just looked out the window at school. My car is there, but you are not in it. This furlough was as perfect 18 days I've ever spent. It has been so long since I saw you – almost five hours!

November 30, 1945

I realize just how much we mean to each other.

December 1, 1945

Today I asked Mom to look for my ID and liberty card only to discover that you has already mailed it to me – thanks a million! It is optimistic to believe I will get out before February. I am dreaming about you, our home, our future, and those pleasant memories.

December 3, 1945

My typing students are typing really well. One typed 60-0 on a one-minute and 44-0 on a five-minute test! She's a first-year typist. We need lights for our

Christmas tree – none work. Does the PX have any? While you're there, look at the silverware.

December 3, 1945

I'm still here, but I feel that I'm motionless – neither coming nor going and halfway in between some reality and a ready-to-be-forgotten past. I even enjoyed the PTA meeting and especially your talk, I should say *speech.* I can think of no other wonder that would surpass the love and enthusiasm that grow and grow in my anxious anticipation for our happy future.

December 5, 1945

I am living from one school event to the next, and I am happy every day. I can't imagine that you liked the PTA meeting – it was "corny," and I was unprepared to speak. The saying, "kiss and make up" doesn't apply to us. We prefer to straighten things out first, and I like that. Have you seen any Roger's silverware?

December 5, 1945

Don't send any more mail here; we may be sent to Quantico, VA. I don't want to be sent to Cherry Point again! I'll try to find Christmas presents for your family and mine.

December 6, 1945

Did we spend $30 when you were on leave? How did you get your watch back? Did you threaten him? Did you use a Marine hold and just take it from him? I'd like to know.

December 7, 1945

Here is the $30 I owe you – I'll have to get used to the idea of pooling our money. Can you buy Christmas gifts for my family? I'll send you some money. I have a few suggestions.

December 13, 1945

It is snowing very hard, and the temperature is zero. Many kids and teachers are absent – they should close school. My car is okay, and I am having no trouble in the snow. My cousin, Walter, has given Pat a ring. Pat is Erv's cousin. Her ring is not so nice as mine and not half as big, but it is nice. They plan a June wedding – Walter wants to beat me. Gay is planning a wedding in July or August. WHERE ARE YOU?? Quantico, I hope. I am making stuffed animals for the little ones in your family. The kids put snow in the overhead study hall lights before I arrived there, and as it melted, I thought the roof was leaking. I went shopping and purchased all the gifts. I spent $16.69 in total for all of them.

December 14, 1945

Our trip to Quantico was long, dirty, and boring. It took two days and three nights; we have not yet been assigned to duty. Our barracks are the nicest to which I have ever been assigned. It would give your dorm a run for the money. It is three stories high with a huge basement and marble floors. My window overlooks the Potomac which is about 1 1/2 to 2 miles wide. There are 500 men here. Quantico is just 38 miles from D.C. We have a PX, barber shop, rec room, and mess hall plus facilities for washing our own clothes. It has been ages since I saw you.

December 15, 1945

The PX is beautiful and large; there is a full-sized library, Marine Corps museum, bowling alley, and several bar rooms serving beer and milk shakes. The movie theater is beautiful; I asked about the silver and was referred to the order department which was closed. Luck is still with me; I will be home for Christmas. A friend is buying me a ticket for the train out of Washington for the 20th – I want a reserved seat! No one has received any mail, for we were here for a day and a half before they told us our new address.

December 17, 1945

When I ever get out of here, please don't ever let me leave you again!

FURLOUGH December 20 – December 25.

December 26, 1945

I am sorry I left you waiting for the train, but I just couldn't stand there any longer; I know I would have cried again. I'm crying now as I realize again that someone loves me as much as you do.

December 27, 1945

Today is so long, and those days at home were so short. Why must time be like that? Time seems to hasten the end of pretty things in life. There were no

seats on the train, but I thought of the baggage car, and the baggage man was kind enough to allow me to ride with him. We were soon surrounded by 245 others in the same predicament. It was a long, tiresome 16 1/2 hour ride.

December 27, 1945

I plan to make myself be very busy for the next several months. Mother washed, and I ironed all day with the new iron you sent me. All of your other boxes arrived too. The mailman knows what's going on! I ironed six of your shirts and six of Bob's. I'm slow! It takes me a half hour to iron one. My cedar chest is almost *full!* I try to imagine the day when our time will no longer be rationed. We have $572.26 in the savings account.

December 29, 1945

I am waiting for the Secretary of State, Jimmy Burns to come back so I can return to the barracks and finish this letter. He flew in three hours ago from Russia, just before my quitting time, and now I am standing by waiting to send his plane off. He is this very minute conferring with the President on his yacht in the Potomac. He was due back at 6:35, but it is now 7:45, and he has not yet returned. The PX is no longer taking orders for silverware. Maybe things will change when the excess profit tax is lifted.

December 31, 1945

All my aunts and uncles are amazed at how much fun you were at the party at Aunt Lil's. They didn't really know you until then. They all like you; you made a very favorable impression. Now, maybe they can understand my attraction to you! In an hour and a half 1946 will begin – I can think of a million things to make it the best year we have ever known.

December 31, 1945

We shall share 1946 wholly and *completely,* experiencing a happiness, an understanding and an overall love which we not yet had an opportunity to know.

The other night while I was on duty, waiting for Secretary Byrnes to come back, I wrote a poem. It's corny, but here it is:

WAITING

This could be a night for history
After all is said and done;

And Mr. President and Secretary
Have traded pun for pun.
But to me it's hours of waiting,
About which I'm not too keen,
An ingratiating feeling –
Hidden from sight – unseen.
Now I stand and watch the clock
And wonder just when
Mr. Secretary will return
From spinning his important yen.
It's not for me to guess
Nor even wonder why
Men have to keep others waiting,
While time is flying by.
There is a concession, however,
About which there is no debating:
That the man who has the most
Invariably keeps the others...waiting.

Goodnight, my darling – my honest and most sincere wishes for the happiest new year of all your years.

Love ever,
Bud.

One cold winter's night, the leave of S/Sgt. Marvin F. McCollum was unexpectedly canceled because of the arrival of Secretary of State, Jimmy Byrnes, from Russia. Being an aircraft engineer in the United States Marine Corps, Bud was assigned to prepare the airplane to fly Byrnes from Quantico, Virginia, to Washington, D.C. – when the signal came from the Presidential yacht in the Potomac that their conference was completed.

Time passed. While waiting and waiting, Bud penned this poem as the hours of his canceled leave ticked away.

During the endless delay, Bud informed the pilot that he should be allowed to de-ice the plane, but the pilot always replied that it would be just fine. More than once, Bud requested the de-icing. "No," was the answer.

When Jimmy Byrnes saw the plane – well, he blew his top. I don't know what happened to the pilot or to the plane. At least Bud was not reprimanded. Jimmy Byrnes ordered a limo and continued to D.C. by automobile.

And a nameless young Marine forfeited his leave.

"Soon I am coming home for good! It's hard to realize that this isn't just another furlough."

January 1, 1946

I dream about the day the separation officer shakes my hand and bids me fair sailing! Then can my dreams of becoming a civilian, going to school, being married, having a family, home, and happiness become a reality.

January 2, 1946

My pride dictates that you must *allow me* to purchase our first set of furnishings, even if it means cashing some bonds. I have always been independent financially, and it is hard to accept your financial help. I shall carefully blend dependent and independent. Happiness is the heartbeat of a home, and you to me *are* happiness. I am very proud of you, and I want you to be proud of me, someday. I am putting a new engine on a ($35,000) plane.

January 3, 1946

We butchered Old Friday; Mother has canned 28 quart jars of meat from the front quarter.

Let's save our New Year's celebrating until you are discharged. I am thinking of you as a civilian.

January 4, 1946

When you tell me you are arranging all of your things to be ready to move out, I have a good feeling all over.

January 4, 1946

I have all your letters in order; this is #440.

January 4, 1946

The discharge situation is very disappointing.

January 7, 1946

Tomorrow you will be 24; Happy Birthday!

January 8, 1946

It's that car again! I'd like to buy a new one before you are discharged. That car will be your *responsibility.* Millie was married over Christmas; the diamond ring was from him.

January 8, 1946

The PX has a very limited amount of silverware. We'll have to wait. I accidentally went out for the basketball team. Today I am 24, and I miss you with all my heart.

January 9, 1946

I have a letter from Bill McDulin paying you quite a compliment – "one in a million," he says. He's looking for those qualities lacking in Millie. He isn't telling me anything I didn't already know. Long before my feelings were aroused, I knew you were nice, had a strong sense of morals and values. The dynamic character traits you possess blend to make you YOU. Kindness, tolerance, understanding, and ambition give you a strong, sincere love for me – I like it, because it is *you* who stirred the most powerful of feelings which are mine.

January 11, 1946

I am not going to China.

January 14, 1946

The price of solid sterling is $23 for a 6-piece place setting. A 4-piece place setting would cost $15. Eight 4-piece place settings would cost $125. We could always buy more.

How is it possible to go out for the team *accidentally?* Tomorrow Eisenhower and Nimitz will speak before Congress concerning demobilization plans.

January 14, 1946

I've been playing a lot of basketball. Tonight at supper the guys were talking about the disadvantages of being a civilian. I listened for a while, and then when I had heard enough of their squawks, *I began on them!* They make me sick! They are a bunch of parasites panning their laziness off on the people of this country. Our national debt is $262,000,000,000 and at the present time we can't pay the interest on it. They choose to add insult to misery. They are the type of guys who can't stand the competition which is present in civilian life. Here a guy doesn't know what it means to be independent as to food, clothing, and lodging – everything is provided for him. After the Service I shall say, "Life has its ups and downs, but it's mine, and I can truthfully say I have been happy." They are too weak to accept the responsibility that Old Man

World has placed on them. Thinking of you is so reassuring and exemplary that my confidence gains momentum with each thought.

January 15, 1946

Chester left this morning; I hated to see him go. I may never see him again. All over the country there are men with love and gratitude for memories of sincere and needed friendships. Buddies take the place of mothers, sweethearts, fathers, and brothers – I'll miss Chester. It's nice to have friends, but nicer to love you.

January 15, 1946

Does Eisenhower plan to have all three-year men out by April 30? Does it apply to you? A new universal joint for *that car* will cost $15 to $20. I can hear you telling me, "Oh, I love you so much."

January 17, 1946

The government has taken $257 in taxes from my wages this year. I shall get back $28.

January 21, 1946

A big piece of glass cut a hole in my new tire!

January 22, 1946

I am looking forward to spring. April reminds me of Easter when I wore my "blues" and met all your cousins. There were so many! I am remembering the ocean at Morehead City, the porch swing complete with mosquitoes, and dinners at *Sea Shore Dinners*. For 3 1/2 years my life hasn't been my own – my plans have, but not my life...

January 24, 1946

I am busy 24 hours a day with work and basketball. Mr. Edington will write to Sid Gillman about me.

January 28, 1946

Just as I was pulling into the barn lot at home I heard air leaking from another tire. A wire had punctured it, and now I have no spare.

I'm glad Mr. Edington will write to Sid Gillman about you – that'll give you a big boost if you go to Miami. It's hard to enroll – there are so many returning veterans. No girls will be accepted until 1947. We have $630 in the savings account. I AM SO TIRED OF WRITING LETTERS; IT JUST SEEMS SO ENDLESS – SO FAR AWAY.

January 29, 1946

Eisenhower says he'll keep his promise to the Army boys, but says nothing about the Marines.

January 30, 1946

I am glad that noise was only a broken bolt. I have already missed the second semester of college; maybe I can get out of here for summer school. There are so many lonely minutes, hours, and days; it can't last much longer.

February 1, 1946

We have a basketball game again tonight. Shall I purchase our wedding bands at the PX?

February 2, 1946

I am so glad you have decided to go to college.

February 3, 1946

We shall have a nice life together, because we are truthful and tolerant of each other's weaknesses. I shall write to Miami about transferring my Wake Forest credits and enrolling in summer school.

February 4, 1946

Having you mention our wedding rings makes me very happy.

February 5, 1946

My biggest challenge is wanting you – *now* doesn't matter, *tomorrow* doesn't matter, but the day I am discharged and I am free…

February 7, 1946

Today a card came saying the nylons for which I had registered were available. I have been waiting and not able to purchase any for a very long time. Waiting would be easier if only we knew when you would be discharged. Two more of my cousins are home. Everyone seems to be home, except *you.*

February 7, 1946

We have another basketball game tonight – I catch the bus in 15 minutes. My love is stronger than ever before, and my heart and soul are sincerely devoted to protecting and sheltering something so young and alive – our love.

February 10, 1946

We had basketball games two nights in a row, and tonight we play Baltimore. I have ideas for a team if I am ever coaching.

February 11, 1946

The P.S. "I *like* you" makes me very happy. I want a plain wedding band – just plain so as not to take anything away from my perfect diamond ring. If we had any sugar, I'd bake you some cookies.

February 13, 1946

You will be a wonderful coach – the boys will like you, and you will have very good teams. I predict it! You will teach them character in addition how to play the game. You already know so much of what you may learn in college.

February 13, 1946

Did you ever notice how much we depend on each other at times – we unite forces and place a little of our lives in each other's hands. I like being dependent on you for some things that I lack. May the day speed when our feelings are kept alive by more than our memories.

February 14, 1946

A poem for Valentine's Day.

CUPID

Cupid's aim was straight and true
And bore a seed of love from you.
It grew and grew until Heaven above
Towered its roof to house our love.
His arrow left scars
That were quickly healing
And left closed within
A wonderful feeling.
Since then I have guarded

Each and all my memories.
I'll house them all
So please don't stop, please.

February 15, 1946

Even my students are asking when you will be home. Mr. Finkbine, your mother, and even your brothers are asking. Bill says to tell you that if you don't come home soon, he'll marry me – fat chance – he's too young and wild for me.

February 18, 1946

I like the thought that I mean more to you than all the basketball games in the world.

I would need to remember that later, in 1962, when Bud's high school team won the STATE CHAMPIONSHIP!

February 20, 1946

I am planning my civilian wardrobe. I can feel a pent-up touch in me as a direct result of 3 1/2 years here amid all these restrictions. It is as though I have been pushing against a solid wall, and when I finally break through and come home, I am… I have recently wondered if our souls don't need rest, too. I am debating endlessly with myself, and right now I need a glass of water – something that will refresh me as I begin a new start. You are that *glass of water.*

February 23, 1946

We now have $800 in the bank.

February 24, 1946

I went window shopping today for clothes.

February 24, 1946

I shall be that refreshing *glass of water* you need. You have been pushing against that wall for such a long time – 3 1/2 years. The next time you have free time, do NOT write to me – just rest and *sleep.* Looking at my Shakespeare book, this quote came to mind: "Sleep knits up the raveled sleeve of care." So just take a long nap. SO many others are coming home; it makes me miss you more. You haven't been home since Christmas.

February 27, 1946

What other people think, what other people say – this does not affect me. It is what I think and say and do that interests me. We have always been able to change each other's point of view fairly and deeply and found an answer satisfactory to both of us. You said, "We shall live quietly and simply and be happy; that is all it will take to make you forget the unpleasant part of having been in the Service for so long, I hope." To me that is *everything!*

March 3, 1946

Counting our bonds, we have $1400, and this week is payday. That should buy our first few rooms of furniture.

March 3, 1946

That car is making a big noise again! Is there no discharge system for Marines???

March 6, 1946

Today I lost half my paycheck – gambling! After all these years of resisting being a Marine, I had one weak moment. I am sorry and ashamed. I considered not telling you, but I must tell you. I swore a solemn oath that that would be my first and last gambling adventure. And now I don't know what you will think of me. I am punishing myself.

March 6, 1946

I thought you'd be out by January, then February, then March, and now maybe June? I HATE THE MARINE CORPS. I think I'll hunt a summer job. If you can purchase towels and washcloths at the PX, please do. When a store gets some, the ladies tear the store and each other up, trying to be first in line.

March 8, 1946

I have had my teeth cleaned and several cavities repaired. I read each letter you write three or four times. Each hour of our lives will have to make up for all the lonely years we have missed. I cannot come to your prom; you and your seniors have planned it so carefully. All leaves have been canceled.

March 10, 1946

I suppose a new car is out; we want so many new things – a new house, furniture, new clothes, going to college and, I forgot the most important thing of all – a new life together.

March 10, 1946

According to the newspaper, I should be discharged by May 1.

March 12, 1946

My first reaction to your letter about gambling was tears. I have so many reactions; I prefer to talk to you instead of writing. I am unhappy and ashamed as you are. You have always displayed will power! Just once in 3 1/2 years you have become a Marine! That's not too bad. You are forgiven, but I can't say I have forgotten. You knew how much I have always hated gambling. You wanted to know how I feel. Everything will be just fine as soon as we can talk about it. I love you with all my heart.

March 13, 1946

The state inspector came today; he talked with some of my students. I was not the least bit nervous – not at all. He had no criticism of my teaching. Some of the faculty were scared to death, and a few had harsh criticism.

March 15, 1946

I've been almost afraid to receive your letter; I just knew your first reaction would be tears. I feel awful to have put you through my sad tale. I was concerned about your feelings. I wondered what position your faith in me would take. I knew I must tell you. I am not happy, but I am glad that I told you. We'll talk about it when I come home.

March 16, 1946

They need me to teach at the Hamilton Business College two nights a week for three hours. I won't do it unless they give me at least $1 per hour. What do you think? They also want me to teach in day school this summer. If you take the job at camp with Mr. Edington for the summer, I could teach. What do you think?

March 17, 1946

I have neither the words nor the power to tell you how grateful I am for having someone write to me as you do. The bugle sounds to remind me that this is *today* and not *tomorrow*. Goodnight.

March 19, 1946

LETTER FROM YOU

I went from talking to letter writing
In the shortness of a day.
I found it wasn't nearly as exciting
As the things your lips could say.
There were many letters, however,
With many different types of prose;
But the ones from you –
Well, I "kinda," "sorta" liked those.
Days went by a little faster
And each held some new thrill,
Just thinking that a dear, dear friend
Might have written a letter
And remembered still.
You can never guess the pleasure
That each and every letter brought
Nor will you ever realize the portion of my happiness
Those thoughtful letters brought.
The real power lies behind the hand
That sent to me the things to write.
And, Dorothea, in all the land
I'm glad that you are the one I love tonight.

March 19, 1946

Please don't feel awful about the letter I wrote – you wanted to hear the truth; that's how I felt. Be glad we can talk things over – anything, anytime, forever.

March 20, 1946

Here is a sketch of the formal I am making. If you don't make it for the prom, I'll wear it for class night.

March 26, 1946

The sketch of the formal looks nice. Is this your own creation? I'll explain the poem when I come home.

NATURE

Nature's beauty has no bounds
Given to our God-sent looks.
And the trickling of her glory
Rounds the earth in endless little brooks.
They wander through untouched beauty
In endless little streams
And add a song of Heaven
To our earthly dreams.
Theirs is a privilege to go there
And take a solid peek
Into the realms of beauty and
Peace for which we seek.
If only we could flow around
And gather into our hearts
A portion of Mother Nature's love
Which she cautiously imparts.
Then we would all attain
The maximum of a thrill
Drifting like a little stream
Through valleys, rocks, and rills
And when they flow into the realm
Of quiet, peaceful air,
They can be proud
For they have been somewhere.

March 26, 1946

I think a day job is quite enough without your working nights too. You are also so busy with the senior class. You don't have to work this summer, either. If I go to school, we'll receive $90 per month, and on June 11 I shall get $100. If I don't go to summer school, I'll find a job. Do as you want, but not because we need the money.

March 27, 1946

Your letter was too late. I am teaching at the business college two nights a week, until May 1. When we are married, I'll let you do all the worrying about money – if there is any worrying to do. So if you prefer, I shall not work this summer. I think I'll have a full-time job learning to cook, take care of a house, and *you,* without teaching people how to type. How would Mr. Edington's offer at camp fit into our plans? Shall I send him a wedding invitation; then he'll know what you are planning. I am so proud of my seniors – we have $600 in our treasury.

April 1, 1946

YOUR RING

My problem now is to say "Goodnight,"
So that you can remember
With all your might
That I love you.
Remember, my Dear, that night last fall
When I gave you your ring
And received a kiss.
That was the best night of all
Because I loved you.

April 4, 1946

Today there was a lump in the envelope – out fell my wedding ring. Why didn't you tell me you had purchased it last January? You let me describe over and over what kind I wanted – and you had it already! It is perfect!

Two ladies will help with the chaperoning – all our plans for the class trip are coming into focus. That will be the climax of all our senior activities. I can't get used to the idea that this discharge isn't just another furlough that will soon end like all the others.

April 7, 1946

Soon I am coming home for good! It's hard to realize that this isn't just another furlough.

April 8, 1946

Today I made a blouse to go with the white suit. My formal is finished. I visited at your home today. Bill wants to know when the wedding will be. I told him it depends on how soon you could find a house, and he replied that that would be impossible. There was a picture of some Army huts they were installing at Miami for returning veterans. They looked awful in my estimation – worse than a trailer! I will send you a picture. Maybe you can find a nice place in Oxford. Even if we have to pay $50 per month, I want something nice. But that's your problem, and it won't be easy. THE END IS IN SIGHT!! Once you told me the Marines have a motto: "If it can't be done, we shall do it right away; if it is impossible, it will take a little time."

April 9, 1946

Today I finally had the feeling that it is spring. It is as if an April shower were being born within me, giving my soul a drink of life. And now the saying, "In the spring a young man's fancy lightly turns to thoughts of love" flashed through my mind. Spring and love go hand in hand, but they are different – spring is *temporary,* and love is *enduring.*

April 10, 1946

Today I signed a three-year contract for $190 per month. I can break it, but it guarantees me a job at Ross School for the next three years.

Are you able to purchase any sheets and pillow cases at the PX? It is impossible to purchase any here. Ruth and Mother both need pens – can you buy any good ones?

April 11, 1946

Our school paper has a different version of your quote: "In the spring a young man's fancy lightly turns to thoughts of love and spring, so you see that's why I am hoping that we have an early spring."

April 14, 1946

Last December when I told you I'd rather you didn't come home anymore until you were discharged, I didn't realize the discharge would be five months away. That is a long time. THERE ARE 16 DAYS UNTIL MAY 1!

April 16, 1946

My alarm clock is broken. Are there any in the PX? There aren't any in town.

April 16, 1946

Tonight holds the handle that opens the door to tomorrow.

I will be able to go with you on the senior class trip, but remember – we are chaperones!

Bud did purchase my wedding ring on January 21, 1946, for $7.30; he just sent the receipt!

April 21, 1946

I'm sorry I missed your telephone call. Mother told you she would be happy to see you. THERE ARE 11 MORE DAYS UNTIL MAY 1.

April 21, 1946

I remember another Easter. When I was free, I didn't know my heart; then I found my heart, but I was not free. Now I shall have both! Once again I talked to your mother instead of to you. I didn't send any flowers for Easter – I did not have enough money for an ice cream cone. They pay us when we are discharged.

April 24, 1946

I am glad that you were visiting my home the last time I telephoned. I was happy to tell your mother that I would be coming home to stay! I am happy when you visit my family. When you like the people you love, it makes me happy. Now all I can think of is you, college, discharge, and finding a place to live.

1946, APRIL

Of all the little things I have enjoyed
For the past 3 1/2 years,
It gives me the greatest pleasure, now
To bring to a close another page of my life.
Sgt. McCollum is now a memory – the past.
Although his was a short life,
It was made, in one aspect,
Beautiful by you.
This aspect, this beauty
I am personally returning to you
In the personage and care of "Bud."
I am sure that no effort,
No return of friendship
Was ever more dear.
I hope you will find in "him"
Life as you would and have always wanted.
He, too, has waited,
He, too, can now realize a dream –
Our dream – dream built on hope, tolerance, and understanding,
And a very strong appreciation of your love.
What could offer more security for a lasting happiness?
Who has a greater right to that happiness than you?

May 1, 1946, brought all that we could have hoped for. Bud was officially discharged – and by May 3, he was home. Our lives changed drastically. From that day on, our love only continued to grow. Once Bud called it a fairy tale, and for the most part, he was right; we really did live happily ever after.

However...

Postscript
1946 and Beyond...

"On June 4 my appendix ruptured, and I was nearly dead by the time Dr. Stafford found me lying on a wooden bench at Mercy Hospital."

Nearly one thousand letters passed between us during our four years apart – letters filled with love, plans, joys, frustrations, and fervent hopes for the future.

We were so tired of the War, of writing back and forth, of waiting for furloughs, and finally, after the Armistice, for Bud's discharge. We did not want to be married until all of that chaos was concluded – too many challenges – and we resolved that there would be no children, either, not until we had a real home of our own. Although we still agreed on everything, I told Bud that he was in charge. Of course he accepted that responsibility calmly, knowing we had already seen enough upheaval to last a lifetime.

After he came home, I remember our walking together down High Street, when he abruptly inquired about setting a wedding date. What else had I expected? Yet I was speechless! He had finally returned for good, something I had longed for – so what was wrong with me? I still find no words to describe my reaction – not surprised, not upset, not afraid, just the utter strangeness of no longer saying, "No." We decided on June 6; school would be out, and there would be enough time for the necessary preparations. Mother had a lot to do.

Bud's entrance to Miami University was difficult, but Sid Gillman, Miami's football coach, used his influence to hasten enrollment. He began classes and football practice early that summer.

Then Fate, as Bud had mentioned a long time ago when 12 Marines were killed in a plane crash, reared Her ugly head. We had waited and waited for the perfect time to be married. Now was that time.

But on June 4 my appendix ruptured, and I was nearly dead by the time Dr. Stafford found me lying on a wooden bench at Mercy Hospital. I was too ill and in too much agony even to sit up. One look at me, and the doctor called a surgeon – before knowing exactly what was wrong. I didn't care what they did to me, as long as the intense pain stopped. Two days before my wedding, and there I was, clutching my right side, too sick to care.

And Bud? He must have been frantic!

In one of his letters he'd written that it is in wartime that most medical advances take place. Penicillin was one of the most recent – and without it, I would have died before my wedding day. In one of my letters I wrote, "You never know what might happen." A premonition?

Those army "huts" that I had once thought so ugly were the only available housing in Oxford. Bud applied for one, but was turned down because he had no certificate of marriage. Even when Dr. Stafford went over to explain our situation, the stalwart secretary Mrs. Mann shook her head.

Dr. Stafford sat in a chair in one corner of my recovery room. It reminded me of his sitting in a smaller chair before my surgery, holding his head in his hand; I think he was praying for me.

This time he joined us to offer advice. I had been in the hospital for nearly a month. If we could not find housing, we could not be married, for we'd have no place to live. If I were still too ill to get married, we couldn't have the housing. Years later, Bud joked to his students that we "had" to get married. That's all he said - then the bell rang. Shocked, they rushed to me for an explanation. Class could not begin until I'd revealed the entire story.

So the doctor suggested that we be married as soon as I was dismissed from the hospital – and on July 5, I was almost too weak to walk down the aisle. That morning when I visited the surgeon to have my incision checked, he placed a big gauze bow over the taped patch.

Our reception was held in the church rec room; someone had decorated it with crepe paper. We took off the top layer of our wedding cake and ate it in our motel room with the ice cream Bud had bought. I think we finished the cake for breakfast. Then Bud drove me home, and I stayed with my mother for the next two months. But he at least had the proper certificate to show to Mrs. Mann, and we got our little house.

By the time Ross School began in September, I was well again and ready to move in. Bud had completed both sessions of summer school; football had become too demanding.

Vet Vil, as we called it – short for Veterans' Village – turned out to be a fun place. Many couples were newlyweds with the husbands attending college, so we grew very close. We lived there two years. The sides of those 200 square-foot units (one bedroom, one bath, divided by a curtain!) were made of a thick cardboard-like material, and when the wind blew, the walls shook. We had a village grocery store, and Paul Dietzel, later of Louisiana football coaching fame, was our butcher. Bob and Ferne McDade shared the other half of our house; he was working on his master's degree, and we could hear the click-clacking of two typewriters day and night. We stayed in touch for a long time afterward.

Across the boardwalk, Randi and her husband often quarreled. It seemed incongruous to hear him exclaim, "Damn you, Honey!" One day I used the village washing machine after someone had dyed a rug purple. We had purple towels and underwear for months. Bob and Copie Davis were special buddies. Copie made enough spaghetti sauce to feed all of their neighbors – we really did have many good times.

Bud lettered in baseball, pitching for Miami for two years. Ara Parsegian and many other later-to-be-famous coaches were also on the baseball team.

After graduating in 1948, Bud played semipro baseball for a number of years. As a pitcher he earned $25 if the team won and a lesser amount if they lost. Other returning Servicemen joined him on a Grange basketball team which won the State Grange Title two years in a row.

With a B.S. in education, he found employment with Mr. Needles (his former high school coach) at Seven Mile High School. He taught seven classes a day in history, health, physics, and chemistry, and then successfully coached football, basketball, and baseball. Years later, when a news reporter asked why all three of his children had December birthdays, he replied slowly, "Well...

there's this lull in March after the end of basketball season...before baseball season begins."

Hanover Township's West Park subdivision was a unique undertaking by veterans seeking permanent housing. When we decided to apply for inclusion in the project, there were only two lots remaining. Don Fitton, Sr., was president of First National Bank when the board had to evaluate our application. We owned a cedar chest, an electric fan, and a radio, with only a small amount of money in our savings account. Mr. Fitton told the board that he knew us, that Bud had played ball with his sons, that I was a friend of his daughter, and that he personally would approve our loan! The lot cost $850, the house $10,821. At 4% interest, we committed to $60 per month, including insurance and taxes, a princely sum back then. But we never missed a payment, even paid off our mortgage early – and I still live there today.

Once again a hot tear rolled down my cheek on Christmas Eve, 1949, as I studied God's awesome gift and a perfect symbol of our love – a beautiful baby boy with a dimple in each cheek. We named him Marvin, Junior – but we always called him Buddy. My doctor had been astonished to find me pregnant at all. He'd predicted that I might be childless, due to the poisonous infection that had permeated my body.

Yet, somehow, our dreams had come true; we had accomplished everything as planned – love, marriage, two college degrees, a new house, all new furniture, a new car, and now, finally, a wonderful little son.

Two lovely daughters would follow – Pam in 1952 and Melanie in 1953 – along with two successful careers. After five years of teaching at Ross, I resigned to become a full-time mother for the next 11 years. I returned to teach at Fairfield, Harding Junior High, Taft High, and finally at Hamilton High, retiring in 1982 with 30 years of service, having "bought out" several maternity years.

One spring day in May of 1950 found Bud admiring the beauty around him as he drove up Eaton Road toward Seven Mile. Somehow he veered to the right in the dewy grass, ending up in a severe collision with a tree. Having just taught in health class that the steering wheel kills more drivers than any other auto part and seeing no way to avoid the tree, he leaned away, broke off the steering wheel, and smashed his face into the right hand metal dash about eight inches. Gene Steed, right behind him on his way to school, pulled him out, and rode with the ambulance to the hospital. Gene called me, and then he called his own wife. I called Bill McDulin, who was at that time a car salesman. June and Bill took Buddy to my mother's house, where he stayed for a month – I don't even remember seeing him during that time. Mother learned to sterilize bottles and make formula; she and JoAnn had a great time with a five-month-old.

Bud's jaw was broken in eight places, requiring the skill of a dental surgeon. Dr. Stafford remarked that if he had not been an athlete, accustomed to seeing pitches coming toward him at perhaps 90 miles per hour, he would never have seen that tree.

Schools did not offer health insurance in those days. We did have Grange Insurance, which even paid for a private nurse who carried snippers with which to cut his wired jaws in case he vomited. Otherwise, he would not have been able to open his mouth. A dentist pulled a tooth so that a straw would allow him to sip liquids.

When young people marry for love, vowing, "in sickness and in health," they have no idea what they are promising. Sickness will invariably become the ultimate challenge to anyone's devotion.

After a month of hospitalization, Bud finally came home – to bills. No car, no money. Just the obligations of a new home and a new baby. In 1950, teachers were paid only during the nine months of the school year; during the summers, they scrambled to find temporary work.

My secretarial skills came in handy. I quickly found employment at $1 per hour at Southwestern Steel, and I rode to work with a neighbor who was treasurer of that firm. JoAnn came to live with us to help care for Buddy. One afternoon I arrived home to find that my husband had filled a baby bottle with Kool-Aid, and a wide-eyed Buddy was enjoying it immensely. "What are you doing to *my* baby?" I demanded. "Well," came Bud's reply, "it is hot today."

In the spring of 1953, Bud's younger brother Bill had purchased a boat and wanted to show it to him. Due to April's showers, the river at North "B" Street's dam was high, but they went for a ride anyway. On the second trip they took Buddy along – no life jackets, no life preservers, too young and naive even to *think!* After Buddy's ride they decided to go once more up the river. This time, on the turn by the dam, the boat swamped. Bill stayed with it, and Bud went over the dam into the muddy swirls. Bill's wife ran to the riverbank, leaving me in the car with her child, Buddy, Pam, and Melanie not yet born.

Being young and very strong, Bud gave one mighty push when his feet struck the bottom of the dam, and he swam to a pile of rocks in the middle of the river. He later revealed that only the thought of the children and me gave him the extra strength to propel himself away from certain death. The fire department and the police came to his rescue. I must have been more angry than frightened – it all happened so fast. I wanted the police to arrest them both, and I scolded all the way home. What if Buddy had been in that boat?

All was quiet (except for me), and Bud stayed a long time in the shower, regurgitating muddy water. I think he stayed so long to give me time to cool down. I was angry at Bill, too; what a tragedy that might have been! When at last Bud held me in his arms, my anger melted into praise and thanksgiving, for once again God had been with us.

Life resumed. Seasons passed.

Grocery shopping with three small children could have been difficult, but it was not. I plopped Melanie into the shopping cart, strapped a harness on Pam, gave her leash to Buddy, and told him to keep his other hand on the cart. He was a big help to me; nobody was running wild through the store – no problems with such obedient little ones.

Those years are now a blur of baths, diapers, formula, high chairs, and oatmeal, along with cooking, cleaning, sewing, and the companionship of a husband who completely and faithfully loved me. We were a very happy family.

Years later, Buddy remarked, "Mom and I really used to go places before we had you girls!" And once, when a visitor asked how he liked having sisters, he replied, "I get so tired of carrying Kleenex."

To this day all three are good, productive citizens. All were involved in sports. The girls were Girl Scouts, and they took piano lessons from Jean Wright. Pam played the piano for Sunday School, and Melanie accompanied Taft's Treble Aires for two years. I sewed all of their dresses as well as my own while supporting the family's varied activities.

Buddy was an excellent three-year varsity baseball catcher in high school and also played for his dad on the basketball team. At Earlham College, he was the varsity catcher for all four years.

He now teaches chemistry and physics at Hamilton High. His wife Peggy is an attorney. They have two sons – Jim, who works with computers, and Mike, who is attending law school in Virginia.

Pam heads the emergency nursing department at Fort Hamilton Hospital. Her husband Bill Klaber is associated with Klaber Enterprises. The Klaber Band, organized by Bill's father in 1930, still plays at weddings, parties, and Oktoberfest celebrations throughout Ohio. Pam is a devoted stepmother – and now step-grandmother to 13!

Melanie is a widely admired Hamilton High mathematics teacher. Her husband Larry Allen, her high school sweetheart, was one of Bud's highest scoring and most talented Taft High basketball players. In one of Fate's delightful full-circles, he eventually became Hamilton High's head basketball coach and established a winning tradition of his own, which included a state championship in 2004. Their daughter Heather and her husband Peter Farnham are both teachers pursuing their masters' degrees – and they just welcomed Jackson Christopher into the world last fall. Our first great-grandchild! Daughter Holly is working on her master's degree on-line. Son Billy Bud has graduated from the University of Albany (NY) with honors in leadership, math, and physics. He has been nominated for Scholastic All-American. He is a gifted athlete, just like his father Larry, his uncle Buddy, and his grandfather Bud. Billy's recent engagement to Cait Nevins means a very welcome addition to our family.

In my mind, I can still see Bud holding a basketball hoop in his hands and instructing Billy, then age three, how to practice shooting.

A master's degree became Bud's in 1952. He coached basketball and football for Hamilton's Big Blue, and when Taft High opened in 1959, he coached all three major sports for a short time.

We were invited to a New Year's party at Sis and Gay's. Their children and ours were more than just cousins; they spent many, many hours together on vacations and swimming. Gay had flooded his basketball court for ice skating. Bud purchased four pair of beautiful white skates and proudly showed them to the children and me. Four pair! That surely cost a lot of money! I was so irritated that the only "fight" (yes, in quotes) we ever had occurred. I threw a box of toothpicks at him. Bud didn't even move from the table; he just sat there, grinning at me, while I crouched on the floor, gathering them up. How could I call that a fight? Well, I think you need two people for a fight, and he refused to join. Bud and the kids all wore their new skates and had a grand time that evening, while I watched from the window of the warm house.

Bud's good friend, Ara Parsegian, offered a coaching job alongside him at Miami. At that time, I wasn't working, and Bud was earning $2400 per year at Seven Mile. The job paid only $2000. As much as he would have enjoyed coaching with Ara, we could not imagine living on so much less.

More than a dozen plaques and awards still grace our living room and family room. Bud's Taft High basketball team won the Ohio State Basketball Championship with a 27-0 record in 1962. Many years of successful coaching in all sports (one year while teaching at Seven Mile he had a table tennis champion of Butler County), earned him the enduring respect of his peers. In elementary school he had become the marbles champion, and at Fairfield High School he'd won the Butler County tennis championship. Whatever the sport, whether player or coach, he managed to become a winner. He was a true all-around athlete.

But of his many awards, Bud valued most his being selected in 1980 as "Taft's Top Teacher." It was, in fact, the highlight of his career.

And Miami University honored him posthumously in 2003 by electing him to Miami University's "Cradle of Coaches."

Over the years Bud built several additions to our home. He opened the living room's hall entrance and the stairway with a hammer in one hand and a carpentry book in the other. He remodeled the upper level to include two bedrooms with built-in drawers and a second bath. He ceramic-tiled both bathrooms with only a magazine article as his guide. The garage was enlarged, and he planned a new family room with the skill and intricate drawings of an architect to guide Jack Arent, our builder. Inside and out, he took complete charge – although I did nail a few boards in the upstairs sub-flooring.

I never needed to carry out garbage, put gasoline in the cars, mow the lawn, or do anything else outside the home. Bud took all of that responsibility in addition to spending sometimes 10 to 16 hours a day at school.

After our mortgage was paid off, and the children had completed their post-high school education, we spent many happy hours boating on Lake Cumberland. We shared a powerful ski boat and a houseboat with family and many friends.

Keeping a houseboat in working order was no simple task. But as a former aviation engineer, Bud found it interesting. Once, when our gas oven would not work properly, I wrote to the manufacturer, telling him that I was certain that my mechanical husband could follow his instructions.

As I read his detailed notes aloud and tried to show Bud the diagram, he retrieved a hatchet from his tool box. The Lunsfords had come with us to enjoy the boating. Bud was in the oven with the hatchet while I tried to guide him. No hatchet was mentioned by the manufacturer. My voice grew louder and louder. When he had heard enough from me, Bud stood up, at 6' 1" tall, raised the hatchet, and spoke to our friends: "You'd think a tongue would wear out with age!" What a clever way to shut me up! He said not one word to me directly. I can laugh about it even now.

Bud went back to the oven, gave it one tap with the hatchet, and it was fixed. I never asked how he'd repaired it. The day we sold the houseboat, that oven was still working just fine.

A motor home later carried us to faraway places – mainly East and South. That was an easy way to travel, with all the conveniences of a regular home.

Bud had had high blood pressure and diabetes for quite some time, but a ruptured disc turned into a disc-space infection, which is quite difficult to treat. He'd already had bypass heart surgery in 1981. Then the Fate he often spoke about dealt him two more low blows – Paget's disease (a rare bone disorder) and prostate cancer. Through it all, his attitude was calm and philosophical: "We'll just do whatever we have to do."

He died in June, 1991, at age 69, ten years after his heart surgery.

The night before he passed, I awakened at 3:00 a.m., checked the house, and hurried back to bed so I could rise early to go to the hospital. Sitting on the edge of the bed, I suddenly heard a voice: "God will take care of you." It gave me quite a jolt. Knowing that these words were in a church hymn, I searched every songbook upstairs and down for the remaining verses, but couldn't locate the right one. I slept no more that night.

I know that God does not lie, and I hold Him to His promise. I have had several additional experiences in which His promise has been true.

On October 30, 2000, I was carrying two large "care" packages to the post office for the grandkids away at college. I couldn't see where I was going, tripped, fell, and broke my left arm (the humerus) near the shoulder joint. My shoulder was completely shattered, with small pieces of bone going everywhere. The doctor actually used the world "shattered," and sent my X-rays to a specialist in Cincinnati – who returned the film and said he couldn't fix it.

Pam, her husband Bill, and a spirit-filled group from church came over after their regular Wednesday-night meeting. They (no, Jesus) have been responsible for a half-dozen healings in our church family – so I was glad they came to anoint me and pray. The anointing oil is the symbol of the Holy Spirit. I needed not one of the pain pills prescribed, although the break was very bad.

During the night I became aware of a quivering tingle moving up my arm, but it was not enough to wake me completely.

My next appointment and x-ray left the doctor all smiles. "I don't understand this," he remarked. "All of the broken pieces are returning to their correct position, and the humerus has lined itself up."

"I believe it!" was his reaction when I told him of the prayers and the anointing. After just six weeks of physical therapy, today there is only the slightest difference between my arms.

A year later when I was having lunch at the downtown Hamilton hotel, I decided to walk across the street just to show Dr. Zancan how it had all ended. I threw both arms into the air as he came down the hall; a big hug from the doctor! He was delighted to see me, for he admitted, "I expected that your arm would hang uselessly at your side forever."

In 2004 my right forefinger was hurting, and two different shots had not relieved any of the pain. I couldn't even pick up a coffee cup and was unable to do any needlework. Dr. Zancan said he could fix it only with surgery.

Once again, it was Pam and Bill to the rescue! We sat together, and they prayed. In the middle of the prayer we heard a tremendous crack. It scared us all! My finger had never made that noise before. After we recovered from our shock, they continued the prayer.

I am now doing needlework (cross stitching) on another baby quilt, and I can do anything necessary with my index finger.

Several bouts with manic-depression (sometimes called bi-polar disorder) since 1972 have been more than unpleasant. Psychiatrists know to prescribe the proper brain chemical, so my issues had been under perfect control since 1988. In April of 2005, however, a medication change caused my depression to return. None of three different drugs worked. It was now October, and I was extremely annoyed at finding no relief.

On October 28, as I awakened, I began a prayer that ended with more of an admonishment. I shouted, "Where are You? You promised to take care of me! I hold You to Your promise. I'm not even sure You hear me – or even care. So I'd like to see some kind of a sign."

Suddenly I remembered my appointment with Dr. Helen Holtman, a psychiatrist. I'd been seeing her every week – she was trying so hard and was very supportive.

It was scheduled so early that when I returned home, I decided to take a nap. I don't know if I slept for one minute or for one hour, but when I awoke I thought that my granddaughter Holly had arrived and was standing near the chair in the family room with her back to me. Then I realized that it could not be Holly – the figure was too small. She wore a light green skirt and an off-white blouse; I saw her legs, but no shoes. As I sat up to get a better look, she slowly faded from my view. An angel! God had heard me, and this was His sign. When I rose, the horrible depression was gone, and I have had none since.

I shall never forget what the angel looked like. Had I needed to shout in desperation to be heard? The parnate and lithium have balanced my brain chemistry, and I now have back my enthusiasm and energy. But more than that – I know that an angel is not far away, and that God does keep His promises.

My overall health has remained remarkably good; all of my siblings eventually had false teeth and assorted ailments. Ruth endured epilepsy, cancer surgery and heart problems. Bob was diagnosed with Parkinson's disease and eventually took his own life. JoAnn's problems began with a stroke from high blood pressure. My mother died at age 76 of a heart attack. My father lived to be 83; he died in a nursing home of hardening of the arteries and a stroke, which left him blind.

Here I am, at age 88, mowing the grass, planting and trimming bushes, shoveling snow, painting the basement, wallpapering the back hall, painting my bedroom, climbing a ladder, scrubbing the garage and attic, paste-waxing and polishing the family room's hardwood floor, driving my car, swimming at the "Y" twice each week, cooking, sewing, cleaning, washing, and ironing – doing everything I can to keep this place where I have lived for more than 60 years in good shape.

Yes, I continue to reside in our "brand new" home with our "brand new" furniture. Every room in the house contains Bud's handiwork or some structural addition. In that respect, he is still here, still making my life as pleasant and serene as possible. And his strong spirit still surrounds me. I am alone, but never lonely.

My Christian faith and the nearness and love of my children, grandchildren, and great grandchild have enabled me to exist happily without Bud. I am used to it, but I still don't like it. Making decisions is hard; he always knew exactly what to do. I will always bask, however, in the reflection of his accomplishments as a husband, father, teacher, coach, and a man of enormous influence in our community.

The players still speak of Bud with such awe and reverence. The oldest of them are now in their late 70s; the youngest in their late 40s. The possibility of coaching becoming his career had beckoned during his Service with the U.S. Marines – since he had a talent for getting the best out of his teams even back then. But he couldn't have predicted the phenomenal stature he would attain, not only for producing record wins, particularly in basketball, but also for molding young men's characters.

His gentle philosophies regarding hard work, gentlemanly behavior, and moral integrity, which had impressed me so much in Bud's Wartime letters, also made an enormous impact on the teenage boys whom he coached. They soaked up his motivating peptalks laced with humor like little sponges – and then quoted him to their friends and families for decades afterward.

One short rhyme that originally appeared in our English grammar books, used to illustrate comparatives and superlatives, became his hallmark:

Good, better best,
Never let it rest,
Until your good is better,
And your better best.

One former player told me he often repeated that over and over to himself when he went on sales calls.

At the same time, Bud could be a stern taskmaster, with five hours of laps and whistle-drills during weeknight practices. "We often beat teams that were technically more talented than we were," one player reported, "only because we were in such great physical shape."

One of his most non-negotiable demands was to ignore what he called "uncontrollable variables." Screaming spectators, unfair calls by referees, and any efforts to rattle someone attempting a free throw – all must be tuned out. Those things were not controllable. That's why Bud's teams almost never indulged in shows of temper, and anyone who did was immediately sent to the locker room – no matter how loudly the fans protested.

Bud often quoted the philosophy espoused in Machiavelli's *The Prince*, a handbook for young rulers, which asked, "Is it better to be loved or feared?" "It is safer to be feared than loved," Bud declared. "But a skillful prince will try to make himself feared without making himself hated by those who are forced to submit to his power."

His strength, his dignity, and his genuine affection, however, made fear a non-issue. Somehow he had found the two ultimate keys to stellar coaching: First, he selected boys who were "coachable," receptive to what he was able to teach them. Second, he made them *want* to become better through experiencing what success felt like. Winning games, league titles, and championships created a feeling of triumph which his teams would remember all of their lives. "I don't know if we always made them want to *do* their best," Bud remarked in later years. "But we did accomplish showing them the value of what their best could *do*. I only knew one way to play myself, and that was as hard as I could play. I learned that there were factors other than God-given talent that contributed to success or failure."

The results still speak for themselves, even today. "We'd have run through a brick wall for him if he'd asked us to," said one player.

One of the most powerful and endearing duties Bud took on was his tender protection of me. The only time our children were ever in trouble was if they caused me to worry; he insulated me even from them! It was reassuring to feel so safeguarded, and even today he continues to cushion me, as I still receive 1/2 of his pension check each month.

Re-reading our letters has pulled me backward in time. Immersed once more in events from 65 years earlier, I was startled one afternoon by the telephone ringing. It was Melanie. "What are you doing, Mom?" she inquired. My voice was thick with tears. "I'm 21 years old," I responded, "and I've just received my engagement ring."

Yesterday and today are forever intertwined. I can return instantaneously to 1943 or 1952 or 1981 whenever I wish. And now that I have the twin benefits of both age and hindsight, I see everything more clearly.

One particularly compelling read is a 13-page letter that Bud wrote on August 4, 1943. He told me that as a young teenager, he'd made friends easily with male classmates, possibly because he was so good at sports – but that girls terrified him. He didn't believe that any of them found him attractive. Insecurity became resentment, which turned over time to bitterness.

"But *you* were nice," he added. "You seemed different."

He was determined to do something admirable with his life, so that those who had once snubbed him (particularly girls) would sit up and take notice.

Then when the War broke out in Europe in 1939, and he saw so much world suffering, his focus changed…

…to greater and better things – but not for myself. For all of the people subjected to the cruelties of War.

Can you see now why I didn't want you to like me? I wanted to prove to myself and the world that I was good enough for what it had to offer. Since coming into the Service, I have seen so many fellows with attitudes different from mine, fellows who had their way with women. I decided that my life would be cleaner and greater than theirs. It may sound strange to hear me say that I still have not satisfied myself. But I know now that I do not matter as much as I thought I did. What I had to do was a job that required all of me.

That day we talked about not going steady anymore was the day I realized that you really did love me for who I was. And when you kissed me, I knew that I was in love with you. But I could not tell you the whole truth. I only knew I did not wish to hurt you – and that I wanted you very much.

Thinking back to that painful time, I couldn't help thinking about how off-base my sadness and confusion had been. Bud had simply been unwilling to draw me into a real relationship until he was able to sustain it. First, he needed to understand himself.

I marvel now at the poetic language, the beauty of Bud's words and phrases. Sometimes a construction that might have seemed completely "off" coming from someone else, conveyed his meaning perfectly. By comparison, my own letters sound so dull and practical! On the other hand, practicality was essential during such a long wartime separation. I'd been given wonderful parents, a solid, loving upbringing, and an excellent education. So intellect and common sense were never issues.

However, Bud had a depth and a wisdom that I didn't see in other young men his age. Sometimes after a movie date, I'd say, "Bud, talk to me." I didn't care what subject he chose; he'd go on for hours, and I was always riveted. How did he know so much about history, politics, psychology, sociology, religion, and ethics? Of course he was a voracious reader, but he often had time for little more than *Reader's Digest.*

Our pastor, Dr. Minor, has two doctorates, one in psychology, and the other in divinity. He teaches us that the soul, which leaves our body at death, is indestructible. It houses our intellect, creativity, personality, behavior, and emotions. It is eternal.

One day I asked him to substantiate this, since I could not find it anywhere in the Bible. He responded that he'd studied Greek for three years, and this information is available only in the Greek translation.

Yet in 1944, Bud wrote to me: "My soul is the holder and absorber of all my love. The soul is the living part of us."

How was he able to verbalize that at age 22?

Is it possible that some of us come to earth still retaining the knowledge that we acquired while on the other side? Is that why so many people were so drawn to him and his simple yet timeless philosophies at every stage of his life?

I am often asked what made our relationship and our marriage so strong and long-lasting.

First, I believe that those War years, which involved so much waiting and longing, wrenchingly endless at the time, guaranteed that we would never take each other for granted. Through our letters, we grew to understand each other extremely well. There were no surprises. We always felt blessed to be finally married, settled, earning a living, and rearing a family. Bud never wanted to see me unhappy – and he did his best to make certain that I never was.

Second, we genuinely respected each other. Neither of us ever took a back seat to the other in terms of power, control, privilege, or entitlement. Before we were married I told Bud that I wanted him to take full responsibility for making certain that we would always be secure. And he did. One reason we never fought was that he was completely in charge, and we both liked it that way. All I had to do was mention a problem, like needing additional square footage in our house, and he would resolve it. I had complete faith in that ability; I trusted him.

We had so many traits in common: high standards, energy, ambition, dedication, enthusiasm, a strong belief in God, and a firm commitment to each other and to our children. In areas where we differed, we seemed to dovetail each other for the best possible outcomes. He was thoughtful and deliberate; I was more spontaneous, organized, and punctual. He was calm and rational, even when expressing a personal opinion; I was much more emotional.

Third, we had the solid support of both families. None of our parents ever interfered or disapproved. They were always proud of us and our accomplishments, just as we were of our own children. I must add that Bud's family absolutely adored me. When I visited, all six sisters and four brothers argued over who would sit near me at dinner! His mother was eager to the point of pushing to see us married, with me a permanent part of their family. It's impossible to resist the blazing warmth of such all-encompassing love.

Fourth, Bud's values, his character, and his devotion to duty were all unwavering, the core of who he was. Even as a young coach, he once gave his team the following admonition at their basketball banquet: "Live your life in such a way that the weight of your influence will be a golden stream of exemplary behavior reflecting God's goodness."

That's what *he* did. Always.

Rereading those letters we exchanged reaffirm for me that I wasn't imagining or idealizing this fine young Marine. He was truly wise and caring beyond his years – qualities widely recognized by his friends, and later on, the boys he coached.

Two specific lines he wrote in 1943 still leap off the pages to grant me so much comfort:

Dorothea, don't concern yourself with things over which you have no control. Turn your memories into feelings; be happy.

Love,
Bud.

I was, and I still am – especially whenever I start remembering.

About the Author

Dorothea Fant McCollum still lives in the same Hamilton, Ohio, home that she and her husband Bud bought in 1949. They were happily married for 45 years until he passed in 1991. Remarkably healthy and active at age 88, Dorothea is a doting great-grandmother who remains close to her children and grandchildren as well. She admits that she is still deeply in love with that handsome, athletic young Marine, whose poetic Wartime letters transformed their friendship into passion.

Index